EXPLORING AND MINING FOR GEMS AND GOLD IN THE WEST

54 YEARS OF PROSPECTING, DIGGING AND GEM-CUTTING

By Fred Rynerson

Paper Edition ISBN 0-911010-60-2
Cloth Edition ISBN 0-911010-61-0

DEDICATION AND APPRECIATION

I dedicate this book to my wife, Beulah Bonfoey Rynerson, and my old-time friends, dead or alive, who were in the gem mining or lapidary business in San Diego County, California from 1901-1925.

Naturegraph Company, Publishers, Healdsburg, California 95448

MINERALS ON COVER

Top is jade, the three on left are tourmaline, the blue is turquoise in matrix, the large crystal on right side is kunzite, as is the large cut stone in lower middle, the small cut stone is spessartite garnet, the small greenish and red crystal is tourmaline.

TABLE OF CONTENTS

INTRODUCTION

I have left this manuscript of my husband, Fred J. Rynerson, almost as he left it a year before he died. He was so enthusiastic about his gem mining, locating mines, seeking other products from the ground, as well as the making of many friends he worked with, that he wanted to make this record - - and as faithfully as he could. He got so much joy out of those fifty-four years that he had to crystalize these experiences into some permanent form.

Hence it did not seem right or wifely for me to change any idea or conclusion or anything else of meaning in the whole work. I was obliged to shorten the paragraphs here and there and give more directness to the action, so as to meet the conditions of the publishers and make the whole more readable.

The manuscript was written from memory largely; although he took notes and kept a running account of the various experiences, and of his associates from day to day. He greatly appreciated the human contacts he made, for he liked people.

If he has omitted any major incident or any names of those who worked with and for him in mines or in shops, I am sure he would remedy that at once. But with all the carefulness I can muster, I cannot find such omissions. I am having this work of his published for I want it to be a Memorial to him for the benefit of all who knew and loved him. This Memorial is erected by my two sons, two daughters and myself.

Beulah Rynerson

PREFACE

To fulfill a promise, made at the bequest of some friends, I have recorded here some happenings in my life during the early days, when tourmalines, kunzites, beryls and other gem stones were first found and mined in San Diego, Imperial and Riverside Counties in California. I have also reported some "lost mine" stories and experiences of others.

The "lost mine" stories, except those silver finds of Mr. Westover's, the Old Mexican, and Bill Trenchard's uranium find, are "just stories"; I cannot vouch for them. The experiences of others and those of myself, as I relate them in this book, are all true.

Fred Rynerson

Dr. George F. Kunz and Frank Salmons standing in front of the Pala Mission Bell Tower at Pala, California. Pink, lilac, and purplish to amethyst-colored examples of spodumene are named Kunzite. See pages 16 and 25 in this book.

CHAPTER I

BOYHOOD DISCOVERY OF AN OLD MINE

About 1896, my father and Billy Likens, who owned a livery stable on the northwest corner of Second and E Streets (San Diego), located a copper claim on a hill about a quarter of a mile west of the old Encinitas Copper Mine and a little north of the town of Olivenhain in San Diego County. My father took me up there with two men to do the assessment work and to build a road up the hill to the mine.

One of these men was a Swiss, a short, heavy man in his fifties. The other was a young fellow between twenty and twenty-five years old, a collector of minerals and Indian curios. We called him "Jack." I was fourteen and supposed to keep the pot full of meat and help on the windlass. This was during the first week of my school vacation in summer.

We went down in the shaft about twelve feet and started a drill hole in the corner of the shaft. Jack was holding the drill and I was tapping the drill lightly with a doublejack, or a long-handled hammer of eight or ten pounds. One does not start throwing the doublejack over his shoulder when he starts a drill hole, but taps the drill lightly until he has a hole about an inch deep, then hits the drill harder. It was when I was tapping the drill that my father appeared at the top of the shaft with another man, a mining engineer.

My father taught me how to strike with a sledge hammer so I could hold my own with men five to ten years older. Being only fourteen, I was proud of my ability to hit the head of a drill with an overhand hard blow and never miss it and avoid smashing the miner's hands.

How long they had been standing there I didn't know, but just as they were leaving, this reincarnation of a burro (all due respects to the burro), leaned over the top of the shaft and said, "What you got down there, Billy, a Woodpecker?" Now that remark at that time, was a gross insult to my ability to handle a doublejack. My young blood boiled over and I meant to see him when we finished that hole. But he and my Dad were gone when I climbed out of the shaft.

I spoke to my father about it when I met him again and he said the engineer was just joking. Then he said, "Fred, you'll have to learn how to take jokes. You'll have a lot of them poked at you during your lifetime. Laugh as much as the joker does, and he won't get so much satisfaction out of it."

The country round about the mine was full of game - quail,

rabbits and a few deer. Every evening I got enough birds and rabbits to last a day or two. We always had a pot of beans on the fire so I cooked some of the birds and rabbits in with the beans until we could pick the bones out; leaving the meat in with the beans. What was left in the pot for the next meal was a gourmand's dream!

A thunderstorm came up one day and turned into quite a rainy spell. The afternoon of the second day, the rain slacked in the evening so I took the shot-gun and walked down the hill to some long low mounds covered with large sumac bushes. I had often wondered how they came there. They seemed to radiate from a point at the south end of the mounds.

As this place was alive with rabbits and quail, I made for it first and shot two rabbits before I arrived at the mounds. Swinging around to the south end, I came upon a round hole about eighteen inches across. I couldn't see down into it very far for night was coming on. Going back to camp, I walked in a wide half circle to the left and picked up another rabbit.

I had told Jack about these mounds before. He thought they might have been made by the Indians. When I arrived back at camp that evening it was quite dark. I told Jack about the hole at the south end of the mounds. He jumped up from his bunk, letting out a whoop and said, "That's what it is, it's an old mine! Maybe a lost mine!"

He lit another lantern. We had no flashlights or gasoline lanterns in those days. Down the hill we walked again. Jack held the lantern down into the hole as far as he could and found that it was an old tunnel and the floor of the tunnel was only five-and-a-half feet below the surface. We made the hole a little larger and Jack let himself down into the tunnel. Then I slipped down too.

This tunnel led up toward and away from the mountain, in a northerly and southerly direction. The northerly end had a solid rock breast, but the southerly end seemed to be backfilled with rock which was packed in solid. The over-all length of the open tunnel, as we found it, was not more than twenty-five feet, while the width was three-and-a-half feet. How deep it was we couldn't estimate, for the floor was filled with dirt washed in during the years. We had to crawl on our hands and knees to explore it.

The walls of the tunnel showed no pick or tool marks, and were a low grade copper ore carrying a little gold. We did not assay this ore, but could pan a color or two out of it. It was about the same as we got out of my father's mine farther up the hill, running from three to seven dollars to the ton in gold.

There must have been other workings there for the mounds

would account for ten times the amount of work we could see. Those who last worked the property must have covered the workings well, for brush covered the place and all except the mounds looked like the surrounding country. Digging into the mounds produced the same copper ore we found in the tunnel.

Later, I heard that two Frenchmen living in what was called "Frenchmen's Valley", a little to the northwest, probably had made the tunnel in the late 1860's or early '70's.

In the spring of 1919, Mrs. Rynerson and I drove up to the old copper mine. The country was beautiful with all kinds of wild flowers. The place where the old tunnel was located, showed that someone had been working the old diggings for a windlass stood there in a large pool of water.

My father and Billy Likens had sold their mine to two men by the names of Withem and Kelly. When the shaft was twenty-five or thirty feet deep, the two miners working in the mine cut through some material much like aluminum paint of several colors, from silvery white to dark bronze. I never discovered what that material was.

My father was a blacksmith by trade and came to California in the early 1870's, dressed tools at several mines, ran a shop in Colton, California, then went on to Wickenburg, Arizona and opened the first shop there. He knew the miners and prospectors well.

He set the heavy iron tires on the wheels of freight wagons, fitted the jerkline teams' shoes which the teamsters nailed on the mules and horses. He hired several Apache Indians to get wood and help him set the big tires. One day, while several Indians were in the shop, a drunken miner came in and tried to pick a fight with them. My father spoke to him several times, but he persisted in his efforts. So Dad took a red-hot iron, pushed it against his belly and drove him out of the shop.

After a year's time he made plans to sell the shop and go back to Clayton, Indiana and marry his sweetheart, Emma Hall, who later became my mother.

He had bought a horse and saddle and a six-shooter and was about to leave when Mr. Wickenburg came to him and said that no Indians had been around for several days, no freight or stages had come, even the Indian girl that worked for him had disappeared, so he should not leave until they got news of what was going on. After a day or two Dad became impatient over the delay. An old Indian scout who knew the country well, told him about the best route through to Prescott, one that probably would miss any marauding Apaches.

Dad packed the saddle bags full of food, tied his blankets on back of the saddle and lit out. The old scout had told him to make his fire in a depression, or hole, so the light couldn't be seen, and never build a fire in the mornings, for the smoke would be noticed.

On the morning of the second day, he saddled up and started out. He had camped in a little gully which cut into the edge of a little mesa. He said he had hardly stuck his head over the edge of the gully, when they spotted him. There were about thirty Apaches, all mounted. They let out a yell, then split, half going off to the right and half to the left. In the next two minutes Fate decided whether I would write this or not!

Dad never ran, but rode straight ahead. They all turned and rode toward him, forming a circle around him. Not a word was said. Dad said the cold chills played up and down his back so fast that last minute, he was about frozen, and his scalp felt it was already starting to slip! He said those fellows were painted up so grotesquely he couldn't tell one from the other. He sat on his horse trying hard to force a smile, when one of the Indians, a big fellow, slid off his horse and came over, put his hand on Dad's horse's neck, looked straight into Dad's face and asked him if he had any "sug" (sugar). Dad pulled out of his saddle-bags a small bag of sugar and handed it to him. The Indian poured about half of the sugar into a buckskin pouch and then handed the rest back to Dad.

Right then and there Dad said his scalp stopped twitching and his hair lay down, for he knew they were not going to harm him. The Indian asked for some tobacco, and Dad handed him all he had. The Indian gave him back half of it, then looked at Dad again full in the face and finally walked over and mounted his horse.

The horsemen parted on the side Dad was heading for, and without a word, rode away. Dad said he was sure some of those fellows worked for him in the shop at Wickenburg, though he wasn't absolutely certain. What other reason would they have had for sparing him?

Next day about noon, he crossed the road leading south to Wickenburg and saw two freight wagons that had been burned not long before he arrived. There was no sign of the swampers and skinners (drivers); they and the horses and mules must have been taken away.

Still following the directions the old scout had given him, he came to a creek in a shallow canyon. Since it was dark when he arrived there, he dismounted and led his horse down the slope to the creek. When within twenty feet of the water, the horse snorted and jerked back. Making his lead rope fast to a small tree, Dad walked back to the creek and saw what he took to be a log lying along the edge of the water. On closer inspection he found it to be an Indian who had died of smallpox. Walking up-stream, he found another one. Going back to his horse, he mounted and rode about a half mile up-stream before he made camp.

Next morning he continued on his way. Arriving at Prescott, he threw in with some others and all made their way up to the Union Pacific Railroad. Here he sold his horse and outfit and boarded an eastbound train for Clayton, Indiana.

In 1885, Dad left Clayton and headed for California with my mother, her sister, my sister and me. We came straight through to Sacramento, on the Union Pacific Railroad, then on down to the little town of Riverside. Dad built a blacksmith shop on the south side of East Eighth Street, about where No. 2944 is now. In the northeast corner of the shop were set two chairs and he made an L-shaped bench that fitted into the corner and extended six feet each way from it.

His forge was twelve feet back from the front door and close to the east side of the shop. Under and around the benches were rock specimens and ore from several mines. Some he placed up against the front of the shop on the same side.

My father liked to talk rocks and mines, and it wasn't long before he had a number of old prospectors and others bitten by the same bug, sitting in that corner, or in the chairs. Dad never stopped swinging that hammer. He could talk and never lose a minute's time of his work.

I was just a kid of seven or eight years, and was all ears when those old prospectors told of their experiences, fights with Indians, and big "strikes" they ought to have made, but at which they arrived too late.

ORE VEINS

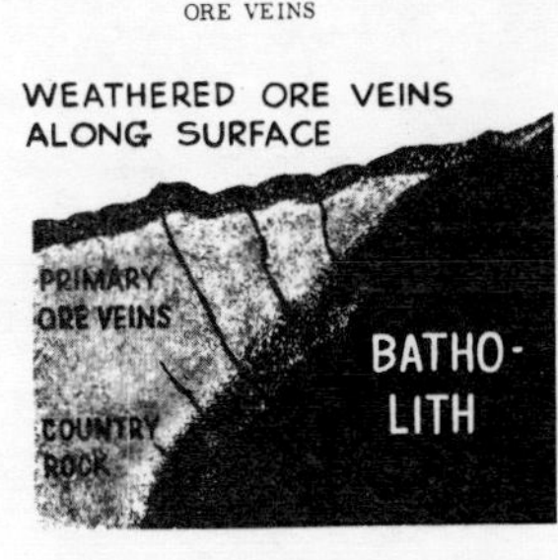

William Rynerson,
father of Fred (p. 1).

Fred Rynerson at age of 36.

CHAPTER II

MY START OF A GREAT ADVENTURE - MOSTLY UNDERGROUND

In the year 1895 when I was thirteen years old, I first saw a crystal tourmaline. One of our neighbors invited me to his home to hear their new Edison Gramophone. It was before loud-speakers came out and you heard the music off the records through ear-phones, which you placed in your ears.

After hearing all the records played, one of the daughters, who was several years older than I, and who was interested in rocks and minerals and knew I was too, brought out some rock specimens. She picked one out and held it up for me to see. It was dark pink in color, about one and a half inches long, by an inch in width. She said it was a tourmaline a friend had given her when she lived in Hemet, Riverside County, California.

It was the first tourmaline I had ever seen, and I didn't know then that during more than half of my life I would be interested in, and working with tourmalines and other native stones of San Diego, Riverside and Imperial Counties in California.

In the 1890's, the Damerons, Ingram and Angel children picked up the pretty crystals when they visited each other, or walked to and from school. They took them over to the Mesa Grande store, where they traded them for marbles or candy.

It was Mr. Verlac (or Mr. Gettney) who sent some of these crystals to New York City to learn their value. Some got into the hands of "Tannenbaum". He at once sent a man named "Highway" out to Warners Hot Springs, San Diego County, to investigate the sources.

When Highway found the locality, he also found that a Mr. Orcutt (and others) had located a claim on the vein. Whether Orcutt's claim was valid or not we do not know. Something was wrong but evidently Orcutt didn't think it worth fighting about. Highway was tough; he drove the others off and took possession of the property.

One morning Highway found Orcutt and another man seated on the steps of a little cabin where the old bunkhouse now stands. One had a shotgun. When Highway walked up, he grabbed the gun, jerking it out of the other man's hands, and ordered both of them off the place. While Highway was staying at the Angel Ranch, some men in a buckboard, all armed, passed the house, going in the direction of the mine. Highway saw them, then picked up one of the Angel boys' 30-30 rifles, ran out the front door to the opposite side of the house. The road passing the house made a long quarter-circle around an apple orchard and across a creek. Highway took a short-cut trail from the house, below the orchard. On the run, he met the men in the buckboard as they drove up. At the point of his gun, he ordered them to go back; which they did. After that Highway had no more trouble with them.

MY INTRODUCTION INTO THE GEM BUSINESS

During 1900 and 1901, I lived in Kern County, California, working in the oil fields. In February of 1902 I came back to San Diego, California to visit my parents. After a short time I decided to return to Kern County. On my way back, I stopped in Los Angeles to see a friend, but he was out of town. As it was Sunday, I bought a newspaper and went to my room. On opening the paper I discovered a full-page account of the "Great Gem Discovery" at Mesa Grande, California. I had known tourmalines were found there. I had seen Highway on the property but I wasn't interested then.

At the top left corner of the page was a picture of an old-time San Diego Booster, Charley Collier. In his hands were pictured crystals of several colors. The article stated that C. O. McCarroll was among those interested. I knew McCarroll as an oil well superintendent, for whom I had worked, at one time. So, after reading the whole page, I decided to return to San Diego and look him up.

Arriving in San Diego the following morning, I didn't find McCarroll but left word with a friend of his where I was going and that I wanted to see him next day. In the meantime, I went out to see Harry Dougherty, who lived and worked near La Mesa, a little town eleven miles east of San Diego.

I told Dougherty of the gem find at Mesa Grande and that I might go up there to work. I spent the night with him. While we were away from the house the next morning, McCarroll drove up, inquired for me and left word to see him first thing next morning.

Next morning I saw McCarroll and found he had already planned to have me dress tools at the mine. He told me to meet him at his house early next morning and we would drive up to Mesa Grande. He was taking another man along, Mr. K. C. Naylor, a jeweler. Next morning he asked me to drive, so he could talk to Mr. Naylor. Since driving would take the monotony out of the trip, I didn't mind.

We started about nine o'clock, picked up Naylor at his home and drove out to El Cajon Road, now El Cajon Boulevard. It was then a dirt road thirty feet wide. The horses "Mac" had hitched to the two-seated buckboard were good so we made good time.

We drove by way of La Mesa, El Cajon, Lakeside, Fosters, then up the Mussy Grade to Ramona. After we pulled into Ramona about 6:00 P.M., Naylor got a room at the Adams House, while McCarroll and I rolled up on some hay on the east side of the barn.

McCarroll had a large, all-white Navajo blanket about an inch thick, which he threw over us. In the night a drizzling rain came. I knew Mac was awake so I told him we would get his nice white blanket wet if he didn't get it into the barn. He only grunted; saying, "That's what it's on there for." When morning came he got up, took hold of the side of the blanket, held it up and shook about a gallon of water out of it. Another shake or two and it was apparently dry.

McCarroll was a big man, weighing over three-hundred pounds. He had a marvelous memory of places and names, also a capacity for raw eggs. While I was harnessing the horses, Mac was foraging in the horse stalls for eggs. After a short while he came to me and said, "Fred, do you like raw eggs?" I said, "No." He had his big hands full of eggs, and started cracking them on the end of the stall, letting them slip down his throat as he threw the shells back towards the manger. He got on the outside of ten eggs before we went into the Adams House for breakfast. Then, to my surprise, he dished himself three fried eggs and two pieces of ham!

We got away that morning around seven-thirty and made it to Mesa Grande about noon. Then we drove over to Mac's prospect where he had two men working, whom I knew. One was Verde Angel and the other was Frank Moore. Verde went home at night and Frank and I bunked together on the ground close by the workings; cooking our meals over a camp fire. McCarroll had his meals with us when he was there; also a cot to sleep on when he stayed overnight.

Several days after I got there, one of those drizzling rains blew up in the night; but this time the Navajo blanket wasn't over us. Instead, Moore had a red, yellow and green colored comforter that he threw over us. In the morning we were printed all over with the designs off that quilt!

Two men by the names of Tach and Meyers were working a prospect just west of us. I don't remember that they got anything worthwhile out of their workings for they quit the place shortly after I came. For that matter, we didn't do any better. After two weeks, McCarroll said, "We're going to put some Lapidary equipment in the back of Naylor's store in San Diego, and want you to help us set it up." He said they had ordered the outfit

Old-time Mesa Grande Post Office, about 1903.

Old-time miners and wives at Mesa Grande.

from Frank Marcher of Los Angeles, and that they were going to organize a company and would be cutting tourmalines, shortly.

The Himalaya mine at Mesa Grande had been in operation for some time before I came. The help was drawn from the surrounding country, and I knew most of the men working there. Tannenbaum had his man "Friday", by the name of J. Goodman Bray, who called himself "The Black Millionaire". He was a colored man.

Felix Lochr was the foreman but after a short time Bray and Lochr got into an argument and Bray discharged him; putting Vance Angel in his place, which position Vance held til the closing of the mine in 1912.

The early mining operations on the Himalaya were done on the northwest end of the vein. This vein had been broken off at this end and had slid sixty feet or more to the west; breaking up into slabs and lying like a house roof shingled the wrong way. The lower edge of the upper slab pushed under the upper edge of the lower slab. Great quantities of tourmaline were taken out.

After working out a large portion of the vein in this section, the vein was worked in an open cut up and over the mountain. A tunnel was opened on the vein and put through about five hundred feet to a point below the top of the mountain. A shaft was sunk that connected with the end of the tunnel. In working the cut to the top of the mountain, hundreds of pounds of tourmalines and other mineral crystals, such as morganites, stibiotantalites and pollucite specimens were taken out. The latter three were not well known, and hence large amounts were lost.

After a few days, Mac and I drove down to San Diego to set up the lapidary equipment, but found it had not arrived. I told Mac I wanted to learn how to cut stones. He said, "All right Fred, but we can pay you only three dollars a week to start."

I had made a little money in the oil fields, and I felt I could afford to learn another trade. I started cutting turquoise on an outfit Naylor had. The inactivity of this job almost got me down. Every so often I would have to go out and walk around the block. I had been accustomed to more active exercise and it was hard for me to do without it. After a month we heard that there would be another delay in getting the equipment, possibly several months. Why, I do not remember.

In the meantime, Gail Lewis had made a strike in his diggings at Mesa Grande, on the south half of the main vein. The north half was the property of the Himalaya Company. But it was Gail's property that McCarroll had in mind when he told me they were going to organize a company, which resulted in the San Diego

J. Goodman Bray on horse.

Gail Lewis, Fred Rynerson and Frank Trask looking at tourmaline.

Cameron Family at home (see p. 31).

Tourmaline Mining Company. The years 1903 to 1909 were the big ones for mine and prospect discoveries. The years up to 1910 were bonanza years for the lapidary.

Our lapidary equipment arrived and we set it up. For practice cutting, we used quartz crystal, but it wasn't long before we were on the tourmalines. Naylor and I were the only cutters in San Diego at that time. In about five weeks I was cutting three to five stones a day! In four months I could do six tourmalines in eight hours. I was sweating blood doing that much when one day McCarroll came in and asked me how many I was cutting in eight hours. I told him "Six." He said Marcher had a man that was cutting eight stones in eight hours.

I almost called Mac a liar, but thought maybe someone had lied to him. Before the end of the year, I knew it was possible; for I was cutting that many and better in eight hours. This was made possible by roughing out fifty or sixty stones at one time, sticking them all on the plugs, cutting and polishing the tops, and then turning them over and cutting and polishing the bottoms.

The tourmaline crystal is about the most easily cut and polished of all the native stones. I would mark the crystal with a little notch, at about the length of the depth of the stone the crystal would cut, and then clip it off with the nippers or chisel. After that came the polishing.

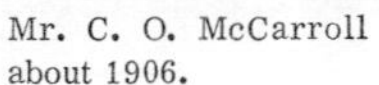

Mr. C. O. McCarroll about 1906.

Mr. Mit Dameron and his two daughters, Lola and Mamie.

CHAPTER III

EXPERIENCE IN THE MINE AT AGUANGA MOUNTAIN

It was in the later part of the spring of 1903 that Naylor sent me to the claim on Aguanga Mountain which he had bought from Bert Simmons, to open any likely-looking vein. I contacted a friend, Ben Boone, and we travelled by train to Fosters, the end of the line; then took a stage to Ramona, changed to another stage for Mesa Grande. Here we picked up Harry Dougherty, some provisions and tools. Ed Morris of Mesa Grande hauled the outfit, with us, to the mouth of Koaler Canyon at the foot of Bert Simmons' trail.

When we arrived it looked like it was going to rain, so we unloaded everything from the wagon and Ed Morris headed back to Mesa Grande. Dougherty had ridden his horse over also. We met an old friend riding through who offered to take one load up for us. Some of the stuff we didn't want to get wet we packed onto the horses and took up to Bert's first camp, a nice spot where two canyons came together. Water flowed down the right hand branch and made an ideal camp spot.

Now it was raining a little. We packed some provisions, the tent and blankets on the horses and we left Boone there to put up the tent. He said he knew how, and would get everything in out of the rain. Dougherty and I started on foot for Bert's place at Oak Grove, three miles away.

With Bert's two burros and pack-saddles, we started back to pick up the rest of the outfit at the foot of the trail. By this time it was raining hard, so we hurried up the trail to camp. We wallowed through and we were pretty wet. When we saw the tent partly up and Boone inside but our blankets outside in the rain, we got angry. Dougherty, who could swear "beautifully", made the atmosphere blue, for a while.

I had left San Diego with a sore throat that had developed into pains in the chest so that I could hardly talk. In spite of this, I piled onto a burro and started down the trail, leading the other. But it was too slow going, so I got off and drove them on ahead of me. When I got back to Bert's house it was almost dark and still raining steadily. When I got back to camp I was soaked to the bone.

Dougherty had the tent up and a big fire going. I tried to dry off but was not successful. I soaked up rain on one side and was steaming on the other. I got the water warmed up in my clothes, so I took off my coat and shoes, rolled up in my blankets, taking a tuck under my feet, pulled my head in like a turtle and shivered myself to sleep.

Something pressing on my head awoke me early next morning. After using my right hand to investigate, I found that six inches of snow had fallen on the tent and pushed it down on my head. I rolled over toward the center of the tent and found, to my surprise, I didn't have a sore throat; so I pulled the blankets over my head and went to sleep again.

Anyone who has camped in half-melted, slushy snow can understand our feelings that morning when we got up. For my part, I had lost my cold and pains in my chest and hadn't felt better in days. Dougherty was tough and used to that kind of life; but Boone never lay still long enough to get warm. He said he did not sleep all night.

There was fog in the canyons and about the camp, but no wind. Most of the snow was gone by late afternoon, leaving everything soaked. We put in the day getting wood for the fire, cooking up some beans and fixing camp.

The next day we tackled Bert's trail - and what a trail! He had picked out all the high places to get over before getting to his claim. One place was so steep Dougherty called it "Past-Redemption". We didn't use that trail long before we cut out another one. Starting from Bert's first camp, we went up the left hand canyon, making an easy grade to the claim.

Most of the places we worked proved to be only pieces of vein matter. Only one place produced tourmalines, but they were in very beautiful colors. The pinks, blue-greens and yellows were very bright. The crystals were not large; one-fourth inch was about the thickest we took out. This work was all done on the southwest side of the flat.

From what we could make out, considering the amount of the work, the vein was not in place but had been moved down-hill and left a dump, broken up and scattered. Many of the topazes found later were on the up-hill side of pieces of vein matter or on large pegmatite rocks.

Before we built the new trail, Boone decided to leave us so I took him down to San Diego and got him a place at Naylor's, learning to cut stone. Then I went back to camp where I'd left Dougherty.

In the past week I developed a good case of poison oak, and as the days were hot, Dougherty and I decided to leave in the evening for Mesa Grande. This was best for me, for the poison oak didn't bother me so much when it was cool. I rented a saddle horse from Mit Dameron of Oak Grove, and rode a cool eighteen-mile ride that evening. (Too cool, sometimes.) Occasionally, we got down and walked for a while to keep awake and warm up. But mostly to keep awake, since we had worked hard all that day.

We reached the Shoulder Ranch about two A. M. the next morning. This is about two and one-half miles from the store where the stage left for Ramona at eight A. M. We decided in the meantime to get some sleep if we could. We had no blankets other than the two saddle blankets and each a single wool and cotton blanket five by six, unfolded. We lay down on the side of the road next to the bank and both of us went to sleep at once. About dawn, I dreamed that thousands of ants came crawling up the hill toward us. They got to my feet, then half way over me, and, I thought, since they hadn't started to eat me, they might be harmless. So I lay very still.

After the ants had completely covered me, they started biting me. With a yell to Dougherty, I made one big jump, landing almost on the opposite side of the road. When I jumped, I took the blankets with me, leaving Dougherty lying uncovered on the ground. He came to life at once and sat up with, "What the Hell's the matter with you!" I looked at my clothes, but could see no ants. Then I knew what had taken place. I had been cold when I lay down, but when I started warming up, that rough, stiff, saddle blanket started scratching my face and hands. About that time all the poison oak in me started going to town. I told Dougherty my dream but got only a sarcastic comment. It wasn't a "nice" way to wake him up. Dougherty rode back to Oak Grove the following day.

Shortly after, Dr. Waldemar T. Schaller visited us. He was fresh out of the University of California. It was while he was with us that all three of us saw kunzite for the first time.

Bert Simmons came up to camp one day and wanted to know the name of a crystal he had; showing us a lilac-colored kunzite crystal, two inches long. None of us knew what it was. Bert said they had found it at Pala, and mentioned the two Basque Frenchmen, Pedro Paleche and Bernado Harriot. The spodumene crystal, later called "kunzite", after Dr. Kunze, had been found several years before, but no one thought it of any value until the Mesa Grande mines were being developed. It was the two Basque sheepherders who brought some crystals to Frank Salmons, who, in turn, started interest in the stone. Large quantities of the material were mined out by those two Basques from a claim called the "Pala Chief."

Dr. Schaller was with us for some time, but it wasn't long after Bert showed up with the kunzite that he left for Mesa Grande. It was pretty hot. We got a horse from Mit Dameron, while I rode Dougherty's horse. We set out for Mesa Grande, eighteen miles to the south; arriving at the Angel Ranch in the afternoon. I fed the horses, and rested until dark before starting back, leading Schaller's horse. I bade Schaller goodby and didn't see him again for a year.

There was a half-moon shining when I got a third way across Warner Ranch. It set behind Aguanga Mountain. I stopped and reset the saddles, for I had come off the mountain by way of the trail instead of the road, where some places had been very steep. The trail led off from the foot of the Warner Ranch-Mesa Grande Grade, to the east side of Monkey Hill, then on to what is called "Puerta la Cruz", where it ran into the Oak Grove-Warner Ranch road, now Highway 79.

I had climbed out of the wash into a grove of oaks, about three miles from Oak Grove, when a large meteorite burst out of the southern sky and streamed across the north, making a loud hissing noise, like a steam boiler blowing off. It lit up the whole country. The smoky appearance of the tail could be plainly seen for some time afterwards, and was very luminous. Later, I heard a meteorite had been seen to fall in southern Nevada.

Going to and from work on Aguanga Mountain, we had to keep our eyes peeled for little rattlesnakes that climbed up in the brush, probably to catch birds. These snakes were about eighteen inches long, and a very light gray in color. We would thresh the brush ahead of us, sometimes, before proceeding through it. I found afterwards some people called these the "Wilson Rattlesnakes".

Later, we moved up on the flat from Bert's first camp, and made camp on the claim, until the water dried up. We got our water on the flat out of holes dug for that purpose. Rain and snow filled these holes with dirty, red, muddy water. We warmed up some and added a little tomato juice, which settled out the dirt and cleared the water, "some". When the holes were all dry, we moved down to Bert's first camp again.

I asked Bert why he had all the ashes around his camp. He got a far-away look in his eyes and said, "Fred, when I was looking over that mountain I was pretty low in cash, and had only a little flour and salt, so I lived mostly on deer meat. You no doubt found some bones in those ashes. I couldn't put all the bones in one pile, so scattered them around".

There was always something happening around Bert's first camp that livened things up a bit. One day I was going over to Aguanga for the mail and some grub and thought I would drop Naylor a line. So I made myself comfortable under an oak tree just outside the tent about twenty feet. I had just started to write when I heard a cry far up the right hand canyon. I thought nothing of it for it sounded quite far away. After about ten minutes, I heard it again, this time so loud it got me to my feet at once.

There was a game trail that led down that canyon and past our tent. I looked past the tent and up the canyon. Coming over a small rise were two large animals I took to be lynx. They were a hundred yards away and seemed to be black in color. I made a run for the tent, got my 44 Colt six-shooter, and ran to a small oak tree about seventy feet up the canyon from the tent. The trail the cats were on led across a gully and up over a log about eighteen inches in diameter. From where I was standing, the log was twenty-five feet away and about twelve feet above me. I pulled down my gun on a point about two inches above the log, where the trail led over it, and waited about thirty seconds. A large head appeared, rising, until half the chest was exposed.

The cat saw me at once and the hair on its jaws started to rise, making his head look a foot wide. I pulled the trigger! He went down back of the log, then I saw the other one, which was a female. She made two leaps up-hill into the brush. As soon as I shot, I ran to my left, and up the hill, cocking the gun at the same time. Out from behind that log sprang the first cat. It sailed three feet above my head and to the right about six feet; landing to the right of where I was standing when I shot. It made one more jump and was out of sight.

That was a long jump, even if it was down-hill. But the funny part of it was, I didn't think to shoot! I just stood there with my mouth open. That cat looked as big as a three-months-old calf. I had never had one sail over my head before and probably never will again. Whether it intended to put up a fight, or tried to distract my attention from the female, I wouldn't know; but I believe, from past experience, it was the latter.

In working the claim, we got very few topaz, but the tourmalines were of very good color. The pink was a rose-pink, and the greens were more of a blue-green; both colors being very bright. The total amount of gems taken out came to only a few pounds. We continued to work until after the Fourth of July, when I left for San Diego and Dougherty went back to Mesa Grande where he worked for the San Diego Tourmaline Mining Company.

Several years later, K. C. Naylor let the claim go and Dr. C. C. Valle of San Diego relocated it. After a few years Paul Valle, Dr. Valle's son, told me his father was giving it up and told me to locate it, for he heard that J. W. Ware was going to open it up. I struggled up to the old flat, looked it over, but figured it would be money in my pocket if I left it alone. J. W. Ware got the property and patented it. He called it the Blue Topaz or Emeralite Mine and took out some fine stones of blue topaz.

I don't think Bert Simmons discovered anything worthwhile or we would have heard about it. Bert told me the reason he prospected the Aguanga Mountain. He said when he was a small boy and had first moved into the Oak Grove Valley, his uncle had been looking for a section corner on the mountain. When he returned he had a crystal three inches long and one half inch thick, of a greenish color. He said he always remembered what that crystal looked like, and when he heard of the strike at Mesa Grande, he decided to look the Aguanga Mountain over.

Dr. C. C. Valle (p. 18)

John Wesley Ware, partner in Mesa Grande Mine (pp. 18-19).

At camp on gem hunt.

CHAPTER IV

FASCINATING AND DIFFICULT WORK OF A LAPIDARY

Back in San Diego, I stuck with the cutting end of the business for several months. Ben Boone and I worked together. When we moved the shop to F Street, I started teaching cutting to an Indian boy, Sipreana Pachito, from Mesa Grande, who had been working for C. O. McCarroll. I also taught another boy, Orten Dimond. Dimond wasn't with us long, but Pachito became a good cutter, later working for both Frank and George Marcher of Los Angeles.

After several years Pachito became tubercular and passed away. He was a good steady worker, and I remember he was the one who coined the word "Breweryite", meaning gem-cut pieces of beer bottle. The rough broken pieces sometimes were sold to jewelers by prospectors who mixed them with the rough of spessartite garnets. Boone turned out to be a good cutter also.

I cut only tourmalines at the shop for several months, then took in some custom work as prospectors were bringing in everything from beach stones to higher quality native gem stones; also gold ore and picture rock, to be slabbed and polished.

The years 1903 to 1909 were big years for gem prospecting and locations. W. H. Trenchard (Bill) had been busy locating essonite and spessartite garnet claims, also called hyacinth. He located several claims north of the Mexican line. He found a violet-colored chalcedony that he called "Violite". He discovered a large vein near Tulley Mountain which produced one beryl! I saw part of a crystal he had taken out that was over twelve inches in diameter. Bill Trenchard also discovered and located the marble on Coyote Mountain, Imperial County, and the nickel deposit on the same mountain.

It was in 1903 that C. O. Johnson and W. H. Trenchard started a lapidary shop in two of the old Horton House show rooms on Third between C and D Streets, in San Diego. They later took Doc Wilson in as a partner and organized the San Diego Gem Mining Company, moving to 1529 D Street (now Broadway).

It was in one of these Horton House show rooms that the cutting plant of Johnson and Trenchard was located and where I saw a large black tourmaline three inches in diameter and five inches long. I called to Johnson, who was in the next room, and asked him where he got the large tourmaline. He said that Frank Salmons had brought it in to sell for ten dollars for what was in it.

I looked the crystal over and detected a dark pinkish tint through the outer surface. The top was a perfect termination, but the other end was a dirty-blueish white. I had had experience with smaller crystals of the same color and kind, but none as large as this one. Some of the smaller ones would cut very fine rose-pink colored stones.

I marked around the crystal about one inch below the terminated end and broke it in two. I expected to find a pink core but not one and one-half inches in diameter of the most beautiful rose-pink with the greater part of it flawless!

Now I could have left the ten dollars with Johnson, taken the crystal and walked out. Instead, I called C. O. to see what I had. He in turn phoned to Salmons, and Salmons came down and walked away with the crystal. I heard later that he sold the crystal to the American Gem and Pearl Company of New York for $500.00 and they, in turn, sold one cut stone out of it for that amount! Frank Salmons told me years afterwards that the black crystal was taken out of the Pala Chief mine vein, but down the hill from the kunzite workings.

TWO MEN WITH THE PEARLS

Two men came into the shop one afternoon looking as though they had been on quite a rough trip. They were bewhiskered and their clothes were dusty and dirty. One said they had some things they would like to sell, and pulled from his pocket a cloth wrapped around some pearls. Some of those pearls were almost black, some pinkish and some pure white. One was about a quarter inch in diameter, almost perfectly round, and blue-black in color. All the pearls were almost perfectly round.

I asked what they wanted for them, but they replied that they wanted to find out their worth first. I told them to go to Ernsting's Jewelry Store and see Ernsting personally.

They had some garnets and beach stones said to come from the east coast of Lower California, Mexico. From things they said, I figured it was about a hundred miles below Yuma, Arizona. Then they told me of an experience they had which gave me an idea of how they got the pearls.

They had been camping close to the beach when a wind storm came in from across the Gulf. After a while the wind became so strong that it blew spray from the breakers into their camp, so they pulled up stakes and moved into a small canyon a hundred yards from the beach. This position offered some protection from the wind.

During the early morning hours of the next morning the wind died down and they heard, coming from the beach, growls and noises which told them that coyotes and other animals were near.

When they left camp to investigate, they found coyotes, coons,

Old lapidary shop on F Street in San Diego (see page 15).
Fred Rynerson at right front; Cipriano on near left.

C. O. Johnson, Burr Porter, Doc Wilson and horse and buggy, front of San Diego Gem Company store.

wildcats and other animals feeding off of tons of shell-fish and giant shrimps. Some of the latter named were ten and twelve inches long. The heavy seas that night had broken loose tons of oysters and other shell-fish and in gouging out the muddy shore bottom had cast shrimp and shell-fish of all kinds upon the beach. They said they ate shrimp and oysters until they became almost sick. After several days in the sun, the stench became so bad they got away and came back to the California line and on to San Diego.

Ernsting bought several pearls from these men. One was four-tenths of an inch in diameter and of a blueish-black color, which I hadn't seen before. This led me to believe they had more gems than they let me see.

Evidently these men were well equipped with knowledge of the desert, to venture into that country and get out alive.

Bill Trenchard and Bill Hill were all over the desert and the desert slope east of the Laguna Mountains, from the Mexican line north to the Banner gold district. Ralph Jasper and his father, J. A. Jasper, also had some claims around Dos-Cabezas. I have cut some very fine hyacinth colored garnets for Mr. J. A. Jasper. (He was with the San Diego Gem exhibit at the St. Louis Fair in 1904.)

Bert Simmons had located a vein over in Coahuila, that was later sold to a Mr. Fano of San Diego, California and was from then on called the "Fano Mine". Bert told me, after he had sold the mine, that he had been afraid the sale wouldn't go through. When Fano came out to look over the claim, he, Fano, climbed upon the vein, took out his check-book, looked around and said, "Bert, what do you want for this claim?" Bert said he had made up his mind to ask $2500.00 so he told Fano that was the price. Bert said Fano looked around again and said, "Bert, I'll give you $1250 cash." When Fano drew out that one-thousand-two-hundred-fifty dollar check and put the cash on the end of it, it sure sounded good to Bert. So he said, "Sold for cash."

Back in the shop on F Street, I was making $25.00 a week, when one day the Secretary of the San Diego Tourmaline Mining Company, A. L. Ross, came in and said, "Fred, we're turning the shop over to you. We'll give you our cutting and pay you a fair price. You will keep the shop open and pay the expenses of running it."

That sounded good to me so I said, "O K." and "Thanks." That first day I couldn't help thinking that there was a catch to that bargain somewhere along the line, for the custom work was paying the expenses of the shop and then some, which cut down

Fred Rynerson in doorway of lapidary shop.

Bill Trenchard and Spotty (see p. 21).

James Jasper with gem display at St. Louis World's Fair.

on the company's cutting bill, or cleared it all.

After the first two weeks I was averaging $40.00 a week. In another two weeks I found that Mr. Ross wouldn't pay me for the cutting of the company's stuff, but I didn't like doing business that way! In the meantime I had been working on a new facet-cutting hand piece. The name "Hand Piece" was passed along to us by Frank Marcher of Los Angeles. Some lapidaries now-a-days called them "facet heads" or "cutting heads". (See picture on page 26).

From 1903 to 1907 there were new-fangled facet cutting machines invented. Some that have been invented since 1925 are identical to those invented in the early 1900's. I lost a lot of sleep over three before I got the one I wanted, and still have.

I was still keeping the shop open. Boone had gone into business for himself. Pachito stayed on a while, then left for other parts. That left me alone. I had about completed a new shop next door, when Frank Salmons and C. W. Ernsting came in one day.

Mr. Ernsting was a jeweler on Fifth Street (now Fifth Avenue between Broadway and E Streets in San Diego). Mr. Salmons had interested him in the kunzite and tourmalines. They had sold a lot of kunzite to the American Gem and Pearl Company of New York City. They also had a considerable amount cut for themselves by the same firm.

When Salmons and Ernsting entered, they had a large cigar box full of kunzite crystals. Ernsting asked me if I knew how to cut kunzite. I told him I had never cut any but could try. Ernsting said, "Suppose we let you try." They said I would be paid the same as they had paid the American Gem and Pearl Company, which was $5.00 a carat.

The material they gave me to practice on was the best. One crystal was about four and a half inches long by three inches wide and three-quarters of an inch thick. This crystal was a perfect piece without flaws or checks, and of a beautiful lilac color. Another piece had the end sawed off and I detected that it had been sawed with a diamond saw. This crystal was about three-quarters of an inch thick, but slightly imperfect. It would not cut full width of the crystal perfect, but would produce many smaller size stones that would be perfect.

On this crystal I decided to start. I tried the mud saw, using 200# grit and cut the crystal half off, when I saw that the mud saw was out. Where I should have had five carat stones, I got only three carats roughed out.

I was doing this experimental work in the evenings, for I had all I could do in the daylight hours with regular cutting. At the

Frank Trask (see p. 39).

Fred Rynerson with favorite hand piece.

Bill Trenchard with horses.

end of the first evening, I had four kunzites roughed out, ranging from two and a half to four carats when cut. That wasn't very good. I could have roughed out much larger flawed or imperfect stones of the pieces I sawed up, but flawed stones were poor sellers those days and we always strove to get the best out of the crystal, unless we were given other instructions.

The next evening, I started on my first kunzite. I cut three tops that evening but didn't polish them. I did that next day, running them through with the same work. I found them as fine to polish as beryl. I turned the three over so I could cut the bottoms. Before I started on the bottoms I cut the top of the fourth stone.

The first two stones never got to the polishing lap. The third, I did, but in the morning I found it too had gone the way of the others. That left me with the one with the top cut and one side scaling.

I knew I would have to get a diamond saw some place, or make one. Diamond saws were not as easy to get, those days, as they are now. That next morning, as if I had a good angel watching over me, a young man came into the shop. He wanted to know about the tourmalines and where the mines were located. After talking a while, he said he had worked for Frank Marcher in Los Angeles, and some places in the East. I told him I needed a diamond saw and asked if he knew where I could get one. He said I could get one in New York, but why not make one?

That was really good news. He told me to get a flat piece of stovepipe iron less than one millimeter thick, cut out of it a disk the size I wanted, then notch it with a dull knife every eighth of an inch on the outer edge of the disk and not over one sixteenth of an inch deep. Crush some diamond bort in vaseline, rub some into the notches, then take a roller and roll the edge of the saw, crimping the notches around the diamond.

That was the extent of the information I got on home-made diamond saws. I made a roller out of a bed caster, grinding a groove about one-sixteenth inch deep around the circumference of the porcelain roller. After getting the material for the saw, I cut a disk four inches in diameter. In cutting, I stretched the outer edge and caused it to wobble when running. I took it to a machinist, who had been turning off my laps, and found he was a sawright by trade. He showed me how to put a tension in the disk when straightening it so it would run true.

This is done by placing the disk on a true-surfaced piece of cast iron, or any hard metal that has a true surface. Then with a light hammer, I tap lightly from the center out to the edge, turning the disk about a half inch each time the outer edge is reached. If the outer edge wobbles too badly, tap the disk from the center to about two-thirds of the way to the outer edge. Keep turning the disk! After making one complete turn of the disk, turn it over and repeat the operation on the other side. If the disk is cupped, tap the disk from the outer edge to half the way to the center. Do this on both sides. This was difficult for me to do at first, but it wasn't long before I was keeping my saws running true.

I went to Mr. Ernsting and told him I had to have some diamond bort and asked if he knew anyone in New York who could supply me. He looked through several jewelers' catalogues and found the address of a firm from whom I bought several carats of rough diamonds at eighty-five cents a carat. Some of the largest of these crystals would have perfectly made a fifteen point stone. Some were quite yellow in color and others, very light pink.

In crushing the diamond, I didn't get the proper size the first time. Nevertheless, that first load in my saw made a complete cut across the crystal, which was two and one-half inches long by three-quarters of an inch thick. It was a nice clean cut too, without shattering the cleavage planes on the sides of the crystal. I gave the slab a good looking over and studied the cleavage planes. I decided on a plan and tried it out on the last stone I had left of the four. To cut a kunzite is interesting, but as a lapidary I had to compete with other lapidaries in New York; else I wouldn't be cutting long for the miners of kunzite. It took a full evening to cut the bottom of that last kunzite. I let the polishing go until next day and looked it over the first thing in the morning. Finding it still all together, I believed I had hit on a plan to cut it. I altered this plan later when I became more familiar with the stone.

When I had decided on the width of a slab I intended to saw, I put the crystal to the edge of the face of the grinding wheel and ground a mark across the crystal where I intended to saw. That is, I ground off the sharp edges that would cut away the metal of my diamonds. Grinding with the cleavage planes and not against them, is the key. To save gem material, figure what the depth of the stone will be from the width, or diameter, the stone will be when roughed out; then add one-sixteenth inch for sawing.

The kunzite crystal is made up of cleavage planes similar to those of mica. These, in a complete crystal, are double and lie like a V, or the roof of a tent. Where they come together, there's a distinct line like a ridge pole in a tent.

I never start sawing a crystal with one of these cleavage planes heading into the saw. It's hard on the saw and I might have trouble with my stone later. The larger crystals are much safer to handle than the smaller sizes, which, as a rule, are more fragile. It is best to let the saw hit the flat side of the plane, or off the edge of the plane.

I have heard that stones cut with this seam, or "ridge pole seam", would come apart. This is not true. I have cut hundreds of kunzites with this line, or seam, crossing over the tops and sides but have never known any to come apart, nor have I ever had that line, or seam, cause me any trouble.

When I rough out any shape kunzite, I grind with the cleavage, as I would plane a board with the grain of the wood, not against it. Do not grind parallel to, and on the edge of the cleavage planes, but diagonally across them. This prevents the abrasive on the wheel, or lap, from opening the cleavage planes which, in some cases, will split the stone in two. This is the cause of most casualties in roughing and cutting kunzite. Even though the split is just noticeable at first, with damp and then warm weather, or, on coming in contact with body heat, they may split on through.

This plan applies to cutting kunzite on the lap, too. When cutting a stone at any angle across the axis of a crystal one will probably run across one facet that does not polish. If you have a wide swing to the arm that holds the hand piece, lay your stone on the other side of the center of the polishing lap, and the facet will take on the desired polish. In other words, polish the facet from the other direction.

When cutting the bottom (or culet) of the kunzite, do not let the culet come to a complete point. Take out the plug that holds the stone, hold it in one hand and between the thumb and two fingers with the culet down, then grind off, near the center of the lap, what you think should come off. This will leave a suitable sized culet when the bottom is finished. Twirl the stone with the fingers when grinding off the culet.

I used a roughing wheel of 180 grit, and the same number grit on a lead lap, polishing on a tin lap, using chrome oxide, rouge and tin oxide. The chrome oxide was the best polishing powder I ever used. After the first thirty pounds I used, I couldn't get any more that was worth keeping in the shop.

It is best to start by cutting round or rectangular stones-round, oval or marquis-under twenty carats. It is best to use eight main window facets around the stone; from twenty-one to forty carats, add two more, or ten main window facets; from forty-one to one hundred carats, twelve to sixteen facets. Make each main window facet the same width around the stone, no mater what shape stone you cut.

Mr. Fred Schoulder with wife, Joaquina Nawlet Schoulder, and her sister (far right), Tamasa Nawlet Anderson.

Men of Angel Family; father on left and 8 boys with rifles;Fanny and Molly in background.

The old Twentieth Century Cut and the Rose Cut, we found, were not suitable for rings and other jewelry since the pointed top is too easily marred, not being protected like the culet (or bottom) of the stone.

During 1904 to 1906, I ran my own shop. I cut a great many native stones from all the known mines in San Diego, Imperial and Riverside Counties. Most of the material from Trenchard's locations went into the San Diego Gem Company's shop. The San Diego Gem Company had locations of their own. Later, Trenchard sold out and went on his own, and then he brought to my shop some very fine specimens of essonite garnets, some of which were quite large and wonderfully brilliant when cut.

These stones came from several different locations around Mountain Springs, Tulley Mountain and Dos Cabezas; all in San Diego County except a few locations in Mountain Springs District.

Old Bill Hill, Sam, Charley and George Cameron, who lived near Campo, San Diego County, had some very nice garnets cut. Some came from Lower California, they told me. Charley gave me a dozen and a half nodules, which I still have.

H. W. Robb of Escondido, California and Dan McIntosh of Ramona made a strike east of the McIntosh ranch house and brought in some yellow tourmalines and some small topaz crystals. One yellow-green tourmaline, about one and a half inches in diameter, had a bright red spot, about one half inch down from the top of the terminated flat top, and a little to one side of the center of the crystal. This spot was about one-quarter of an inch across and seemed to be round. As the years have gone by I have deeply regretted not buying that crystal.

In all the hundreds of pounds of different colored tourmalines I have handled, or have seen, I never ran across another like it. Those were the days when something new in the gem line turned up almost every day. I suppose we all thought this was going to last forever - or we would probably have done something about it.

Robb and Pray, of Escondido, had a location near the McIntosh ranch. They brought in a large specimen of quartz crystal with two large yellow-green tourmalines, close to three inches in diameter by four inches high and solidly crystalized into the quartz mass. The whole specimen was about sixteen inches across by six inches thick. It had numerous other tourmalines of the same color sticking to the quartz. These ran in size from one-fourth to one inch in thickness and to one and a half inches long. Robb wanted twenty-five hundred dollars for it. I do not think he got it.

CHAPTER V

INTERESTING STORIES OF GEM-HANDLERS AND CUSTOMERS

Answering questions of prospectors and others who were interested in the native stones, took up a lot of my time. Some were sincere in their quest for information, while others wanted to settle a bet, or brag about what they had.

I remember two men who came into the shop. Both had been celebrating their big find. One wasn't as far "gone" in drink as the other, and took it upon himself to be spokesman. He said, "I have a stone in my hand." He was holding the stone behind him. "And we want you to tell us what it is. We have a bet up and agree to take your word for it. I say it's a tourmaline and my partner here says it's a kunzite."

Then he handed me the rock. It was a very dark piece of rose quartz. I told him it wasn't a tourmaline or a kunzite, but was a very good piece of rose quartz. The other man, who had been quiet, came to life about that time with a, "You're a damn liar!", and headed for the door. The spokesman smiled a little and he too went out, not even thanking me. Both headed back to the saloon on the southeast corner of Fourth and F Streets, to drown the bad news. Rose quartz wasn't of much value, those days, but I wouldn't mind knowing where those fellows got that piece. I have seen some good quality stuff in my time, but nothing any better.

There was a saloon-keeper, Bridgewater, who had been taken in by some prospector for a grubstake. He came into the shop one day, after I had come from lunch. I hadn't started to work, so sat down and talked with him. He told me he had some very valuable gem stones and had located several claims covering the discovery. They were more valuable than diamonds because they were harder, he said. I had heard that line before, so many times I could guess what was coming. After a little more talk, he showed me three round pebbles about one-half inch in diameter. He asked if I was equipped to cut stones as hard as they were. I told him I was, and got up to change into my shop apron. He said he wanted to keep the stones he had with him, but would bring in some later for me to cut. He never came into that shop again. The pebbles were quartz!

Another saloon-keeper, whose name I have forgotten, ran a saloon on the northeast corner of what is now Broadway and Front Streets, across from the old Court House. He came in one day, handed me a chunk of rose quartz and asked me to cut a stone out of it. I could see that a part of it had been sawed off and told him I didn't like to cut a stone out of it as he wouldn't like the stone - and it wasn't wise to cut a faceted stone, anyway.

He said, "Man, you're crazy! Look here!" Then he took from his pocket a paper of several cut stones of clear, colorless quartz.

I said, "Sorry, Mister; but those stones never came out of that rock."

He said, "Oh yes they did!"

I told him I would cut a stone out of it and if it turned out clear, or looked like those he had, I wouldn't charge him anything; but if it came out a pinkish color, he was to pay me $1.50. I was charging $1.00 those days for single stones up to two carats.

He said, "Okay! Go ahead."

I knocked off a small piece and roughed it out to about a carat size. All this time he never let that stone out of his sight. He asked me if he could watch me cut it. When I finished the stone, he never said anything but "Thank you.", paid me the money and walked out. I never knew who did the cutting and panned off on him the white, clear quartz for the rose quartz. I often wondered what the saloon-keeper did about it.

About this time, April 1904, I took a week off to drive up to Mesa Grande. There, a friend asked me why I didn't locate a tourmaline vein that Gail Lewis once had found, but had given up. He told me about where it was but as my time had almost run out, I told Harry Dougherty to locate it for me, and we would go fifty-fifty on it. He named the claim "Esmeralda".

When I arrived in San Diego, I prepared for a trip into the unknown. I had been keeping company with a young lady by the name of Beulah Bonfoey, since October and on May 23, 1904, we married, Beulah was a "natural", when it came to camping out and prospecting, so we have had some very interesting rock-hunting trips, and later worked the mines at Mesa Grande, together.

Along with all the kunzite I could cut, I had been working on two different facet-cutting hand pieces. One of these I decided to keep. It does not get out of order. You can cut any number of facets around a stone, or any shape stone you desire, without removing or moving the plug into which the stone is cemented. This piece is fast to operate, since it can be used right-or-left-handed. Two of these hand pieces (the original two) I have now, after cutting hundreds of stones of all sizes, from less than a millimeter to an eighty-one carat tourmaline. The small stone had fifty-eight facets, counting the table and culet (base). The large tourmaline had seventy-eight facets counting the table and culet. This large tourmaline had come from the Tourmaline Queen Mine at Pala,

Going after gems

First work on Esmeralda Mine (see pp. 34-35).

California. I have also cut several large kunzites of over one hundred carats. In the spring of 1953, I cut one pear-shaped kunzite of one-hundred-forty carats, plus several thousand stones of different kinds - all on a hand piece, or facet head, now over fifty years old. (See picture on page 26.)

The stand, or elevator, has a six-inch arm, onto which is attached the facet hand piece. This gives a wide swing so the cutter can use the right or left side of his lap when cutting or polishing.

In 1905 Dr. C. C. Valle, an old timer of San Diego, Harry Dougherty, a native of San Diego, Callahan and I organized the Native Gem Mining Company. Dr. Valle was President, Harry Dougherty was Superintendent and I was Secretary of the Company.

Shortly after we started working the Esmeralda Mine, two large quartz crystals, with several large morganites crystalized on their sides, were found. The largest of the quartz crystals stood about thirty inches high with a diameter of eleven or twelve inches! The largest morganite was the size of a teacup, or three inches in diameter, and was about that length protruding from the quartz.

This large specimen was sold by the Native Gem Mining Company to a Mr. Wilkey of Palo Alto, California for $500.00. The smaller one, about two feet high with one morganite on it, belonged to Dr. C. C. Valle's collection. After Dr. Valle passed away, the crystal, and a portion of his collection, I sold to Mr. Ernest Schernikow of San Francisco, for Dr. Valle's son, Paul.

Some very nice pink and blue tourmalines were taken out of this mine (the Esmeralda). Some of the crystals were bi-colored, dark pink and blue. Both colors were very bright and clear when cut.

At one of the directors' meetings it was decided that Dr. Valle and I should make a visit to the mine. To my knowledge no automobiles had ever ventured into that country so we thought we would put on style and make it in one and possibly save some time.

We contracted with a local mechanic to take us to Mesa Grande, or as far beyond that point as he could go. The reason for the contract was that automobiles those days were not dependable, and we had only two days to make the trip.

The road out through La Mesa, El Cajon, Lakeside, Fosters and on up to Ramona, wasn't paved but was a good dirt road. Mussy's Grade was at times very dusty, with a few chuck holes. From Ramona up to Mesa Grande, by way of Graves Grade, wasn't what anyone driving an automobile would consider a "good" road. In fact, the road really ended a half mile from the mine.

We left San Diego at noon and chugged along on our way. I say "chugged". The engine had two cylinders and we often moved along by jerks. We passed Ramona about six miles, when the engine got so hot we had to camp for the night. We rolled up in our blankets in a peach orchard. Next morning, we found two tires flat and something else wrong. After several hours, however, we chugged on back to San Diego, arriving there late afternoon.

The next try we made was with a better car, although its owner was bad luck. We took along the same mechanic we had on the first trip. We reached the cabin Dougherty was staying in, and spent the night. Next morning we looked over the mine and after lunch we started back to San Diego.

We drove back by way of Santa Ysabel. When we arrived at that point, the owner of the car asked us if we would wait there while he drove to Warner's Hot Springs to see his wife. Dr. Valle told him to go ahead, but to get back in time for us to make San Diego that evening.

On our way over to the hotel, Dr. Valle said, "Fred, you'd better get some sleep. I have a hunch we may have to walk back to Ramona tonight and get an early ride into town."

I parked myself in a chair on the porch where I had a good view - a mile of the Warner Hot Springs Road. About five-thirty P.M. I made out a car trailing along back of a four-horse wagon, about three-quarters of a mile away. I awoke Doc and told him I thought the car was coming, but it was back of a freight wagon and might be some other car. He walked out on the porch in his night shirt, took a long look and said, "Get ready, Fred, for that walk I was telling you about!

It wasn't long before the car arrived and we heard from the mechanic that the battery had gone dead and there wasn't another to be had until the up-coming stage the next afternoon. So Doc said, "Let's go!"

After a bite to eat, we started the walk to Ramona. We were four miles on our way when Tom Davis, the mechanic, over-took us with a horse and light wagon and carried us into Ramona. We stayed the night at the Ramona Hotel. Next morning at six Doc awoke me. George Roque got us some breakfast and we caught an early ride back to San Diego. It was four or five years after that before we again tried the automobile. We always played safe and took the horse-drawn stages or hired horses and a buckboard for the trip!

Most of the history of the Esmeralda Mine was written shortly after the second pocket was taken out. Later on, a tunnel was run to tap the vein lower down. The tunnel passed under the vein. Digging up in the roof of the tunnel, at a point where the miners should have contacted the vein, they found it, about a foot above the roof of the tunnel. The vein lay across a ridge and struck northeast and southwest about three-hundred feet long.

Before the Esmeralda tunnel was started, I had traded my interest in the company for property in San Diego and had no more to do with this property or company. About 1913, I did some work on the southwest end, but ran into what I expected, a broken vein; so I quit.

Down below the Himalaya Mine, and scattered all the way down to Temescal Creek, were pieces of pegmatite vein not in their original places. I had worked several and found them unproductive. Yet, some had highly mineralized portions, such as are found around pockets or pocket zones. Some pieces I worked had been broken right through a pocket, dumping the contents out, leaving the quartz and spar lining, sometimes studded with stubs of tourmalines and beryls.

A term used in the early 1900's (and even to this day), to describe these small chunks, or pieces of vein matter, was "blow-outs". I cannot conceive of a piece of pegmatite vein being a blow-out. A piece of vein matter detached from its original position, does not have definite walls on the ends of the veins. They are broken and irregular, some ends being pinched off, and ending in a scattered, broken mass, like the southwest end of the Esmeralda Vein. The northeast end is broken too, but the smaller pieces have been washed away, since it faces a canyon on that end. None of these pieces of vein have any depth to speak of. One long vein near Pala went in about forty-five feet. The end showed a clean break along the vein.

In the early days of gem mining in San Diego County, we worked over a lot of these pieces of vein, also deposits. The deposits in my experience have never produced any good indications of being gem bearing. These deposits are not pieces of vein matter but are a local mineralization concentrated from the surrounding formation.

CHAPTER VI

ERNSTING AND SALMONS - LAPIDARY SHOP AND ITS EQUIPMENT

The first of 1906 I went to work for Salmons and Ernsting, building lapidary equipment for a shop in the rear of Ernsting's jewelry store on Fifth Avenue in San Diego. I moved my lapidary plant to my home and did my own cutting when I had time. The material was tourmaline, garnets and beryls. I took some "no rush" jobs too.

When the shop was completed at Ernsting's, I had nothing but kunzite to cut for a long time. Some crystals were beautiful pieces, some, very dark pink or lilac color, some as large as my hand. I hated to saw them up, even then, when all of us thought there were plenty more.

The time I was building equipment, Gail Lewis came to my house and wanted to know what I would charge to teach him how to cut stone. I knew Gail had a piece of property on the east side of the San Diego Tourmaline Mining Company's property. I asked him about it and, after some talk, we made a trade. He was to give me an undivided half-interest in the land which, not being surveyed, might be a foot wide or a hundred feet wide; he did not know. I took a chance and accepted his deed.

There was a small vein that ran parallel to the main vein; and, about one hundred feet below, it outcropped on the hill side. This vein connected with the main vein at different depths, getting deeper as it led northwest. Gail and I worked it at different times, but it was a poor producer. Maybe we picked a poor place.

I had, in the meantime, gotten the shop going at Ernsting's and had Gail Lewis working with me. He became a good cutter and later went into business for himself.

Nickelson and Harsch were two men who organized a company called the "Mesa Grande Consolidated Gold and Gem Mining Company". They also had several pieces of land around Mesa Grande.

Mr. Harsch asked me one day as I was leaving work at Ernsting's, if I had any property in Mesa Grande. I told him I had and described the property; telling him I also had a partner. He wanted to know what we wanted for it. As Gail and I had never talked of selling, I told Harsch I would have to see my partner first. Lewis and I talked the matter over and decided to sell an undivided half interest, providing the buyers would survey the land for a thirty-day option. We did this to prevent us from getting into a jam. It also gave us our lines around the property.

How Lewis acquired this property probably wouldn't happen again in a lifetime. There are two surveys in that district! The Washburn of 1854 and another by Wheeler in 1873. The difference of surveys is quite considerable.

Lewis had already sold his mining property to the San Diego Tourmaline Mining Company. It wasn't long before trouble started. During a mining boom, there is always someone snooping around to find a loophole to make easy money, or get land that doesn't belong to him. This was true in Gail's case.

This "party" got a mining right on a ranch in Mesa Grande, east of the mine, telling the owner of the wealth that would come to him, or his; the man signing the mining right being then on his deathbed. As soon as this party got his mining right, he notified the San Diego Tourmaline Mining Company to get off his property. (In doing this, of course, he was attempting to take advantage of the old Washburn survey.)

In turn, the San Diego Tourmaline Mining Company came back at Lewis with, "Settle with this man or give us back our $10,000." Lewis got busy. So did the ranchers in Mesa Grande. A man by name of Kidder, from the Land Office, came down and looked the situation over and called a meeting of the ranchers at the Mesa Grande store. He told them if they moved their lines to a certain survey, some would lose and some would gain by it. So they decided that all the ranches and lands would be held to the lines originally bounding them, which was according to the Wheeler survey.

The decision blocked the efforts of this party to get hold of Gail Lewis's property. In settling with this man, Gail told me he made a bargain with him to settle the expenses of the legal advice by flipping a coin. Gail won.

The attorney for the San Diego Tourmaline Mining Company then made out a meets and bounds deed to the property and asked Lewis to sign it; which he did.

To determine the boundary lines of our property, Nickelson and Harsch hired a surveyor by the name of Wheaton who, as I remember, was a government mineral surveyor, or had been. We were all there when he finished the job, which gave us an L shaped piece of ground and 122 feet of the main vein.

We were hauled into court at once, but the law decided in our favor. McCarroll and I had some lively arguments over that decision, but all in good fun, for Mac was a swell fellow. Too bad we cannot have those fellows with us always.

According to our agreement with Nickelson and Harsch, work was started at once. We had Frank Trask doing the work of sinking a shaft on the vein. He had hardly started the cut when he struck some crystals of tourmaline in the dirt. When he cut the vein and started down, it was almost one continuous pocket down to the sixty-five foot level. A large amount of nodule and pencil tourmalines, also some stibutantalites, were taken out of this shaft.

In the office of Nickelson and Harsch was a man by the name of Rockwood. About the time Nickelson and Harsch took an option on our property, they sold to Mr. Rockwood one-half of their interest, or one quarter of the whole, for as much as they had paid us for a half-interest. Rockwood put his deed on record before Nickelson and Harsch had received ours, though it was in escrow. This made Rockwood hot under the collar.

Several months went by and we were down in the shaft to about the sixty-five foot level, when Earl Rockwood, Mr. Rockwood's son, came to me and said that his father was selling out to the San Diego Tourmaline Mining Company and that they were going to close us down, or stop us from working.

I went to K. C. Naylor, who had control of the company at that time. He told me all about Rockwood's troubles and said that he had bought Rockwood's interest and would buy mine, if I wanted to sell. I told Gail Lewis he'd better sell too, as I was. I sold my interest to Naylor and shortly afterward work was stopped on the property. I don't remember if Lewis sold to Naylor or not.

Naylor later drove on through our old shaft and on over to the Himalaya's south side line; taking out a great quantity of material, tourmalines and beryls.

Along about this time, on my way home one afternoon, I met Bill Trenchard and he told me that Worth Merritt, who was working for the San Diego Gem Company, had gone out on the edge of the desert to work the hyacinth-colored garnet mine that the company owned and they feared he had become lost. This was in 1906. Doc Wilson told me afterward that he sent Merritt out there to do the work, and he was to go over to El Centro, Imperial County, to pick up Bill Hill and return to the mine.

It was about this time, also, that I went up to Mesa Grande to look at a prospect a friend had and wanted me to look over, and tell him what I thought about it. It turned out to be a detached piece of vein matter carrying some quartz crystals and indications of pocket zones, but the whole piece was so small I doubt if it contained anything worthwhile. It looked like the pocket, which no doubt had been a part of the vein, or joined it on the side, had broken off and was lost in the debris.

As I had walked down there from the Angel Ranch, I walked

back by way of the Himalaya Mine; cutting across from the old Ingram ranch house to the office of the Himalaya Company. When I arrived there, they had just cleaned up several hundred pounds of tourmalines which were being put into fifty-pound powder boxes for shipment to New York.

On the ground under a large oak tree was a twelve-by-twelve foot canvas which was spread out and covered with tourmalines. The largest was about one and one-quarter inches in diameter by three inches long. The average size was about three-fourths inch by two and a half inches long.

These crystals drying on the canvas had been taken out of one pocket and were of a different color than I had seen before. All had a flat termination on one end. The cap, or terminated end, was a very bright blue color, and in a crystal one inch thick by two long. This cap was about one-quarter inch thick. Next and below the blue was a bright canary yellow about three-sixteenths inch thick; the rest of the crystal being a dark, wine red.

All the crystals on the canvas were of the same coloring and there must have been four barley sacks full in all. Vance Angel and several other workmen, including J. Goodman Bray, were there and they seemed to take no notice of these beautiful crystals other than just another batch of tourmalines that was to be boxed up and shipped away. I examined a number of these crystals and found some slight imperfections in the blue caps; but the yellow band and the most part of the red was perfect.

Several months later, a jeweler sent me one of these same crystals to cut. He wanted a blue, a yellow and a red stone cut out of the crystal. The blue and yellow came out all right, made beautiful stones, but the red was too dark to be brilliant. All these stones were cut across the crystal or axis.

Later, in 1914, when we had a lease on the Himalaya Mine, I asked Vance Angel where he took that pocket out, and described the crystals. But he had forgotten. He thought it might have been in a certain place, which we worked but found no crystals of the kind I had seen on the canvas. The value of this find was far greater than even we imagined.

CHAPTER VII

HOW GEM STONES ARE MARKETED

Leo Schiller, K. C. Naylor, Ernstings, San Diego Gem Company, Jessops' Jewelers, and Burnell's were the principle local retail markets for native stones in southern California. Burnells and Schiller had no lapidary, but the others did. The San Diego Gem Company had as cutters Harvey Samuelson, Burr Porter, Fanny Wheat and Ben Boone, all excellent cutters. C. O. Johnson and Doc Wilson of the San Diego Gem Company were also good cutters. I remember one cutter at Jessops'. Gail Lewis and I worked at Ernsting's, cutting the gem material from both the Pala Chief Kunzite Mine and the Tourmaline Queen Mine. Both mines are close to Pala, California.

Burnell's had a young cutter, Miss Rose Guetelli, who was a ''natural'', when it came to selling the native gem stones. She was saleslady for Salmons and Ernstings, and later, for Frank Salmons in his Gem Mine store on Broadway, in San Diego, up to the time of Salmons' death. Then she became interested in turquoises in Nevada and has some beautiful stones.

Harvey Samuelson is still in the lapidary business in Salinas, California where he has a fine home. He and his wife, Daisy cut large quantities of jade and other gem stones. Burr Porter is still cutting in Oakland, California. Fanny Wheat still lives in San Diego, California. I have lost track of Ben Boone. Doc Wilson lives in San Gabriel, California, and heads the American Gem Company. C. O. Johnson lives in Lemon Grove, San Diego County, and is interested in the packing business. Harry Dougherty is still interested in mines. Gail Lewis lives in Mission Hills, San Diego. W. H. Trenchard last resided in Bard, Imperial County, California. These persons were the first in the gem mining and lapidary business in San Diego, Riverside and Imperial Counties in California.

W. H. (Bill) Trenchard cut for K. C. Naylor, over a period of years. K. C. Naylor and Bill passed away, the winter of 1949. I have received word that Burr Porter, of Oakland passed away between Christmas and New Year of 1952.

From 1904 to 1909, Salmons and Ernsting were mining kunzite and tourmaline in their mines at Pala. (Both have since passed away.) The quantity and quality of the tourmalines from Pala were

Footnote: C. O. Johnson, Gail Lewis and W. H. Trenchard have passed away since this was written, also Harry Doughtery, Harvey Samuelson, Fanny Wheat and Doc Wilson.

much lower than stones from Mesa Grande. No kunzite was mined at Mesa Grande other than small valueless slivers.

Quite a controversy was started over the name of the crystal "spodumene" (kunzite). Fred Sickler, of Pala claimed he was the first to discover it and that it should be called "sicklerite". Salmons claimed he told the world about it and it should be called "salmonite". From talks I have had with Salmons, I don't think he cared whose name it followed, but he liked to see Sickler boil over. Probably Sickler did find it first, but he failed to get it into the proper hands to put the stone over under his name.

The Pala Chief was a big producer of kunzite in those days, along with some black-skinned tourmalines. The Tourmaline Queen Mine produced some very fine tourmalines, from which I have cut hundreds of all sizes and shapes. I have cut many kunzites. Kunzite colors ranged from a deep violet to green, the tourmalines from rose-pink to light pink. Only a few of these large crystals would cut a round stone over two or three carats perfect. The imperfections followed a pattern that extended the full length of the crystal. Where you took your first two-carat stone out of the first slab off the crystal, you could get another in the next slab, and so on, down the length of the crystal.

One of those large crystals was sold to Mr. Hom Bing, a Chinese jeweler, for fifteen-hundred dollars! It weighed around eight pounds and was to be cut up into one-piece bracelets. When Hom Bing first asked Mr. Ernsting if he had any rough pink tourmaline he wanted to sell, Mr. Ernsting showed him some stuff I had pawed over dozens of times for cabochon and had gotten out all the good in it. We kept it in a barley sack (one-fifth full) but hadn't bothered to put it in the safe. Mr. Ernsting rolled down the top of the sack so Hom could see the contents. Hom asked, "How much you want?"

Ernsting said, "Oh, about fifteen dollars a pound."

Hom said, "I give you twenty dollar a pound and you sell me all the stone you get like that!" Ernsting almost fell over backwards.

Salmons and Ernsting sold Hom Bing a number of tourmalines after that, running up into thousands of dollars. But Hom Bing bought only the pink tourmalines. I gave him samples of other colored tourmaline to send his father in China, but for some reason they didn't go over with the Chinese. Hom Bing's father was a Chinese jeweler and gem merchant. Before he went back to China, he often came into my shop on F Street to have me grind off some opal nodules or rough pieces of opal, so he could see what they were like inside.

One day I was looking over some rough crystals and broken pieces of tourmaline for bead material, when Mr. Bing came in. He became very much interested in it and asked where it came from. I told him. It wasn't long after that he left for China, leaving Hom Bing, his son, to look after his business here. I don't know if he took any tourmalines with him, but I do know it wasn't but a short time before Hom Bing started buying tourmalines.

The Chinese were not interested in facet cutting material for the China trade; but were interested in what we classed as cabochon material, imperfect, but not too flawed or cracked, and of a pink to rose-pink color. The rose-pink was the color most preferred.

The Chinese were good people to do business with - always square and fair in their dealings with us. I remember a time when Hom Bing went to a certain man to buy some tourmaline. The man weighed the stuff and showed Hom the weight. Then he tied up the sack that contained the material and told Hom to come back in the afternoon, as he would have to see his partner about the price before he could sell. When Hom came back that afternoon, he had his own scales with him. The man said, "All right. Pay me the money and take the stuff along." Hom said he wanted to weigh it himself. He got out his scales, weighed the stuff in the sack and found it to be ten pounds short. Hom folded up his scales, walked out of the office, and from that day on would have no business dealings with that man.

It was while I was at Mesa Grande looking over a prospect called the Burro Claim, that Verd Angel told me Jose Rodrigues visited him to show some fine yellow and pink crystals of tourmaline which came out of a prospect he had near his ranch. I knew Verd recognized quality tourmaline so I decided to have a look-see. Verd couldn't get away to go with me, so I got his brother Fred to go, for he knew where Jose lived. We each got a horse, some provisions to last us two or three days, and left Angel Ranch for the old mining town of Banner, San Diego County. From there, we took off in a southeast direction several miles to Jose Rodrigues's ranch house.

We arrived just about dark. As I dismounted, Jose came out of the house, for he had been informed by his good dog that someone was coming. I asked him if he had found some tourmalines; saying I would like to look over the prospect, if he would let me. He said he'd be glad to show us his mine in the morning. We were tired, so I asked him if he could tell us a good place to bed down for the night, and said we'd turn in. He asked, "Have you had your supper?"

I told him "No," but that we had plenty of food. He said his daughter, his son-in-law and he himself had just left the table and there was plenty left for us, and wouldn't have it otherwise but we sit down and eat. I don't believe I ever had a meal go down with such satisfaction. We had tortillas and beans. The beans were cooked with beef and wheat, seasoned with "just a little chili to make them good", as the Mexicans say. While we were eating, we talked of Jose's mine and he showed us some specimens, which weren't so good, and said he would take us to his claim in the morning.

When we started to leave, Jose said his daughter had fixed a room for us to stay overnight and, as it was late, we had better sleep in the house rather than stumble around in the dark fixing our beds. So we turned in and slept on an old-fashioned feather bed. It was morning, it seemed, before we realized it. We had another swell feed (breakfast), then saddled the horses in about the soupiest fog I was ever in.

Which way we started out, I am not sure, but I think we came back a short way, the way we had come in, then turned to the right on a trail leading through high brush, high as my head, when I was on my horse, and as wet as it could be. We wound in and out of small canyons, and over ridges; ending up at the end of a small ridge. There was a hole about four feet wide, six feet long, and six feet deep. I could see that work had been done on a small pegmatite vein about two feet wide. I don't remember tracing out the strike of the vein. On the dump, which was all around the hole, there were a few small golden beryl crystals, the largest not over a quarter-inch in diameter. Some of them were of good color, but badly flawed. I did not see any tourmalines around the hole or in it.

When we got ready to leave, we asked Jose where we were and he told us if we went out "that way", we'd come to a road, to follow that road to the right until we came to another road, then turn to the left, and then we'd be on the way to the Warner Ranch. After we rode over small hills and washes, "out that way", we did come to a road, but the fog was so thick we could hardly see across it. We turned to the right at about a forty-five degree angle and followed the way until we came to the other road. This junction we recognized as "Scissors Crossing" where the old Butterfield Stage Road crosses the Julian-Borrego Road. I never went back to that place again.

In 1929, I had occasion to go into that district and as my time was limited I made only a few calculations regarding the angle at which we approached the first road. This gave me a line almost due south into the foothills of Oriflamme Mountains. We could have wandered off a straight line to the road "out that way" and still come into the road at the same angle. Anyway I didn't find the Golden Beryl Mine, with what time I had. It must be in Section One, Township 13 South, Range 4 East; or Section 6, Township 13 South, Range 5 East, S. B. M. Anyone going in there to hunt for this prospect shouldn't think he's found it if he finds old workings on the west side of Granite Mountain. This was first found by Bert Simmons.

These workings are not on the mountain itself, but are across a gulch from the mountain proper. The vein lies almost flat and contains lepidolite, amblygonite and blue-green tourmaline, very much like those we mined on Aguanga Mountain. Some have coloring resembling that of emerald. Where these workings are, the vein lies almost flat, but as you go on the strike of the vein south, it continues to straighten up and in about a half mile it stands right on edge. At this point some considerable work has been done. When I was there last, about 1929, there was quite a showing of lepidolite in the vein, also some very good colored blue-green tourmaline, but imperfect. Anyone who knew Jose Rodrigues's son-in-law, if he is still alive, could get him to show them the prospect hole.

Cutting stones from a dozen different mines and prospects, I got so I could tell from stones brought in to be cut, about where they came from. Most of the tourmalines from a certain vein have their own distinguishing color scheme, or build-up, and those from another vein have their own. The assonite and spessartite garnets looked about alike, reddish-brown to a dark red, when found in the Jacumba district, and also around Dos Cabezas. I saw some that the Dagget boys took out of their property northeast of Ramona that were taken out as individual crystals, very light color, almost a straw.

The material brought up from Mexico was either very good, or mostly glass. Mr. Ernsting came back into the shop one afternoon and said to me, "Fred, this is the way to buy this stuff!" And he laid a small sack of stone on my bench. "Looks like they will cut some good stones. Look it over when you have time."

After a short time I looked it over. If I remember right, he said he paid $5.00 for the lot. Looking over the stuff, I found about five or six spessartite garnets in the bunch. The rest were glass, or breweryites, broken pieces of beer bottles! The five or six genuine stones were of no value, being badly flawed. The man who sold them to Ernsting said he got them in Mexico. I don't believe there was a jeweler in San Diego who didn't get his share of brewerites, those days; and some had them cut, either not knowing the difference, or not wanting to.

The tourmaline from the Magee and Dougherty Mine in Riverside County near Sage, was a pink-to-deep-red in color. Most crystals had a blue-black skin of different thickness, when very thin this gem gave the pink or red a purplish color, while in some crystals the blue penetrated into the fractures cementing them together. This is the only mine I know that produced tourmaline with this blue penetrating into the fractures. This blueness, no doubt, came into the pocket after the crystal had been fractured. The Magee and Dougherty Mine was situated on a small block of vein matter where the workings just about used up the whole piece.

About this time I was given a job of inlaying the back and a portion of the face of a watch case with some gold ore from Nevada. This gold ore was of a greenish blue and came from the Bullfrog district. The watch was presented to Jack Dodge, of San Diego, who was an officer of the mining Company that had me do the job.

I have often wondered what became of that watch. The inlays were one-sixteenth of an inch thick (or less). Together with the extra gold work that held the inlay, made the watch quite heavy. I did a considerable amount of this type of work, but this job was the most difficult. Each piece was different, with a different curve. Each piece had to be picked out of a choice piece of ore. This took much slab sawing for only certain spots in the slab were tough and durable enough to use.

Rynerson children in mine car. Elizabeth and Buel in back with their father, Fred. Eugene and Myrna in front, with grandfather, Buel Bonfoey, standing beside them.

CHAPTER VIII

LOCATING GOOD GEM AND VEIN STONES

Bill Trenchard located another large pegmatite vein on the northeast side of Tulley Mountain, San Diego County. Bill and I walked the full length of the vein without seeing any concentration of minerals leading to indications of a pocket, or mineralized zone. Not far west of this vein, and in a draw, was an outcropping he had located. Here, he had taken out some good spessartites. South of these workings were some small quartz stringers that carry very good star quartz material.

There were a number of garnet outcrops in the rough country on the left side of the old Devil's Canyon road that leads from Mountain Springs to Coyote Wells, Imperial County. I haven't been to these deposits since 1912, and have forgotten where to take off from the old Devil's Canyon Road to get to them. It would be difficult for me to give instructions on how to get there. One would have to go into that country and search along the ridges between Devil's Canyon and Dos Cabezas. October and November would be good months to go. He would have to take plenty of good water with him. Besides, the country is very rough and gets very hot at times.

In April, 1954, my son Eugene and I drove out to Mountain Springs, camping just at the head of Devil's Canyon. Next morning we walked down the canyon to within a quarter of a mile of the lower end. Most of the road was washed away and only where it had been walled up did it show at all. We climbed the sides of the canyon twice, but I couldn't find the place I was seeking. The country looked somewhat different, after forty-two years.

The old Devil's Canyon Road was very narrow in places so that at times we had to use a bar to get the boulders out of our road. Bill Trenchard told me that just after he had found the marble deposit on Coyote Mountain, his group went back to San Diego to get some provisions. Going back to Coyote Mountain from San Diego, they entered Devil's Canyon in the afternoon of the third day. They didn't have an automobile. . . Only a buckboard and two horses.

Part way through the canyon they came upon a large rock that had rolled off the canyon wall. It was too big to move, so they unhitched the horses and led them to the rock. They unloaded the buckboard, took the wheels off the wagon, lifted the bed up on the rock, slid it down the other side; put the wagon together, loaded up and drove on!

The road leading out of Devil's Canyon to Coyote Wells was one long stretch of sand, lying off to the left of the present Highway 80, pointing east. This highway is a wide, paved road. Instead of leading down through Devil's Canyon it swings slightly to the right after leaving Mountain Springs and runs down through Inkopah Gorge.

One evening about ten-thirty, I went aboard the Owl Train that left San Diego each morning at two A. M. for Los Angeles. I had dressed about six-thirty and gone into the smoking car and was sitting on the east side of the car. The sun was appearing over the hills, when a man sat down beside me. Fixing his tie and looking past me to the hills, he asked if I had been in Southern California long. I told him I had come to California in 1885.

He said, "Well, you ought to know if any gem stones have ever been found in those hills."

I told him I didn't think so. I hadn't heard of any being found there. I asked him if he was interested in gem stones and he said, "Oh, yes. I collect all kinds of minerals and specimens."

I asked him his name and he said, "Wilke, of Palo Alto, California." For a moment or two I could hardly believe my ears.

"This is quite a coincidence." I said. "My name is Fred Rynerson of San Diego.

He was as much surprised to see me as I was to see him. I had for two or three years sold to Mr. Wilke a good many crystals of tourmaline and other specimens, but had never met him; all business being carried on by mail or express.

During our conversation, he told me he had just broken with his mine partner who had bought him out. Then he told me how it happened.

Both had been working on the vein for several days when they struck a small pocket of kunzite. This kunzite was of poor quality but the find gave their morale a good boost. The next morning, Wilke said, his partner got up sulky and in bad humor.

"Now I've always supped my tea," Mr. Wilke said, "and had done so all the time we've been in camp. This morning, when we sat down to breakfast, I led off with kunzite as my topic of conversation, sipping my tea at intervals. My partner had not said much for the last ten minutes, when he jumped to his feet and said he couldn't eat his breakfast and listen to me sip my tea!"

Wilke told him, "I've supped my tea for the past thirty years; and I don't intend to stop now!"

After more talk, Wilke's partner asked him what he wanted for his interest in the claim. Wilke named his price and his partner wrote him out a check for the amount. Wilke packed up at once and drove to Oceanside, where he happened to catch the train I was on.

Wilke wrote me afterwards that his partner worked two weeks more, after he himself had left, but found nothing, so quit. These workings were on the east side of the Rincon Indian Reservation, San Diego County, and to the southeast of the John Mac Beryl Mine.

The gem belt of San Diego County has been moved around a good deal, both up and down. This is more evident in the pegmatites at Pala, than in any other place along the gem belt. All districts along the gem belt have suffered more or less. This disturbance leaves the veins crushed or broken and, with erosion, has shifted pieces of vein matter all over. Some pieces of veins have been productive to the extent that they contained a pocket of gem material. Some pieces have broken off right through a pocket zone; dumping the contents out. I have seen many such places, but only once have I had the experience and thrill of finding the contents of one of these broken pockets.

The old John Mac Mine at Rincon, San Diego County, produced some very fine beryls. Some fairly good aquamarines were taken out, but most of them were light in color. Mr. Mac brought some into the shop to show me, or to sell, but he never wanted any of them cut. I have cut a number of his crystals for those to whom he did sell.

On one of Mr. Ernest Schernikow's visits to San Diego, we drove out to see Mr. Mac's mine. (This was several years after he had quit work on the property.) We had the good fortune to meet a Mr. Calac who worked for Mr. Mac when he opened up the property and had worked with him during the extent of his time there. He showed us the workings, which were twenty-five feet wide by fifty feet long. Three-fourths of the top of the vein had been off down to below the pay streak leaving the foot wall of the vein in place. Mr. Calac showed us the places where they had taken out the beryls. Some of these pockets were ten or twelve inches across, while others were much smaller. Mr. Calac said Mr. Mac told him he had sold $10,000 worth of gems from this mine. I told Mr. Calac if I had taken that much out of so small a place, I certainly would have done more work on the vein.

The day before Christmas, 1909, I received a telephone call from Vance Angel of Mesa Grande. He said he was going out to Fish Creek Mountain on the desert and wanted me to go with him. I said, "Certainly," for I wanted to look at some land in Borrego Valley, if we decided to come back that way.

I left San Diego the twenty-sixth of December on the Cuyamaca train for Fosters (end of the line), took the stage to Ramona,

Longest stretch left of the old Devil's Canyon Road, 1954.

Bill Trenchard milking goat!

Beulah Rynerson when young.

changed to another stage for Mesa Grande where I met Vance at the store. We purchased provisions for a two weeks' trip. Then we drove over to the Angel Ranch where we stayed the night.

We rented two saddle horses and three pack burros. One burro hadn't had a pack on him for several years. When we threw the saddle on him, we knew there was trouble ahead. We put all the canned goods and heavy stuff, the pick and shovel, two five-gallon cans of water, some grain for the horses on him, then put a big canvas over the whole pack and cinched it down good.

The other two burros were tame, so we packed two ten-gallon cases on each, and blankets, cooking utensils, and provisions.

The road leading away from the Angel House, where we packed, was straight for some hundred yards, then it made a left turn, quite sharp. The burro we expected trouble from, we called "Naylor", because he had been used for carrying water up to the Naylor, or San Diego Mine.

Old Naylor looked pretty mad when we tried to lead him, but no go; so we let him loose and drove him out on the road. Then he took off, but that load was heavy. When he came to the sharp turn in the road, though he tried to make it, the load wouldn't! It went straight on, pulling him with it, down off the road into a gully. We were probably a hundred feet back of him when he went over the bank. When we came in sight of him he was lying on his back up against a scrub oak and couldn't get up. We had a good laugh, and Vance got a rope on him. Then, taking off most of the load, we managed to get him on his feet. I don't know how many times he rolled over, going down that bank; but it surely took all the fight out of him; and we had little trouble packing him, after that.

On our way again, everything went fine for a mile or so. Then, while we were going along a trail that led by the side of a mountain, an old Indian woman with a stack of wood on her head came out onto a big rock fifty feet ahead and above us, letting out a squealing "EE-e-e!" of alarm. Then she turned back the way she came. Vance was in the lead and I brought up the rear, with the three burros between us. Old Naylor was third in line, next to me. When the old woman let out that squeal, old Naylor made a right-about face and almost lost his balance. He no doubt thought of what happened to him several hours before. But, with a little persuasion, I got him turned around and on the way again.

Our course now lay across the north side of the Mesa Grande Indian Reservation to the road leading down the Mesa Grande grade, and then to the southwest side of what is now "Lake Henshaw". We did not closely follow the road, but took off in a northeasterly direction; coming upon the road past the old Butterfield Stage Station, below the old Warner ranch house, and down the grade to the San Felipe Valley.

Vance pulled off the road just before we got to the Banner-Borrego Route. We made camp in some willows near a small hill. Here we met a man by the name of Manuel Dyche. He had supper with us and then left for Mesa Grande where he lived.

It was at this first night's camp, that we discovered we had lost our can of lard. When old Naylor piled up in the gully, it must have flown out of the pack into the brush and we failed to notice it. This loss made it hard on the bacon, for we had to use bacon grease in place of lard when we made bread.

Next morning we got going about seven o'clock. Old Naylor never ate a bite all night, just took on a little water. After leaving this camp, we followed the old Butterfield Stage Route to the old Vallecitos stage station. Before we arrived there at the upper end of the valley, the course led through a narrow wash for some distance. This wash wasn't more than fifteen feet wide. When we were half way through it, the horses showed uneasiness, but the burros became quite panic-stricken for a moment. Since Vance was in the lead and I in the rear, they could hardly get away from us in that narrow place. Vance thought it probably was a lion close by, or possibly one had crossed the road at that point before we arrived there.

The new road into the valley is above and to the right parallelling the old road in the wash. One can look down into the wash from the new road at this point. It is now called "Box Canyon."

In December, 1909, the old Vallecitos stage station, where we camped that night, was in bad shape. One corner of the adobe had fallen out and the whole structure was a ruin. However, the large ridge-pole timber that ran the length of the building was still in place. So was most of the roof. The pole rafters and sheeting of willow poles were tied in place with rawhide strips, or thongs. Then on top of these were laid lengthwise with the roof, smaller sticks, also tied with rawhide. On top of all these was a layer of mud or clay which had originally formed the surface of the roof.

That night was cold, so we got into our blankets early. Old Naylor was still mad and wouldn't eat. Up to that time we hadn't met anyone on the road, coming or going, and the road showed no recent travel.

In the morning we decided to do a little prospecting on the southeast side of Big Piñon Mountain. We rode the horses part way and then continued on foot. Vance had a knack of picking old Indian trails. After a short while, he found one. We followed it for a mile or so, when it became very plain and showed much travel by mountain sheep. One of these sheep tracks was the size of a three-months-old calf. We had a shepherd dog with us by the name of "Muzzy". He had his nose in the air, sniffing all the while we were climbing the trail. In a quarter of a mile we came to a little flat of about two or three acres, where we could look across to another ridge higher up. While we were looking around, we heard some small rocks rolling in the direction of the ridge ahead of us and there, standing in the trail about two-hundred yards beyond us, were five mountain sheep. The old fellow in the lead was the largest mountain sheep I have ever seen. He had an enormous head of horns. Sighting us, the sheep took off at once and disappeared into a deep canyon about two-hundred yards to our right.

Along the trail I noticed quite a number of pieces of broken pottery. Some places, the pieces were in bunches, as if a whole pot had been dropped and broken. No doubt this trail had been used by the Indians during the piñon nut season. The piñon trees grow higher up on the mountain.

We did not find anything in the line of metallic minerals or gem stones on that trip up and down the mountain. The going back down was tiresome and we were hungry for we had only two apples apiece, for lunch.

Next morning we packed up and lit out for Carizzo Springs where, Vance said, were two springs, one alkali and the other pure water. We arrived there about four P. M. and made camp just below the old Butterfield Stage station ruin. There was a lot of good feed here for the animals. After we had staked out the burros and horses, Vance took the canteens and walked up the creek a ways to fill them. While we were cooking supper, another party drove in with a light spring wagon which was made to sleep in. The driver had come in from the Imperial side and camped about two-hundred feet south of us. We found later he had been camping there several days before we showed up and he had another man with him who came in later. They had been locating oil claims over the clay hills around Carizzo Springs.

That evening an Indian with a bad foot rode into our camp. He said his horse had thrown him. I think he knew Vance, for when he saw him, he turned his horse towards our camp. He had passed up the oil locators' camp below us. We had just finished our supper of corned beef and bread, and, of course, coffee made with the water from the good spring. That coffee going down my throat gave me the sensation of swallowing lubricating oil! The Indian got down from his horse and hobbled over to our fire. His ankle and foot were badly swollen. Vance and I had brought along a bottle of medicine just in case of "bug bite", so when Vance was pouring the Indian some coffee, I told him to put in the coffee some of the medicine out of our bottle, to cut the lubricating sensation.

When the Indian had finished his coffee, he said he wanted to get home as soon as possible. He said he lived on the Manzanita Reservation in the southern part of the Laguna Mountains. His horse was a little mustang with plenty of energy. He had ridden in from Imperial Valley and the horse was wet with sweat. When he left us, the horse started off like the wind. I saw the Indian's injured foot go up and over the horse's back and him flat on the horse's side. In another seventy-five feet he was on top and disappeared in the dusk. We didn't envy that fellow his ride home, which was about twenty miles, most of it mountain trail. He was a man about twenty-five years old. The wind was cold off the Lagunas and we looked for a rain. We warmed up a little around our fire and then rolled up for the night.

Next day, an old prospector and his burro came plodding in and camped about seventy-five feet north of us, alongside a little clay hill. He had a small square tent about six by six feet, with no side walls. After setting up his tent, he came down to visit us. He proved to be one of the roving kind. In every place in the West, he had made a stake or two in the past forty years. He was now on the trail of a black-heavy rock, which he was sure he could find. I asked him what it was called, and he said, "Wolf-Ram-Ite. They git tungsten out of it."

I asked him if he had ever seen any scheelite. He said no. I told him it was a tungsten ore, too, and described it to him. He was glad to know about the scheelite and he, like others, said, "I've seen that stuff somewhere." This always boosts their morale, whether they have seen it or not.

The last day of 1909, we planned to go over on the east end of Fish Creek Mountain and re-locate Vance's copper claim; also, to do a little prospecting. After breakfast we packed a lunch, took a good drink of our oily coffee, and lit out for the copper claim.

We rode up to the foot of the mountain and made the rest of the way on foot. The part of the vein we visited lies almost on top of the ridge and at that time, contained some good looking copper ore. I brought home some small, beautiful specimens of copper ore from this vein. There's a wonderful view from the southeast tip of Fish Creek Mountain. You can see up into the Borrego Valley, north to the Little San Bernardino Mountains, east to beyond the Chocolates, across Imperial Valley to Picacho Peak on the Colorado River, south into the Coyote Wells country and on down into Mexico. This, of course, is on a clear day.

From the looks of the mountains west of us, rain wasn't far away. Big heavy clouds were blowing up over the Lagunas, so we wasted little time in getting back to camp. When we arrived, the oil man and the prospector were still there. We had a twelve-by-twelve-foot canvas which we threw over our provisions and our bed. We also piled up some dry wood for a fire in the morning. Since we were going to leave for home in the morning on our return trip, we would have to make two dry camps before we arrived at Palm Creek at the head of Borrego Valley. Hence we filled our six honey cans with water "from the good spring". We also filled the two canteens.

The oil man, the prospector and Vance and I sat a long time around the fire that evening. Our subject of conversation was, as usual, oil, minerals, and some new strikes the old prospector said were being made up in Nevada and which he figured he would investigate in the spring.

There's one thing a foot-loose prospector cannot resist, and that is hot-footing it to a new strike. He will sit alone, staring into his camp fire, and build up a picture of a rich vein that the other fellow never found. A night or two of meditation on the subject - if he has a bottle it will shorten up the time a lot - and then he's off in a cloud of dust!

This brings to mind a story I heard many years ago about a newspaper man called "Print", who had lived and printed a small newspaper in a mining camp. After a few years the mines played out and shut down. Print stayed on, hoping the mines would open up again. He wasn't very well, so he "tied up" with a couple of burros and did a little prospecting. After a short time, the Grim Reaper took him in. Some old pals of his (how they found out wasn't told me) said he went to Heaven along with his two burros and printing outfit.

When he came to the Heavenly Gate, old St. Peter asked his name and occupation. He said his name was Print and he was a newspaper man, had printed the "Golden Nugget" in a mining camp, had always printed the truth and nothing but the truth, covering the mining news; and if he, St. Peter, would permit him, he would like to set up his outfit and print the "Heavenly News". St. Peter told Print to come right in, for he needed a man of his ability to soothe the restless spirits of the prospectors who had arrived before him. Print set up his presses, then went out among the old prospectors, sat around their camp fires and talked of the good old days.

It wasn't long before St. Peter called up old Print and told him he wanted to talk to him in private. When he saw Print, he said, "You've got to help me. These prospectors are digging up the Golden Streets and under-mining the Golden Temples and it's got to stop or the whole place will be wrecked!"

Print said, "Don't worry, St. Peter! I'll stop that over-night."

That evening the Heavenly News came out with big headlines, "Big Strike In Hell". Next morning, St. Peter called up Print, saying hundreds of prospectors were leaving with their burros and packs and he couldn't stop them. Print said, "Don't worry. They'll be back soon."

Days and weeks went by and they hadn't shown up. So one morning, St. Peter was surprised to see, coming toward the gate, old Print and his two burros loaded down with the printing outfit. St. Peter said, "What's the matter? You leaving too?"

Print said, "Well, Pete, I just got to thinking. There might be something to that story after all!"

The oil man had gone to bed and the old prospector had crawled into his tent. The night was cold and disagreeable when we turned in under our canvas. This cover was heavy, but it kept us dry, also anything we kept under it. I had gone to sleep with my head sticking out from under the canvas and my hat over the side of my head, so I didn't feel the light rain that fell during the night. I didn't have long to wait. I unconsciously turned over on my back and was rudely awakened with a bucket full of water in my face and down my neck from off the canvas.

The thought came then to catch some of this water and refill the cans that now contained the water from the "good" spring. I had awakened Vance in my struggles and, as it was still raining, I suggested we catch some of this rain water and fill the cans. After getting into our pants and lighting the lantern, we propped up the sides of the canvas. It wasn't long before we got our first five gallons of rain water. After all containers were filled, we crawled back under the canvas; making sure no water would collect on top of us again.

We would have left Carrizo Springs for Borrego that day if it hadn't been for the oil man. He came over and said he was throwing a New Year's dinner and invited us to share it with him. He also asked me to pass the invitation along to the old prospector. Anyone who has camped in these mud hills when it rains, knows how much of that clay he can carry on his shoes. That morning was perfect for carrying the limit. I walked up to the old man's tent and called to him, telling him he was invited to the New

Year's dinner down at the oil camp. He came back with, "No thanks! I don't go foolin' around, days like these. I just stay in here til she clears up again." He did; and I don't remember seeing him again. The mud had washed down around his tent til only about a fourth of it was visible above the mud. I had heard before of these old fellows sleeping out a storm.

We had a good feed of meat, beans, and Dutch oven bread and spent the rest of the day talking gem stones, oil, and mining. As we were far off the gem belt, most of the conversation centered around oil. Vance had found some float which resembled a black pitch and would burn without leaving any residue. This float was found near Carrizo. Bill Trenchard told me later that he had found a small stringer of it on the north side of the Coyote Mountain not far from Carrizo Creek. It might be possible this float came from what Bill discovered.

This oil claim locator came from Bakersfield, California. During our conversation I found out he had been around my old haunts around Maricopa, Midway and McKittrick, ten years before. I don't think he ever drilled a well out there, but in 1912 Bill Trenchard and I were driving from Coyote Mountain to Carrizo Springs when we saw a drilling rig in operation about three miles south of Carrizo Springs. It was probably him.

We got through the next night without a ducking, had our breakfast, packed up and were on our way by eight A.M. We followed Carrizo Creek almost the whole way down to the point of Fish Creek Mountain, except for short trips off our course to look over the ground.

We camped on the east side of the point that night. Old Naylor was still mad, but had decided that to eat a little wasn't a bad idea. This point of the mountain at one time extended out into an inland sea which was very shallow. Next morning we traveled northwest, along the northeast side of the range. For several miles the old water, or sea level line, was marked by barnacles which had attached themselves to the rocks. This line gradually disappeared into the ground level as we traveled westerly.

About a mile from the camp, at the point of Fish Creek Mountain, and out on the flat away from the mountain, we came across an old Indian storage basket built in an ocotillo. Several of the limbs had been drawn together and left apart at equal distances. Strips of bark, wood, and long grass were woven in and around the ocotillo limbs, making a basket about two feet wide at the top, a foot wide at the bottom and about three feet high. It looked to be very old. What the Indians stored in it out on that flat is hard to guess, as the mesquite shrubs were very small and scattered.

It is possible there were larger trees there at one time that produced a lot of beans.

At another place we crossed over a lot of broken pottery scattered over the ground, covering an area of fifty by a hundred feet. It could have been an Indian camp that had been attacked by raiders and the pots broken.

We did not always stay close to the mountain, but swung out away from it at times to avoid the deep washes, or to look over the land. We made camp that night a little west of a place where the gypsum mine is now, in a field of cane cactus. We gave the horses and burros the last of the water that evening, leaving only two gallons or less in the canteens for us. It was cold so we hit the blankets early.

Next morning it was still storming in the mountains at the head of Palm Creek. The wind was cold, coming from that direction, for the mountains were white with snow. We were heading for a "tank" about a mile southeast of the Narrows. By the time we got there, both horses and burros were thirsty. Every wash we came to, the burros would drag their noses along in the sand. They no doubt could smell the water below the surface.

When we came to the vicinity of the tank, hundreds of doves, crows and buzzards sat perched on the rocks along the hillside close by. The tank was situated in a small gulch. We could not get the animals up to it, although they tried. Vance climbed up, broke the ice that covered the exposed water, and brought some down in his hat for the animals. He made several trips until they had enough for the trip to Palm Creek where the Mesa Grande boys, who were in the cattle business, brought their cattle during the winter months to feed on the desert grasses. They had built a small eight-by-ten-foot corrugated iron building to keep grain for their horses, and also to sleep in during bad weather.

On our trip, Vance had taken his 30-30 Savage rifle and I had taken my shot-gun. The last stretch from the tank to Palm Creek, Muzzy, the dog ran his feet raw, chasing jack rabbits. After we got unpacked, I told Vance I would go out and get Muzzy a jack for his supper. I was gone only about ten minutes when I jumped one and got him. Muzzy had been lying by the side of the house when I returned. I held up the jack to him and he could hardly walk over to me, but turned and lay down again. I threw the jack down on the ground not four feet from his nose and stepped into the shed to put the gun away. I heard Muzzy growl and I quickly looked outside and saw a coyote, with my jack, disappear over a bank into the wash not twenty feet away. I grabbed the gun and ran to the bank, but he had disappeared. Poor old Muzzy was so sore-footed he didn't think it worth the effort. The coyote must have seen me shoot the jack rabbit and followed me to the shed!

The boys there before us had built a small corral of barbed wire around the place where they did their cooking, to keep out the cattle. It took some fifteen posts. On top of each post they had hung four coyote scalps. Vance said this was the work of Arthur Watkins and his partner probably, as it was his turn to be down there and he had left the same day we arrived.

That afternoon, thirty minutes after we arrived, a man with six burros came in and camped a hundred feet east of us. He took the packs off those burros, built a fire, cooked his bread in front of the fire in a frying pan, ate his supper, cleaned things up and finally came over for a visit before we had finished our supper. That bird sure had a system!

He told us he was living with a man by the name of Evans, up in the mouth of Coyote Creek. He had just come down from Warner's Hot Springs with a load of provisions and announced that a blizzard was blowing up on the mountains. For a while he thought he couldn't make it down the trail, which at that time led through Montezuma Valley, over the desert side of the mountains into Borrego Valley. He warned us about trying to go up that way before the weather cleared and the deep snow had settled. We had intended going back that very way, but decided to stay a day or two longer at the camp.

Vance and Old Burro Naylor leaving camp off Fish Creek Mt.

CHAPTER IX

PERSONALITIES MET ON WAY HOME (SAN DIEGO)

In 1912. Mrs. Estella Westover Fewell and her husband, Thomas O. Fewell, homesteaded a claim in the Borrego Valley, hoping to make a living and prove up on their claim. She was the first woman to live there, a real pioneer! There were times when one or both had to be away for several days. Estella tells of once she was there alone for three weeks, and one moonlight night some wild burros came into the corral to drink. She slipped around on the outside and closed the gate. Next morning she had five burros in the corral. She picked out a young one, lassoed it, and let the rest go. She kept the young burro until it was gentle enough to pet, then she tied him to an old burro Fred Clark had left and broke him well enough to drive him up the trail to Warner's Hot Springs.

Another time, Estella says, she drove a team of horses and hay wagon to Westmoreland to get some bailed hay. On her way back to Borrego she had to make a one-night camp. Stopping at the usual camping place, she unhitched the horses, gave them some hay, then made her bed on top of the load of bailed hay. She had a feeling that someone was following her, so she laid her shot-gun alongside of her bed. Shortly after darkness she heard a light buggy and two horses stop near her wagon and someone get out, then she heard him walk over to the front end of her wagon and start climbing up to the top of the hay. When his head appeared above the edge of the bailed hay the invader found himself looking into the business end of that shot-gun and almost fell off the wagon! Getting back onto the ground again, he ran over to his buggy and lit out the way he had come.

The Fewells sold their Homestead claim in 1920 to a Mr. Myers for less than five hundred dollars after all debts were paid. Estella feels that the hours she spent on the desert were wasted, but I don't think so. She helped start a settlement in the Valley, and really pioneered it out there. There was no air conditioning, electricity or gas. Many things they needed she packed on a pack horse or burro from Warner's Hot Springs down through Montezuma over the trail off the mountain into Borrego Valley.

It took a lot of patience and will-power to overcome the hardships of the pioneer and stay in that country. We have had Estella with us on several trips into the mountains and on the desert, and we couldn't have had a better companion.

One morning I wanted to look over this land, so I took the shot-gun and started walking in a northeast direction. Some of the land

Mrs. Estella (Westover) Fewell (now Dayley) and son Orland.

Camp on Golden State Marble Company's Creole Claim, Coyote Mountain. Left to right, Mrs. W. H. Trenchard, Fred Rynerson, Ethel Trenchard, and Bill Trenchard's nephew Hermie. See also p. 97, and Chapter XII.

was very good and some had sand covering a better soil underneath. As a whole it wasn't a bad deal for some young man and wife to homestead. They couldn't very well have children, for those days it was a long way to a school or doctor. Also they had to face fiercely hot summers and icy winter winds. It wouldn't be so bad in winter, but the summers would be a test of anyone's pioneer spirit.

I was quite a way out on the flat and had turned to go back to camp when I ran into a terrible stench that pervaded the air. Thinking it might be a dead cow and I might get a shot at a coyote, I followed up-wind. On rounding a large mesquite bush, I came upon a pile of dead coyotes. The heap was about six feet long and almost that wide, and some three feet high. All the coyotes had been scalped, as near as I could see. Some of the furs were pretty; being yellow, white and black. Some were plain gray color. All were in prime condition when killed. This is where my friend Watkins got the scalps that were on the posts around the corral. He had killed a coyote and another had come to that one's funeral, and so on, until Watkins had built up that pile!

The next day my friend Vance and I walked up the Palm Creek Canyon. Snow was two hundred feet above the bottom of the canyon, and it was cold! Ice covered the rocks where the water from the creek had sprayed over them. We found no rocks of value or indications of gem stones worth carrying out, on either side of the creek.

That evening it looked like the weather was clearing. It turned very cold. Sleeping in that tin can of a house was like sleeping in a refrigerator. In the morning we got up early and packed for our last lap of the trip, hoping to make it through to Mesa Grande that day.

We hadn't gone far when we ran into snow. We had left the camp where the temperature was freezing and now that we were in the snow, the air seemed quite warm. Vance thought it best that we put a rope on old Naylor to lead him up the trail, as he might take a notion to go down-hill if the going got hard. To our surprise, he followed along like a good burro.

We made it up the long trail to the Montezuma Valley by noon. We were met by Hector Angel on horse-back. He was a brother of Vance's and was on his way down to Borrego to do his turn looking after cattle.

The snow in the eastern end of the valley was two feet deep in some places, while in others it was packed hard and frozen. When we got over to the Warner Ranch, the snow was four or five inches deep and we saw quite a number of dead cattle, probably too weak to live through the storm.

I was surprised when I came to a little house just off the road in the Montezuma Valley and saw, sitting on the porch, Mrs. Mit Dameron whom I had known at Oak Grove when I worked the Naylor Mine seven years before. As we hadn't made any lunch before leaving camp that morning, and I was hungry, I thought of the grand biscuits Mrs. Dameron made. I asked her if she would sell me some of those biscuits I remembered her making. She said she would look and see what she had. She came back with six big brown ones and all she asked was twenty-five cents. Three of them were like eating a whole loaf of bread - and Vance and I made short work of them.

We arrived at the Angel Ranch in Mesa Grande late that afternoon, took the packs off the burros, had a shave and cleaned up. I got all my things together so I could get away on the stage in the morning.

I left Mesa Grande on January 7th, arriving in San Diego about three that afternoon. I found considerable work waiting for me, including a lot of repair work. One fishing enthusiast wanted a pink tourmaline fishing pole tip made. He said he thought it would bring him luck. I also slabbed up quite a bit of gold ore and shaped some for mounting, including some just polished specimens.

An old California Mexican came to my home one day, saying he had been told to see me about sawing some gold ore. He was a well-dressed, well-preserved man of seventy or more, and walked with a cane. I asked him what he wanted sawed. He took from a cardboard box a chunk of gold ore almost as large as my fist. It was the richest piece of ore of its size I had seen in a long time.

He then handed me his cane and described the shape and size he wanted inlaid in the head. For my work, he said, he would give me what was left of the ore. I told him I did not do any mounting, but would cut and polish the piece as large as he wanted it. He said that would be all right.

The head of the cane was about two and a half inches across and looked like rosewood. It had a round silver disk about one and three-quarter inches in diameter set in the top. I told him I could remove the disk and set the ore in its place. He said that was what he wanted, and if I didn't mind, he would like to watch me cut it. I told him to come the next day after lunch.

I still had my cutting plant set up at my home. When he showed up that afternoon, I already had the first slab almost off. The ore was so rich I didn't want to grind any more of it off than I could help, so I cut another slab off for the cane. The finished stone, ready to set in the cane, was about a quarter-inch thick in the center and about three-thirty-seconds of an inch thick on the outer edge, conforming to the low curve of the top of the cane.

I made the old man comfortable in a chair and, while I worked on the stone, he told me he got the ore out of the old Comstock Mine in Nevada, years ago. He said that piece wasn't the richest he had seen in that mine. His words: "I was working in a shaft about seventy-five feet deep and was working out a corner, when my pick broke through a hard shell into what I thought was a hole. But my pick seemed to be sticking in some soft metal. Getting the pick out, I looked into the hole and saw I had driven the pick into solid gold! I picked all around this crusty ball and then a solid nugget of gold, almost round and about three inches in diameter, dropped out!"

He continued, "I kept that ball of gold in the shaft with me until almost quitting time, trying to think of some way of getting it out for myself. Just before I was to go off shift, I shovelled it into the bucket and that was the last I saw or heard of it." My shift boss and I lived in the same house and in the morning I told him about it. He said, 'Why didn't you call me? I could have taken that out of there!' "

Man! What a mine!

I have sold and given away sets and small slabs off the piece he gave me, and still have a good specimen left.

FIRST SLACK-UP IN THE GEM BUSINESS

The year 1910 showed the first slack-up in the lapidary business and also in the marketing of rough gem stones. Although the Chinese trade was good, they did not want our gem material or facet cutting stuff. I cut a number of Chinese bracelets which were cut in quarter-circles and mounted together in twenty-two carat gold, as the Chinese did not use fourteen or eighteen carat gold. I also cut some buttons, three-eighths-inch to one-half inch across the top, with a groove on the under side to hold the gold mounting, which in turn had a hole parallel with the top for securing the button to the garment.

BORREGO GOLD

I was downtown delivering the last of the rush work and was on my way home when I met Bert Simmons. He looked like he had just blown in from the hills, and I told him so.

"Yes," he said, "I have been prospecting around Borrego and found some nice colors around on the northeast side of the Narrows."

He took from his pocket a small bottle with about a half

Paul Valle and gold washer.

Otay Oil Well.

teaspoon full of nice sized gold in it. The largest piece was about one thirty-second of an inch across. One of two oblong four-sided pieces three-sixteenths inches long and of a gray color, were also in with the gold. Bert said they were probably iron or platinum. He hadn't tested them yet.

He told me there was plenty of ground out there that could be located, and it might turn into something worth while. This was about late April and as I had put in several months cutting, I was about ready to grab any excuse to go out into the hills or desert.

Next day I happened to meet Paul Valle on the street, and told him about what Bert had told me. He said, "Let's go!"

Paul was a swell fellow to be out with and knew how to take care of himself in most any kind of country. It was the next day or the day after, that we left for Warner's Hot Springs. We inquired there for a man by name of Fewell, who had some burros. I had known Fewell when he was a watchman on the Himalaya Mine property. We found where he lived and arranged to get one of his burros. We bought our provisions at the Hot Springs store, rolled up in Fewell's barn for the night, and next morning we lit out afoot, for Borrego Valley. We went out through Montezuma Valley and down the trail into Borrego. When we were descending into the valley, we spotted the place about where we wanted to go. So when we came to the valley floor, it wasn't long before we were there.

That had been a long hike for one day and after we ate some supper, we rolled up in our blankets in a little wash, the only level place on the cactus-studded hills.

The night was cold and I remember during the early morning hours, both of us were awake, but each was waiting for the other to break out of the blankets to start the fire! I don't remember who started the fire that morning, but during breakfast our subject of conversation brought out the fact that each had been hoping the other would get up first. I do know that we collected no little number of cactus spines in our blankets that night. That little wash was full of them.

We prospected the washes and gullies and decided to build a good dry washer and come back and give it a trial. The third day we traveled back the way we had come, and the next day arrived in San Diego.

Dividing my work between gem cutting and building the washer, we at last got the washer finished and had it shipped to the little town of Julian. Here, we hired old John McCain, who had a cabin and some land in Borrego, to haul us and equipment out to our location north of the Narrows.

It was afternoon before John got away from Julian, and we camped the first night near Old Santinac's shack. Here, the road led up the hill to the right, and at right angles to the Santinac Canyon, then dropped into the Grapevine Wash just above Yaqui Well. The new, paved road, No. 78, leads on down Santinac Canyon and cuts into the old road west of Yaqui Wells. Last time I was through there in 1952, I could see no trace of the old road on the Yaqui Wells side.

Just before we dropped into the Grapevine, old John pointed off to the right and said, "I was riding along here one time and I heard a deep rumbling sound. Off to my right, there was a puff of dust, then a streak of dust came out of the ground, running off to the southeast." Not doubting old John too much, I said nothing about it, but two years later I did see something very much like the same thing, and probably caused by a small local earthquake.

That afternoon, John landed our stuff about where we wanted to test the ground and then drove on over to his shack at Borrego Springs; promising us he would bring us a barrel of water the next day. Which he did.

We set up the tent, made a pretty good camp, then went after the gold. We hadn't done much shoveling before we caught some of the gray metallic pieces I had seen in Bert Simmons' bottle - and a little later a large piece that proved to be the head of a horse shoe nail made of gray Swedish iron!

I don't remember that we got any gold. If we did, it was only a color or two. After a few days, I told Paul I didn't think it worth my time to stay any longer. He agreed, but thought he would stay till the grub ran out and, in the meantime, do some prospecting in other places.

One morning, while we were eating breakfast in the tent, we distinctly heard a wagon moving along in sand and gravel, and voices talking. As we had our tent pitched on a little ridge between washes, we thought at first someone was driving up the wash toward us, so we stepped outside the tent. Once outside, everything was quiet as could be. There was no air moving and not a sound. As we heard the voices coming from Borrego Springs, we looked in that direction. It was several miles to the springs and we could see practically every foot of the way. We were surprised to find nothing that looked like a wagon or people. The sounds we heard from the tent never lasted more than thirty seconds. We never solved the mystery. It is possible that the absolutely still air carried the sounds for long distances.

In my small suitcase, (twenty inches long, and a foot high), I put what few things I had with me and started back afoot the next morning. I didn't go by way of the road through the Narrows, but cut across southwest to the road in the Grapevine wash. This took me over some rough country and a very high ridge. I had gone only a short distance, when I came to a deep canyon with sides almost straight up and down. I had to walk along the edge for some distance before I found a way down into the wash. When on the bottom I had to walk a hundred yards up the wash before I found a place to climb out. When I got to the top of the canyon rim, I set the suitcase down and took my bearings again.

In climbing out of that wash, I had become pretty hot and sweaty. Standing there, wiping the sweat off my face, I looked down at the little suitcase and then at the surrounding country and burst out laughing. It could have happened to someone in the city on a hot day, but out in that desolate country I could have been taken for someone "a little off the beam"!

When I came to the top of the ridge, I could look down on the road south of Yaqui Well. I heard voices calling to horses, and the noise of a wagon, but, for the life of me, I couldn't locate anyone - and I could see the road a long way up and down the wash.

I rested a while on the ridge and then started down the ridge along the mountain sheep trail that led almost to the bottom. In places it was so steep I slid twenty or thirty feet. I walked on up the wash, past Yaqui Wells to where the road left the wash and led over the hills to Santinac's cabin. When I arrived at about the point John said he saw that dust fly up, I stopped and had my lunch, which consisted of one small can of roast beef and some crackers. That can of beef was like a cake of ice for the weather had grown colder as I drew nearer the mountains, although the temperature hadn't been very high that morning.

I walked into the little mining town of Banner about four o'clock that afternoon. Dr. Valle had once told me if I ever wanted to stay the night in Banner, to go to his friend's place there, the only hotel or lodging house in town. I walked up to the door and knocked, but no one answered. Walking around to the rear of the house, I found Mr. Alcot getting in some wood. I told him who I was, that I had walked about eighteen miles, that I would like to stay the night, also get my supper and breakfast.

He told me he was sorry, but his wife was sick in bed and he couldn't take anyone in. I asked him if he knew of a place I could stay, or get something to eat, for I had come a long distance and was pretty tired. Besides, the next five miles, all up-hill to the town of Julian, was more than I wanted to take on that evening, if there was a way out.

"I couldn't tell you where to go." he said.

I was beginning to think I would have to keep walking, to keep warm, and do without nourishment too. Believe me, I was hungry and tired. But just as I started to walk away, Alcot said, "I got a store room over there with some hay and sacks. There's a pile of apples in one corner. If that'll tide you over till morning, you're welcome."

As I started to go over and take a look at the room, I realized I was going to stay there. The few minutes I had been standing talking, my legs had stiffened so badly I could hardly walk. I found the room clean, with plenty of hay and sacks, and a world of big red apples. I picked up three of them and put them under my coat next to my heavy shirt so they would warm up a little. They had the feel of having been in a deep freeze. I made myself a comfortable bed in the hay on some sacks and, with several sacks over me, I figured I wasn't doing so badly. I finished off the three apples and it wasn't long before I blacked out till morning.

As I had slept warm that night, I got up early and found I was neither stiff nor sore. I started up the grade to Julian with a couple of apples in my pocket. When I got two-thirds of the way up the grade, I met Bob Strict and his brother, Julian. I knew Bob when he was working in the gem mines at Mesa Grande.

I had two more miles to walk before getting into Julian, and hoped to catch the morning stage down to Fosters, but I missed it. Knowing I would have to stay that day and night some place along the line, I decided to stay in Julian where I put up at Mrs. McCain's Hotel. Next morning I caught the stage for Fosters and was back in San Diego that afternoon. During my walk from Borrego to Julian, I didn't meet a single vehicle, coming or going.

Shortly after returning to San Diego, a man came into the shop with a chunk of silver ore about the size of my fist. I thought he had made a new find and asked him if he had found it in this county. The reason for that question was that silver ore brought to my mind a happening in Frank Trask's boyhood which he had related to me several years before.

The man said he hadn't found it in this county, but that it had come from Canada. I told him I would like to have a piece of it as a specimen. He said, "Cut me a couple of slabs off and you can have the rest for your trouble." That I did, and still have some of the piece he gave me.

It was shortly before I sold my interest in the Mesa Grande tourmaline mine to Mr. Naylor, that Frank Trask and I climbed out of the incline shaft to eat our lunch, under the oak tree at the entrance to the cut. While we were eating, he told me about an old Mexican prospector who came to Frank's father's ranch near Ballena, which is between the town of Ramona and a settlement called Santa Ysabel, in San Diego County.

Frank said this old Mexican often would bring in some rich silver ore and smelt out the silver on Frank's father's blacksmith forge. The prospector would then leave and be away for four to six weeks. He would always leave the Trask Ranch going in a westerly direction and, when seen coming back, it was from the same direction.

Frank was only a small boy at the time, which would place the date in the late 1870's or early 1880's. At one time the Mexican gave Frank's father a silver mounted bridle for his saddle horse. Shortly after that, the Mexican left as usual, but this time he did not return.

Frank said that after his father died, he and his mother started packing to move to Ramona. He said they had a cupboard, or highboy in the kitchen that reached up to within about ten inches of the ceiling. His mother told him to get up on the stepladder and see what was up there. Frank got most of the stuff down, when his hand touched some leather straps. Pulling them off the top, he found they were wrapped around the bridle the old Mexican had given his father.

Frank said his mother looked at the bridle and said, "Frank, if we could find where the old Mexican got this silver, we'd be rich."

Frank said his mother never looked for the silver mine but, after I had sold out, and the mine where Frank worked closed down, he did try to locate it, though with little success. All he had was a westward direction to follow. He prospected the country clear through to Valley Center and ended up on a small ranch. The last I heard of Frank, he wrote me to come see him. He had lots of fruit on his ranch and would let me take back a wagon load, if I could use it. At the time, however, I had other things to do and couldn't get out to see him. I never saw Frank again for he died shortly after that. He was a good miner.

CHAPTER X

IN SEARCH OF SILVER, OIL, LAPIDARY WORK

On my return from the gold hunt with Paul Valle, I found plenty of work piled up for me. About this time the work did not come in steadily as in months past, but in bunches. Days would go by without a stone coming in to be cut. By the end of 1911, very little lapidary work was to be had. However, I still cut a few kunzite pieces for Salmons and Ernsting and did some custom work for stores.

It was in 1911 that I was offered a drilling job on the wildcat well of the Otay Oil Company, located about a half mile southwest of the old Daneri Winery in Otay Valley, San Diego County. The Bently Brothers, Howard Culp and my father, W. W. Rynerson, were the promoters. Mr. William Bently was President, his brother, Secretary, Mr. Culp, Geologist, and W. W. Rynerson, Superintendent.

The reason I mention this work on the well is that it reveals some interesting things about the geological formation that I drilled through. I went to work on the job before the rig was fully completed. It was what is called a "standard rig", and was the usual outfit used those days for drilling oil wells.

To start off, the country seemed to be alive with rattlesnakes. They were often around the rig, under boards, and under the rig. We had dug a four-by-four-foot hole for a conductor box, ten feet deep, and that evening slid in two two-by-twelve-inch ten-foot planks. On starting to work next morning a tool dresser by name of Charley Culp started to go down the hole when he discovered a rattler in the bottom. I don't believe I ever saw a man his size move so fast getting out of a hole! I came over, looking down into the hole, saw one of our regular friends that called on us every day. It was four-and-a-half feet long and very thick in the body.

I told Culp I would like to catch the snake alive. It was partly hidden behind the boards and, as I was moving the boards, I must have pinched or bothered it; for it opened its mouth, put it over about the center of its body and clamped down. After that it lay still. I got a hook around its neck and pulled it out on the ground in front of the rig. It wouldn't fight back but just lay there till it died - which is usual when they bite themselves.

Nothing but some sticky shales and some water sands were encountered, until we reached the depth of six-hundred feet. Then we ran into some soft sandstone containing what looked like fossil kelp with iron pyrites in it, also dark triangular shell-like particles, probably shark teeth. Next day, right after dinner, Mr. Bently and some others were in the rig and I had just run the tools in and hooked on and run about a foot of screw out, when the bit started hitting something hard.

Mr. Bently, who was sitting on the forge and always optimistic, said, "Fred, that may be a cap over an oil sand." He hadn't more than finished talking when the bit broke through. This was the six-hundred-thirty-six-foot level. The tools hit once and then swung free, then reached out and hit again. I was running out the screw pretty fast, about the end of the screw, when the tools started hitting on something hard again.

On pulling the tools from the hole, I saw no indications of oil on the rope or tools, and there was no gas. I ran the bailer and, on dumping it in the sluice box, a lot of the contents splashed onto the derrick floor. This was as black as ink. Bill Bently jumped to his feet with a yell, "We've struck it!" And we sure had! About a four-foot vein of lignite coal! Pulling the bailer off the peg in the sluice, I found several pieces of lignite and gave them to Bently.

The rest of the way down was shales and stratas of sandstone, until I got to the nine-hundred-ninety-eight-foot level, where I struck rock. I got several pieces of the hard blue stuff from the bailings and thought I had seen similar rock before. So the next day I walked up the Otay Valley toward the east and at about three miles distance I came upon some of the same material in the creek bed. Then I knew what it was. There is a large dyke, with a strike north and south, and a half mile thick, more or less. It outcrops at lower Otay Dam, is worked as a rock quarry at Spring Valley, and lies east of Camp Elliot, San Diego County.

At the one-thousand-foot level, I broke through into about eighteen inches of water sand, and then into hard rock again. I continued on for about thirty feet, when I told Mr. Bently what I had found out and that I thought it was foolish to go farther. He took some samples into San Diego and someone told him they were hard blue shale. I told him to get another driller!

They got another man by the name of Cokley, from Whittier, California, and then another after that. I heard afterward that they had gone over one-hundred feet after I left, and were still in the same rock. I also learned from the driller on the Lo Tingo well, five miles to the west and south of us, that they had struck the same rock at a depth of two-thousand feet. Later, when the well in Mission Valley, north of San Diego, was down around five-thousand feet, they ran into the same stuff. Again, in the nineteen-thirties, a well was drilled over on the north end of Point Loma, near Mission Beach. A Mr. Waggoner who ran an assay shop on Eighth Street (below F in San Diego), who had been their analyst, asked me one day if I had ever seen rock like that before; handing me some of the same kind of rock I had taken from the Otay well. Mr. Waggoner said to me he was told it had come from the sixty-five-hundred foot level. I had previously told Mr. Waggoner about striking the rock in the Otay Well. This proves, without a doubt, that this great dyke pitches down to the west, lies at different depths under the City of San Diego, and extends both north and south of the city.

Several days after quitting the Otay Oil Company, I dropped in to see how Mr. Ernsting, the jeweler, was getting along and who was doing his lapidary work. I found a lot of work for myself. It was a mixture of various kinds but mostly kunzite and tourmaline facet work. Outside of an exceptionally fine stone now and then, I had very little pleasure cutting them. One stone was much like the other, and quite routine.

It was the Spring of 1912, and I had been cutting for several months, when Bill Trenchard asked me to help him in re-locating some marble and oil claims out near, and on Coyote Mountain near Coyote Wells, Imperial County. I notified those I had been cutting for that I would be away for a couple of weeks. At that time, I had about cut myself out of a job, anyway.

Bill and I left San Diego on the train for El Centro, via Los Angeles. After arriving, we purchased some food for the trip, then hired two horses, two saddles, and a light wagon with a top. We left El Centro around 3:00 P.M. We found it pretty hot, driving. We rode by way of Seeley, Dixieland, and Yuha Hill, then on to Coyote Wells. It was dark when we arrived at Dixieland and it became pretty cold by the time we reached Yuha Hill. We took turns trotting alongside the wagon to keep warm.

Arriving at Coyote Wells around midnight, we bedded down in a tent belonging to a Mr. McMann. The open end of the tent was toward the east and next morning I was awakened by a burning sensation in my feet. I looked out and saw through the tent flap, which was thrown back, that the sun was just over the eastern horizon and was getting down to business. Bill was out of the line of fire, and still asleep, so I woke him up and told him to look what was coming into the tent. "Man! It's going to be hot today!" he said, and started getting up.

We gave the horses water and food. Then we made our own breakfast of canned beans, fried bacon, bread, and coffee. We fixed some lunch sandwiches of bread and corned beef, then saddled the two horses and lit out for Coyote Mountain, six miles

Newlyweds; Beulah and Fred Rynerson.

away. It was then about a quarter to nine and that sun was shining hot.

McMann had a toy fox terrier that followed us when we left the camp. We hadn't gone more than a quarter of a mile when we heard him whining. Looking back, we saw him running from bush to bush, as though his feet were sore. We turned around and rode back. Picking him up, we found his toes were blistered. Bill's saddle had saddlebags on it, so we put the dog into one, leaving his head sticking out. Where we worked any length of time, we tied the horses to a rock or pinwood bush, put the dog in the shade of a rock, or made a shade for him. We always found all three there when we returned.

We had three one-gallon canteens full of water. We left two with the horses when we left them. The one we carried would became so hot we could hardly drink the water. But when we got dry, we didn't let a little heat in the water stop our drinking it. The horses always got most of the water but even then, what we gave them was only a teaser.

We followed mountain sheep trails most of the time. Once we saw four ahead of us about three hundred yards. We crossed several deposits containing fossil sea shells and an accumulation of ancient sea bottom material.

We made another trip to the north side of the mountain the next day, which wasn't so bad. We didn't climb much of the mountain that day and got back to Coyote Wells early.

The third day we covered the flat east of Coyote Mountain. The fourth day we went all around Yuha Hill and over to the Yuha Spring, or damp place. Today water has been developed there and it is called "De Anza Well".

On the flat east of Coyote Wells, we ran across an old grave with no marker or name on the rocks. Some poor fellow had needed water badly.

Nothing was left of the old Yuha Oil Company's drill rig but the casing sticking out of the hole. We ran across tons of oyster shells, near Yuha Hill, some a foot long. We managed to carry a few large ones back with us. We saw tons of sand crustaceans, in all shapes, around Yuha Hill. On the east side of Coyote Mountain we found large slabs, two and three feet thick, of oyster beds that were partly marbleized.

The fifth day we started back to El Centro. When we arrived at Yuha Hill, the horse on the right side wanted to stop. Thinking he had something the matter with him, Bill stopped. The horse lay down on the spot. Getting out of the wagon, both of us unhitched the horses from the wagon, then tried to get the horse on its feet again. It only grunted and groaned, like a horse with the colic. After using the whip and twisting its tail, it got to its feet. Bill held the ends of the reins and I took the whip and drove the animal around in a circle at a fast trot.

That sun was hot and I don't know how the horse felt after twenty times around that circle, but for my part I was glad to quit. We put the harness on the animals again and hooked up to the wagon and started out. We had lost three-quarters of an hour there.

We arrived in El Centro, at the livery stable, about five. While Bill was paying the stable man for the rig, he told him about the trouble we had with the horse. The stable man said he was sorry, but he had forgotten to tell us it was an old trick the horse played when out on a trip like that; especially if it were hot weather. We came back to San Diego by train, the same way we went.

Two Frenchmen and Indian at Frank Salmon's Pala Chief Tourmaline Mine.

CHAPTER XI

GARNETS FROM ALASKA. MENDING AN OIL WELL

I stayed in the lapidary business till late in the spring of 1912. One day during that time I was called on the phone by Attorney James E. O'Keefe, who asked me to come down to his office. When I arrived he introduced me to a man who claimed to have come from Alaska.

O'Keefe said, "Mr. ___ has some garnets and I would like to know if they will cut good stones." He put three or four round garnet crystals on the desk. They were from a half to three-quarters of an inch in diameter - what we called in those days, "iron garnets", being a rust color to quite dark. I had seen many of these crystals before and told O'Keefe they wouldn't cut good stones.

Then the man from Alaska took from his pocket two papers of cut garnets, some two dozen stones in each paper. They looked to me like Arizona stuff. He said he had sent two batches of rough crystals from Alaska to Chicago, Illinois to have them cut, and these two papers of stones were what they sent him back.

I told him I didn't know what he had sent to Chicago, but the rough stones he was showing me would not cut and if he would let me pop a couple of them open, I would prove to him that they were of no value and would not cut, and yet looked like the ones he had in the papers.

"Well," he said, "I'll take a chance on two of them." I told him to pick out the two. O'Keefe rustled a couple of hammers and I held a stone on one and gave it a tap with the other. It fell into several pieces and looked worse on the inside than I expected. I did the same to the other crystal with the same results. The man from Alaska said, "How come they sent me these cut stones, after I sent them the same kind you have just broken?"

I asked him what they charged him for cutting and he said they averaged about $3.00 per stone. I told him he could go into almost any curio store and buy them for that price and that they had sold him good stuff for the price of the cutting and probably never attempted to cut his stone. "I can't believe it!" he said, and put his stuff into a bag and left the office.

O'Keefe told me this man wanted him to make out papers to incorporate a company to mine and cut garnets. He remembered what I had told him of a similar case, so thought he would see what I would say about this one.

Soon after that, I received another phone call from Mr. O'Keefe asking me to come to his office. When I arrived he asked me if

I would go up to Sorrento, a small "whistle-stop" on the Santa Fe, sixteen miles north of San Diego, to find out what was wrong with the wildcat oil well being drilled there.

I couldn't get away at the time, but several days later I drove up and met the driller, Mr. Phenix, and showed him my papers. Mr. Phenix had been working only day hours as the other driller had quit or been laid off. I did not make any excuses for my being there, and asked Phenix what was wrong with the well.

He told me they had struck water between six-hundred and seven-hundred feet and had bailed a lot of sand out of the hole. On putting down the twelve-and-a-half-inch casing they had gotten the hole out of plumb. They had worked the casing down to eleven-hundred feet, or better, then had to put in a string of ten-inch and had knocked off the shoe (a protective collar that screws onto the bottom of the ten-inch casing). He had wanted still another string of pipe to go into the ten-inch. He had been drilling on ahead of the ten-inch and the hole was down to about twelve-hundred feet.

I looked at the log of the well and it showed trouble, part of the cause being lack of proper tools to do the job right. When I left, I had a hunch I would be back again, and I was - within another week.

When I got back to San Diego and saw O'Keefe, I told him the hole was crooked, probably started off at the six-hundred foot level, as the wire drill cable showed wear at that level. There was no proof that the shoe was off the ten-inch pipe, so it would be foolish to continue down with the hole in that condition. He asked me what could be done about it and I told him a plan I had.

Later, I had met in Mr. O'Keefe's office an elderly man by the name of McNece who, it seems, held the controlling interest in the well. He asked me a few questions, then sent me up to the well to carry out a plan to get the hole back into proper shape.

Mr. Phenix stayed on the job with me. When I told him I was going to pull the ten-inch pipe, he threw up his hands and said it would pull apart, as it had been driven too much. I told him we would try it anyway.

At that time, the water in the hole had never been shut off and stood some one-hundred-fifty feet from the top. I filled the hole full of water and started pulling the ten-inch pipe. To my surprise, it came up with little effort or trouble. We unscrewed every third joint, standing three joints at a time, back in the derrick. When the last joint came into view, there was the shoe in the bottom, as good as when it was first screwed on.

This made McNece feel good. He asked me if I could pull the

twelve-and-a-half inch. I told him it might be possible, but I would want to put the ten-inch back in to a depth of twelve-hundred feet. I had noticed a scratch on the ten-inch pipe, which led me to believe something was wrong with the twelve-and-a-half. I made a wooden plug to fit into the ten-inch pipe. It had a pointed end about a foot long and was the same size outside the pipe as the diameter of the shoe.

I put the ten-inch down to the bottom, letting it hang on the elevators. Then McNece changed his mind and decided to make some more hole for a while; so I knocked the plug out of the bottom of the ten-inch and started drilling in a soft blue shale. At the twelve-hundred-forty-five foot level, I struck a hard sandstone strata about four feet thick. Under this sandstone was a strata of water sand. The water was highly mineralized and quite hot. When it came in contact with the back of the hands, it caused a stinging sensation at once.

The hole was then bailed out to find out the amount of water this new sand was producing. I learned it was much more than the sand at the six-hundred foot level. It had flowed in with considerable sand too, so I filled the hole full of water again and eased out the sand down to the sandstone cap. Then about fifteen wheelbarrows full of adobe were put into the well, and we ran in the tools and beat that adobe down into the sand strata, keeping the hole full of water at all times.

The drilling was continued on down to the twelve-hundred sixty-five foot level, where I ran into some stratas of sandstone and sticky clays. I asked McNece if he wanted to shut off the water, as I was in a good formation to do it. But he said we would continue to make hole for a while longer.

The drill cable had been badly used and been spliced a dozen times while only some five-hundred feet of new cable remained on the reel. I asked McNece to get another two thousand feet and I would splice it onto the five hundred we had.

After a lot of talk, he promised to get it, also some more ten-inch casing if we decided to carry that size pipe on down. In the meantime I was to continue making hole.

At about the twelve-hundred-seventy-five foot level, we drove into sticky blue clay and here our trouble commenced. The old drill cable couldn't take it. I spliced it and laid in strands once or twice a day. This was work, discouraging work. I was tired.

We worried along until we got below the seventeen-hundred-foot level, when one day McNece came out to the rig. It was after one in the afternoon. He had been up to Los Angeles, he said. He was very talkative, and said he had visited an old friend in the oil business who was drilling in one of the fields near Fullerton, California. I noticed he had his watch in his hand. After a little while he said "Fred, you're running too slow for the depth of this well." I said, "Who told you?" He said, "I was out in the oil field with my friend and asked the driller how deep he was. He told me twenty-five-hundred feet. I counted the strokes of the drill, which were a lot faster than you are running."

We were using a standard rig at Sorrento, not a rotary rig. I wouldn't have cared if he had fired me on the spot, for I burst out laughing, remembering a story I had heard years before in the oil fields up north. It goes like this:

A newly-made director of an oil company thought he ought to have a first-hand "look-see" at the company's new well. Arriving at the rig, he threw back his shoulders and walked in. The driller had been having some trouble with heaving sand and he was sitting on the stool with his left hand going up and down on the tools. His hat was pulled down over his eyes, which were glued to the top of the drill hole.

The director cleared his throat. The driller didn't move. Then the director said, "How deep is this well?"

The driller cocked one eye at the director and said, "G--damn deep!"

The director looked around and, hearing the tool dresser whistling out in the engine house, thought he would find out from him. Going into the engine house, he said to the tool dresser, "You seem to be cheerful this morning. I'd like to know what's the matter with the driller. As a director of the company, I want my questions to be answered promptly."

"What did you ask him?" inquired the tooly.

"I asked him how deep the well was."

"What did he say?" queried the other.

"G--damn deep." responded the director.

The tool dresser burst out laughing and said, "Say! He's a damn liar! He was deeper than that yesterday!"

I came near telling McNece that story but thought of a better way. I said, "Well, do you want me to run these tools faster?"

He answered, "Yes. Increase the motion."

I opened the throttle slowly, and the noise became so great that in about five seconds the old man was on his feet, getting out of the rig. I shut off the throttle and got her running steady again. Then I told McNece not to believe everything he heard in an oil field.

I was a little sore for I just happened to think of the condition of my drill line. McNece said very little the rest of the afternoon until about 4:00 P.M. when I had the screw about run out. I felt a little vibration on the drill line which I knew all too well. The engine started to race and I slowed down to pull out. McNece asked, "What's the trouble?" I stepped over to the hole and said, "No tools. Some time we'll lose them with this old line and won't get them out!"

The cable had parted some fifteen or twenty feet above the rope socket, or top of the tools. I sent down the "Kodac" as it was called in those days. It was a round piece of wood. One end fitted into the bottom of the bailer or sinker bar and flared out at the other end to fit the inside of the well casing. On the under face of the plug, were driven nails about a half inch apart which stuck out about an inch of being driven all the way in. This whole surface was filled with yellow bar laundry soap. When this was sent down the hole and came in contact with anything, it would leave impressions on the soap; giving one an idea of what was down there.

I ran the kodac down the hole and, when pulled out again, I found that the tools were standing in the center of the hole. This had been my luck in the past and I was wondering how long that luck was going to last!

We kept a light string of fishing tools standing in the corner of the derrick for just such emergencies, with either a rope spear or a bell slip socket. As the impression on the kodac was perfect for the bell socket (already on the stem), I sent it down. Then I got an idea and pulled the tools out again before they touched bottom. I figured if this worked right, I would get a new cable - or I would quit.

We were several hundred feet below the bottom of the ten-inch casing, in open hole, and anything could happen. I set the slips high so they wouldn't catch hold, ran the socket down, never got a bit; then the supper gong rang.

McNece said, "Come on, Fred. Get something to eat, and do that afterwards. You'll feel better."

"No," I said, "I stay here til I get them out. You go get yours."

He didn't eat much, I guess, for he was back in less than an hour. We fished for another hour, and I was getting hungry, so I reset the slips again and ran the tools down and felt them take hold. I told McNece I had them and it wasn't long before we brought them up on the wrench. I told McNece then and there I couldn't go on without a new cable. He said, "Fred, I'll order a new cable tonight!"

McNece wanted the twelve-and-a-half inch casing pulled. I was against doing this for it left no protection to the ten-inch which was hanging in a large hole. But my arguments against it went for nothing. I think he wanted to know what that twelve-and-a-half looked like and then sell it, if it was taken out, which he did.

Both Phenix and McNece didn't know, it seems, how I was going to do the job of getting that 12 1/2 inch casing out. Yet it had been done before. We didn't have enough ten-inch pipe to reach the bottom, so had to make a landing around the twelve-hundred-forty-five-or-fifty-foot level.

First, I made what we called a "rats' nest". This was a composition of small green willow sticks about eighteen or twenty-four inches long, tied together in the center with the ends pointing in all directions like the spokes of a wheel. It was forced part-way into the casing with the ends pointing up and was followed by a bundle of soft rope, old gunny sacks, then more soft rope, to make a bundle three feet long and nine inches in diameter. One end of the plug was tied to the center of the rats' nest and was then forced down into the ten-inch casing to the twelve-hundred-sixty-five-foot level.

Then, on top of that, we put several sacks of adobe and a lot of soft rope, building it up to the twelve-hundred-fifty-foot level. Next I got a piece of eucalyptus wood about nine inches in diameter and four feet long and sawed a V, lengthwise, through the center, about two inches wide at the top, coming to a point a foot from the other end. A wedge was then made to fit the V, extending half-way down it, leaving a foot extending above the end of the log or plug.

I tied a small sack of rocks on the bottom of the log, or wedge end to keep it on the bottom, and sent it down the ten-inch casing to the bridge at the twelve-hundred-foot level. I then ran in the tools and set them on the plug, pulled them up about five feet and let them drop, leaving them rest there with a slack line. After a half hour, the tools hadn't taken much slack out of the line, so I pulled them out of the hole. Then I filled the hole up to the twelve-hundred-forty-five-foot level with soft rope, old pieces of rope and sacks. I set the tools down on the lot, pulling them up two or three feet and letting them down slowly, several times. I let the well set overnight.

We pulled the ten-inch pipe again - standing three joints at a time back of the derrick. A plug of eucalyptus about eighteen inches long was fitted into the shoe of the ten-inch, with some six inches extending outside and increasing to about eleven-and-a-half inches at the end, then tapering to a blunt point. The ten-inch pipe was put back into the twelve-and-a-half-inch casing and lowered to the false bottom at the regular level. There I let it rest with the elevator's slack two feet. After twelve hours, the pipe had settled only eleven inches.

To pull the twelve-and-a-half-inch pipe was the next thing we did and it came off the bottom as easily as the ten-inch had. We found that a rock had dented the second joint up from the bottom and that when they had put in the ten-inch casing it had sheared off the dent, cutting a long sliver out of the side of the pipe, down to the collar below. It was about eight feet long. No entry was made in the log of this. The drillers must have known about it and pulled the ten-inch and put a plug in the shoe to get by it. The top end of the sliver extended two inches into the center of the twelve-and-a-half-inch pipe.

This pipe was shipped to Los Angeles, as I expected, and I was asked to get a string of eight-inch to go into the ten-inch. In the meantime, the new cable came and I spliced it onto the good cable on the reel. I then drilled out the plug and false bottom below the ten-inch and cleaned out the hole down to the seventeen-hundred-foot level.

Phenix had left several weeks before McNece came back from Los Angeles where he had been talking with some of his drilling friends at the office. What he told them I do not know. But he said he was advised to put the ten-inch on down and not reduce the size of the hole. I told him that was always the thing to keep in mind, but we had a ten-inch pipe hanging in a fourteen-inch (or larger) hole, and 450 feet off of bottom. If we moved the ten-inch now it might prove costly! The new drill line showed no wear and I was positive the hole was straight.

But he had made up his mind, it seemed, so we took hold of the ten-inch and started to pull. It did not come off the bottom. I told McNece again I didn't think it was the thing to do, but he was adamant.

Max Detrick, my tooldresser was under the derrick floor handling the slips in the spider. This time, the pipe came up a foot or so, then things did happen! The collar under the elevators gave way. The big seven line block flew halfway to the top of the derrick, then came down, smashing everything it hit! I had just looked up into the derrick to see how it was standing the pull. I jerked back under the walking beam as the whip of the cable from the calf wheel grazed my face. If I had been a second slower, it would have torn my face off!

Max Detrick came boiling out from under the floor, thinking the derrick had pulled in. You could hardly blame him when a five-hundred-pound bunch of steel was bouncing around over his head! Max was a fine boy. I liked him very much! I heard some years later that he was killed near Bakersfield in a fall off an oil well derrick.

The pipe traveled fast for a few feet, and got by the spider in the pit, which was only six or eight feet below the derrick floor. Then it slowed up, as the hole below the twelve-hundred-forty-five-foot level hadn't been under-reamed.

We started cleaning up the mess in the rig. In about two hours I ran down an eleven-inch Kodac on the bottom of the bailer. I found the pipe had stopped some two-hundred-fifty feet down from the top, and the bottom of the pipe was some hundred feet or more off the bottom of the hole. The top end was centered in the drill hole.

I had made up my mind I was going to have my way from then on, or I would quit. McNece wanted me to go to Los Angeles with him to talk with his friends, which I did. One man we talked with was an oil well supply house boss, as near as I could make out. All the advice we got from him was to use a bulldog casing spear and jar the pipe out with the drill tools.

I thought the proper way was to send down a die on the end of another string of ten-inch casing, cut another thread on the pipe in the hole, take a pull on it and leave the same in the hole, then put in a string of eight-inch and go on down with the hole.

McNece didn't see it that way, so I told him I didn't want to stay on the job any longer where most of the orders came from someone who knew nothing of the condition of the well. I did want to put that well down because, along the last fifty or sixty feet of the hole, I was getting some showings of oil, and was anxious to know if the dyke that laid to the east, with a strike north and south, was below the surface at that point.

Several months later, I met the driller who took my place. He said he had got out the shoe that had been knocked off the ten-inch casing. I knew then he had been reading the old log of the well, so he wasn't telling me anything. I heard later they had started another oil well and failed - probably drilled from orders sent down from Los Angeles!

CHAPTER XII

THE MARBLE DIGGIN'S IN COYOTE MOUNTAIN

Back in San Diego, I found about three weeks' lapidary work to be done. This gave me some physical rest. A week before I had finished the job, Bill Trenchard showed up and told me the Golden State Mining and Marble Company was going to open up marble claims on Coyote Mountain, Imperial County, and wanted me to go out there and dress tools. He was to build some roads and trails to the claims, also a road out on the northeast side to the old Butterfield Stage road that led from Carrizo Springs to Dixieland.

This, as I remember, was in the fall of 1912, and pretty hot in the day time. The company bought a Model T Ford pickup for us, and Bill and I promptly loaded it up with a tent, grub, picks and shovels, pots and pans, and eating tools, along with a few boards to make a table. The next morning about 9:30, we lit out for Coyote Mountain and the marble diggin's, by way of Dulzura, Campo, Jacumba and Mountain Springs, then down through Devil's Canyon (not used now). The roads were not paved in those days and the going was slow. We arrived at Coyote Wells about sundown and camped there for the night.

Next morning we drove over to where we were to make our first camp. We stopped the Ford a short distance before the road dips into the lower part of the ''Painted Gorge'' wash (not named at that time). The road, at this point, was the same as in 1903. We left this road and took off on another to the left at right angles. We drove the Ford about two-hundred yards over rocks to a small knoll some six feet high. Here we stopped and cleared away the rocks for our camp. Most of the rocks were on the surface, having settled there after years of rains washing the soil from under them, piling up on the surface.

Most of these rocks were limestone and lava. Some were very large, but most of them were small. After putting up the tent and making a satisfactory camp, we shoveled the rocks off the tracks the Ford made, leading back to the road. We cleared each track about eighteen inches wide. In 1950, I could still trace the road to the camp, also the camp site.

That evening we had our first visitor. She came early and within twenty-five feet of our camp-fire. It was a little desert fox, no larger than a small housecat. Her tail was so large and bushy, it was as big as she was. We threw some bread and canned beef to her, which she ate at once. She stayed around the tent for a while after we went inside. We had left a washpan and a cake of

Lava soap on a box outside the tent and the next morning our Lava soap was gone!

The next day we searched out and built small rock monuments along the best route to what was called "The Creole" claim. This road led out through the "Narrows", which is at the lower end of the Painted Gorge wash, then on down the wash about half a mile to the "Elbow", then turned left, back up another wash to the Creole claim. Later we continued the road from the Elbow to the old Butterfield Stage road to Dixieland. It now leads to Plaster City (not in existence at that time.)

We marked out, in the same way, a trail which led up the Painted Gorge to a small canyon leading into the Gorge on the right. The trail here led up the canyon about a hundred feet, then turned left up a small draw to the top of the spur, or ridge, of the mountain, then on up to within some two-hundred feet of a fine white sand deposit. Before we got to this point, the trail crossed what one would imagine was a part of some sandstone sea beach. This sandstone had embedded in it sand dollars and other prehistoric shells.

From near the white sand deposit, the trail led up the right side of the canyon and followed a mountain sheep trail, to the "Siena Claim", which lies on a sloping bench covered with Yucca plants. Most of this Siena marble is scattered over this bench. No quantity was found in place. Some of it was very beautiful. When slabbed up the colors were pink, yellow, red and brown. Some of the yellows and pinks had black veins running through them and would take a high polish. A cave under a large block of sandstone, lies on the northeast side of the flat. The roof has been blackened in the past by Indian fires. In 1949 I took my son Eugene out there to see it.

He screened the floor of this shelter, or cave, and found numerous heads of Chuckwallas (dirt lizards) and at one spot, a handful of Yucca cuds, spit out by an Indian or native of the country long ago after he had extracted the juice. The Chuckwalla heads were found eighteen inches or deeper, below the surface or floor of the cave. He also found a stone rolling pin which was used to crush the juice from the Yucca or mescal agave leaves. This juice could be put into a container of some kind and set in the sun to ferment - which gave to a person some sort of a kick, so I have heard.

Still farther north, past the sandstone blocks, was a dark blueish marble, with hundreds of holes from one-half inch to an inch in diameter, made by rock-boring clams. Some of the shellfish shells were still in the holes.

From a small hill to the right, about fifty yards, is a fine view of the Imperial Valley, looking from the Salton Sea to the north, to the Laguna Salada, twenty-five miles to the south in Mexico. East, on a clear day, one can see the mountains in Western Arizona and along the Colorado River.

The evening of the fourth day, our little fox showed up so we fed her again. We left a small piece of soap that evening, but she didn't take it. She probably had had enough of that kind of food! The wind came up in the early morning hours of the fifth day. Before we had breakfast it was blowing so hard we had to eat our breakfast inside the tent, which we had already guyed down, fore and aft. By evening, we had all our stuff inside the tent, with rocks up to fifty pounds lying on the side walls. This made the tent smaller, but it had to be done or lose the tent. The air was one vast dust cloud, with small rocks and sand flying along like bullets. The air in the tent was full of dust and we were soon spitting mud.

The second day of the blow, the dust cloud shifted more to the east and the air cleared a little. By the end of the third day, the blow was over and we dug ourselves out.

Since we were anxious to get the work started, we had neglected preparing the camp for such a dusty blow, so everything was full of dust and sand. During the whole eight months I spent on the mountain, we had several hard blows, but nowhere near the dust and sand that was in that first blow. Bill called it "A hell of a camp", and was anxious to move over to the Creole where the camp was more sheltered. We had to stay in this first camp until the trail to the Siena Claim was finished.

We had been there a week and needed more help. We drove back to San Diego, got more grub, a forge, blower, and blacksmith coal, two men, two extra tents; and, after five days in San Diego, we journeyed back to "Hell Camp". We stopped at Coyote Wells for about twenty gallons of water and then continued on over to camp.

We made better time going out than we did on the previous trip. The two extra men got the tent up while Bill and I got some supper ready and unloaded the Ford. Canned roast beef fried, bread, butter and coffee made up the meal. Afterward, we all went to bed, tired from jolting over a hundred miles of unpaved roads.

I got up next morning about six. While making some flapjacks, I heard two quick shots coming from the new tent. Looking that way, I saw one of the new men shoot again with a Colt 44 six-shooter. I looked to see his target and found our fox standing fifty feet away. The bullets hit within six inches of it and she didn't move. I called to the fellow not to shoot again, that the fox was our pet. The little thing hadn't been shot at before, I suppose, and, expecting food from us again, had come to get more.

After breakfast, Bill took the men up the Gorge Wash and pointed out the monuments that marked the roadway; instructing them to clear a roadway to the foot of the trail. It wasn't too much of a job, making the road up the wash, but the trail up to the Siena Claim took several days.

While we stopped at Coyote Wells one day for water, two men, John Bodendick and George Hultz, inquired of us if we needed any help. They had heard that the marble deposits on Coyote Mountain were going to be worked. Bill told them he could use two more men and promptly hired them.

The San Diego and Arizona Railroad Survey ran through the Coyote Wells district and several people had taken up homesteads in that locality. Bodendick and Hultz were two of them. They were swell fellows, too. Bodendick was ten years older than Hultz, and had been around. He told me a little of his life when we were on the trail one day, going over to the Creole Claim.

He said he had joined the British army at the beginning of the Boer War in South Africa. One of the first trips he made into the Boer country was with about twenty British soldiers. They surrounded a Boer farmhouse and advanced upon it. Coming to the door, which was open, some of the men crowded in and found an elderly woman working in the kitchen. The British, after finding no men around, demanded food. Without a word the woman gave them all the food she had. Bodendick said the house was as neat and clean as it could be; but, after throwing down some of the food, and spitting on the floor, scattering rubbish all over the place, the British left. Bodendick said it made him sick. He felt he had joined a bunch of thieves and vandals, so he deserted the British and joined the Boers. After the war, he came back to the United States.

Bill put all hands on to the job of building the road to our new campsite on the Creole Claim. We made a road over half way the first day, and almost to the campsite the next day. At lunch time the first day, we ate our lunch in the sparse shade of a large pinwood tree - now called a smoke tree. Bill was feeling good, for we had made good time on the road. One of the men we had brought out from San Diego picked up some little berry-like rabbit droppings and, looking up into the tree, asked, "Bill, what kind of berries are these?" Bill said, "These trees don't often produce berries, but when they do, the old prospectors use them to flavor their beans." About that time, we started again to work on the road.

As it was my turn to get the evening meal, I left the men about 4:00 P.M. and walked back to camp. On my way I picked a dozen of the little "berries". We had cooked up a big pot of beans and this evening we were to get our first serving. When Bill and the men returned to camp, I had everything ready and when they sat down to the table, I dished each two ladles of beans. Bill was getting something out of the car, so I dished him out one ladle of beans and put about a half dozen berries in them, mixing them with the beans. I dished myself two ladles of beans and put the rest of the berries alongside the beans on my plate.

All of us were eating when Bill sat down and was saying it wouldn't be long now until we would be in the new camp. Taking a generous helping for the first mouthfull, he hadn't taken more than two bites when he looked at my plate and then, leaning across the table towards me, with his eyes squinting, spoke through his closed teeth, "Damn your hide!"

I said, "You told us they were good in the beans and that all the old prospectors liked them. I thought if you liked them, I'd try some too."

Bill spat out what he had in his mouth, threw away what he had on his plate, and dished himself some more beans out of the pot. Whenever it came my time to cook, Bill would always give the stuff a good looking over before he started eating! We had to put up another tent for Bodendick and Hultz for we decided to stay in Hell Camp until we finished the trail to the Siena. We took all four men and started building the trail up the mountain from the Gorge.

After two or three days, we finished the trail up to the Siena and threw a big feed that night in celebration of our leaving Hell Camp. To top it off, the fox came too! She was very tame; coming within two feet of me for a piece of ham bone. Then she rushed off into the dark, making a whining noise. No doubt she had some pups back there!

Next morning, Bill took all the men over to the Creole to clear off a bench on the west side of what we called the "Creole Wash", so we could set up four tents and a blacksmith shop. Next day we started moving camp over to the Creole. While the boys were setting up the tents, Bill and I drove back for the bed rolls and other things we had packed. We had everything over in the new camp by evening. Before we left, I painted a sign, "This Road to Hell", and left it at the junction of the camp road and the road to Coyote Wells.

When the camp was in shape at the Creole, Bill set the men to work clearing off the face of a large section of the deposit of white and orange marble. It extended one hundred feet long, fifty feet wide, and forty or fifty feet high. This was a beautiful, translucent marble, the white predominating, with large blotches and veins of orange colors running through it.

Next morning, Bill and I left for San Diego to get blacksmith tools, equipment and other things we needed. We got back on the evening of the fourth day; having been gone four days. We found that the boys had accomplished all that we expected of them, and the face was ready to be quarried out. Most of the marble on the Creole was of a bluish color and how this light-colored marble happened to be there, is something hard to figure out.

There was a lot of waste in opening up this deposit, as it was faulted in a dozen places near the surface. Pieces longer than sixteen feet were hard to get; while, in the blue, which lay next to the white and orange marble, pieces fifty feet long by six feet square could be taken out.

A week after we got the camp going, we had just finished breakfast and the boys had gone to work. Bill expected to go to Coyote for water, but had gone over to the quarry with the men. I was cleaning up things in the cook tent when I heard someone coming up the gravel wash. I looked out and saw two men stumbling along toward the tents.

I came out of the tent and walked toward them. They were in pretty bad shape, physically. At first they didn't say anything to me but made for some boxes and dropped down on them. I could see they were completely exhausted. I didn't say anything to them for a minute, just let them rest a bit, then asked where they had come from. The one who seemed strongest said they were heading for San Diego and had been following the San Diego and Arizona railroad tracks until they came to the end. Then they started toward what they thought was Coyote Wells and ran across our road.

Instead of turning to the left, they turned to the right, coming to the sign, "This Road To Hell". They decided to take that road, since it was supposed to lead to a place with a name. They found it and said it was a "hell of a place, too!" I poured each a cup of fresh coffee, which they wolfed down. Then I gave them a little warm water every ten minutes.

Bill came back in about an hour and said he would take them over to Coyote Wells. We gave them something to eat in an hour or so, then Bill took the lead to the main road at Coyote Wells. I never heard of them afterward, but we were sure they made it to San Diego all right. Both were in their twenties.

Several days after that, Bill took down sick. He told me he thought he had ptomaine poisoning and was going to drive into El Centro to see a doctor. He got to a point about two miles west of the little settlement called Dixieland when he ran out of gas. He discovered a leak in a connection on the gas line. Taking the canteen of water, he started walking. When he arrived in Dixieland he had gotten over his sick spell, so he bought a gallon of gas and walked back to the car, then drove back to Dixieland, filled the car up with gas and drove back to camp. He said he thought a good walk sometimes was good medicine!

We didn't keep the men working steadily on the Creole Claim, but moved them over to the White Marble Claim on the west side of the mountain. The day we took them over there the wind was blowing hard from the north. The deposit we were going to open up was high up on the mountain, and along a ridge. At times it was almost impossible to stand up against the wind.

We could look to the south twenty-five miles, to the Laguna Salada and see huge waves when they broke on the beach, causing a white line to form and then disappear at two or three minute intervals. One could also see from this point an old mountain sheep trail which had, no doubt, been used for centuries. It started leading off a long ridge on the southwest side of Coyote Mountain, then down across the flat, until it was lost from sight in the mountains. This old sheep trail crossed State Highway No. 80 a mile below where the highway leaves the lower end of In-Ko-Pah gorge and five miles west of Coyote Wells. This trail looked as straight as a survey line, or some of them, striking northeasterly and southwesterly.

One evening while Bill and I were cleaning up the supper dishes, we heard the scream of a mountain lion. It seemed to come from the south of our tent and probably two hundred yards from it. The air was still and the canyons echoed with the cry. Several days afterward Bill and I were taking a short cut back to camp from near the Siena Claims, when we ran across the thigh bone of a mountain sheep. Most of the meat had been eaten off of it. This piece had been dragged to its present location by coyotes or foxes. The sheep, no doubt, was killed by the lion we heard.

The white and orange marble quarry was started at the entrance of a small narrow canyon. Most of the material taken, while facing up the quarry, was used as fill in the bottom of the canyon, and to make a level place to square up larger blocks of marble.

In 1951, I returned to this old Creole camp and found all the white and orange marble had been taken out; but they did not take any from the fill we made. Another camp had been made in a small canyon nearer the Creole than our first camp. The old campsite, with the rocks around the tents, was as we left it. The forge I had built was the same, only the ocotillo shelter over it was gone. The fireplace, built of rock, was exactly the same. What little change takes place in the desert in thirty-eight years!

Eugene Rynerson at Indian cave on Coyote Mountain. (See p. 87.)

Mrs. Amy Difley Brown (now O'Toole), and Beulah Rynerson on Coyote Mt.

CHAPTER XIII

THE LOST SILVER MINE AND HOW "DUTCH" LOST HIS MIND

On one of his trips to Coyote Wells for water, Bill picked up a man we called Dutch - a Swede! He had served as a soldier under Pancho Villa, one of the leaders in the Mexican Revolution. He was a strong wiry fellow and a good worker, but a little headstrong. I have forgotten his real name. I'll come to his story a little later, but the following leads up to it.

Several weeks after we looked for the Butterfield well location, Bill and I drove down to the stage road and turned to the left. Bill said he wanted to see what was up at the head of a wash he had located from higher up on the mountain.

When we came to the wash, we parked the car off the road near the bank of the wash, and then walked three-quarters of a mile to a very narrow place. After passing this, we entered an amphitheater of about two acres which seemed to have sunken, or been washed out by floodwaters. The formation was badly broken and had an appearance of being covered with soot on a strip twenty feet wide running through it. The formation showed faulting in a southeasterly and northwesterly direction. This brought back to mind what old John McCain told me about seeing the dust fly up after hearing a rumbling sound. The direction in which the dust streaked along, would lead toward the locality on Coyote Mountain.

Returning to the car from this amphitheater, we walked down the wash about a hundred yards from the car. Then we climbed out of the wash and walked on the mesa for two hundred feet when we saw a twenty-five-pound box of dynamite beside a bush. A box of caps and a hundred feet of fuse were lying by the box. Rocks were placed on them to keep the wind from blowing them away; looking as though someone expected to come back for them.

The powder was in bad shape and looked like it had been there a long time. I took a piece of fuse and lit it. It burned well. Then I put a cap on a piece of fuse about twenty feet long, placed the cap end into the box of caps and then the box of caps into the box of powder. Bill wanted to be sure the Model T would start before I lit the fuse. So, after he got the engine going, and cranked it, I lit the fuse and hurried back to camp. About a block away, we stopped and waited for the explosion. That fuse wasn't so good either, no doubt had runners in it, for we didn't have long to wait when it went off. It made a sharp cracking report, which proved it still was plenty powerful.

In 1940 I told Mrs. Estella Dayley (formerly Mrs. Fewell) about finding this powder. She told me that her father, Morris Westover and her husband were the ones who put it there. She asked me to see Mr. Fewell about it. I was fortunate enough to meet him just a short time before he passed away. I first met him when he was a guard at the Himalaya Tourmaline Mine at Mesa Grande, in 1903. We had been talking about the desert, and he asked me if I ever found any silver ore in the country between Coyote Mountain and Superstitious Mountain. I told him no. He said in 1899 he and his father-in-law, Morris Westover and others drove out past Carrizo Springs to the mesa between Coyote and Superstition, to hunt antelope. Westover was a man who could get lost easily so he never went out of sight of the horses and wagon, while Fewell and the others ranged far afield.

After a time Westover sat down on an outcropping of rock to look around and rest. He noticed the rock he was sitting on was dark and quite heavy, so he picked up a piece and put it into his pocket. After a short time he started walking back to the wagon. Finally the others came in and they decided no antelope were in the district and they started back to Mesa Grande.

Later, Westover showed the rock to Fewell's brother, who was an assayer and chemist and had come down from the north to visit them. He told Westover it looked like a high grade silver ore but he would take it back and test it out. Word got back in a few days that it was high grade silver ore, and that he was coming down to locate the discovery.

Fewell, his brother, and Westover drove out there again, but Westover couldn't remember where that pile of rock was. I don't remember how long Fewell said they were in that locality looking for the silver, but he did say it was hot and their water was running short. They noticed that juice was seeping out of the powder box. So, thinking it was too dangerous to carry back, they took the stuff out of the wagon and left it about a hundred feet off the side of the road.

This was in 1899 but Bill and I found it in 1912. The stuff had been there thirteen years! It was in 1940, forty-one years later, that I learned who had placed the powder caps and fuse there. Mrs. Estella Fewell, whose father was Morris Westover and who, in 1940, was Mrs. Estella Dayley, of San Jacinto, verified the story.

Bill let the boys off for a few days to look over their homesteads and cabins, while we drove to San Diego. When we came back Bill and his wife and two daughters were with us. Before they came, Bill and I had a tent to ourselves, unless one of the company heads came out to stay over-night.

About a week later, on a Sunday, the president of the company and his wife, his brother and another man called Jim, came out. It was hot that day so they stayed only a short time. When the president, Clark Walker and his wife and brother, left for El Centro about twenty miles away, Bill went with them, but in another car. I was to take Jim over to Coyote Wells in the Model T in the afternoon to meet them, on their way to San Diego.

Jim and I left camp about 2:00 P.M. and arrived about the same time that Clark Walker and party showed up. On the road back to camp, there was a long stretch of sand I had to travel up-hill. This was before we got to the Gorge wash. We generally took hills in high gear, but if we slowed down to a stop, it was hard to get back into high again.

I was making good time along this sandy stretch when something I took to be a cap with a red lining, lying in the road, flashed under the car. I knew of no one in camp who had a cap or hat with a red lining. Thinking it might have belonged to one of Bill's little daughters and that it had blown out of the back of the car, I figured Bill could pick it up on his way down to Coyote Wells for water the next morning.

Arriving back at camp, George Hultz came out of his tent and said, "Did you see Dutch?" I told him "No." He said, "He called to you when you were leaving, but I guess you didn't hear him, so he started running across the cut-off to meet you in the Gorge wash. We told him to take some water, but he said he didn't need it."

I told Hultz we would go after him as soon as I unloaded some stuff I had in the car. Then I related to him and Bodendick about the cap with the red lining and bet that it was Dutch's. If so, he was "nuts".

After I unloaded the car, I walked over to my tent and was there only a few minutes, when Mrs. Trenchard called to me in a low voice from close outside, that someone was in the cook tent throwing the cans around. I had an idea who it was and hot-footed it over there. I found Dutch with a stew-kettle in his hand. It would hold about two quarts of water when full but it didn't have a pint in it then. I ran in and jerked it out of his hand. He just stood there with his arms hanging down, like a gorilla, and looking to me crazy as a loon. I called to the boys to come and lead him over to his tent, where he jabbered incoherently about me running over him, of his trying to catch hold of the back of the car and of my just putting on steam and laughing at him.

It was about 140 degrees hot in that tent, but we rolled him in some blankets. He was turning blue and dry as a bone. No sweat.

I ran to my tent and got a bottle of Jamaica Ginger and poured some down his throat. It didn't seem to phase him at first, then he started to groan. In a few minutes more he started to sweat, the color came back into his face, and he lay there completely exhausted. His heart was pounding very hard.

We gradually unwrapped him. In a short time he was resting easier but with a groan every minute or two. In an hour, he was asleep. We gave him a wet rag to suck and by evening he was sitting up. The next morning you wouldn't have known him as Dutch. He looked like a man in the last stages of tuberculosis. But he was tough. He sat around next day like a man in a trance. The second day he asked to go to work.

Bill gave him some light duties and in a short time he was working in the quarry again. But he wasn't the same old Dutch. Something seemed to be bothering him. We came to the conclusion that he remembered what he thought he had seen and done, and couldn't quite connect it with what really happened. Dutch stayed with us about a month longer, then quit, and left for parts not known to us.

We went back the next day, to the spot where I had seen the cap with the red lining, and found by the tracks that Dutch had put the cap in the road, then walked about fifty feet away and lay back of a smoke tree till I passed. We supposed he got the idea that if I ran over his cap, I would run over him. The red lining in the cap turned out to be a red Union Leader tobacco sack!

I don't know what that Jamaica Ginger does to a fellow in that condition, but it seems to help.

Hell Camp near Coyote Mt. marble workings.

CHAPTER XIV

JACK THE RIPPER. NICKEL MINING, PETRIFIED WOOD

I had a similar experience, near the oil town of Maricopa, forty-five miles west of Bakersfield, in 1901. I had been given charge of two flowing wells during a shut-down period and had left the property I was staying on, to walk down to Sunset Post Office. This was situated a mile below, and west of the town (afterward called Maricopa), and three miles from the property I was staying on.

On my return, when I was about a half mile from our property, I saw what I thought was a bear coming over the crest of a hill a hundred feet from our oil derrick. It would move along a short distance and stop, then move on again and stop. Soon I could see it wasn't a bear, but a man on his hands and knees. I got up more speed then and arrived at the derrick at the time he did. To my surprise, "it" turned out to be a fellow everyone called "Jack the Ripper", an Irish character around the oilfields. His tongue was swollen and his knees raw and bloody.

I put him into the derrick, propped him up with sacks and blankets, then I walked up the hill to the office where I stayed. I got a bottle of liquid Jamaica Ginger and some water and returned to the rig and gave him a little water. He was pretty dry, but kept his head and knew how to use it. After a time I gave him a swig of ginger.

Jack was well acquainted with "fire water" and when he got the first swallow down, his eyes started to snap. He didn't grimace in the least when that hot stuff went down. It would have burned a hole clear to my shoes if I had taken that much! I got Jack up to the cook house that next night where he was with me two weeks, recuperating.

Jack told me he had started to walk to McKettrick, twenty-two miles northeast of Maricopa, stopped over-night in an assessment derrick where he had taken a drink of water out of an old tank. He had taken sick and lain down, and couldn't get back on his feet again, so had crawled five miles back to my place. At that time there were no towns between Maricopa and McKettrick, and that whole locality was called Mid-way. Old Jack had quite a crawl!

Bill Trenchard had located a nickel deposit on Coyote Mountain. To get to it we drove up into the entrance of Alverson Canyon, walked half a mile and then took off on a trail to the right side of the canyon which led up the hill to the workings.

Bill sold his property to a Mr. Smith, but Smith gave it up when he found he had to ship the ore to England to have it treated. At that time one could get some nice nickel specimens there.

While he was opening up this nickel prospect, Bill and another man were camped in the canyon. One evening an old prospector with a burro came down to the canyon wash and camped close to them. After he got his camp made he came over to Bill's camp. During the course of their conversation, Bill said, he asked the prospector what brought him into the Coyote Mountain. He told Bill that several years before, he had prospected around and over the foothills of the mountain and had picked up some rocks that he later found to be high-grade silver ore. Did he actually find this ore, or did he know of the Westover find, and was he looking for it? It could have been either one.

Along the later part of August, 1912 at the marble quarry on Coyote Mountain, Wiley Hoover, a director of the company, brought a man who had been sick, out to camp. Hoover said he was driving back that same evening and asked me if I wanted to ride back with him. I had just sharpened up all the drill steel and, since Bill Trenchard had planned to take his family back to San Diego in another week, I decided to go and return before Bill left, so I could look after things while he was away.

Hoover had a Model T, cut down hot rod style, that he used on the desert. He was a big man and when the car got stuck he would pick up one end and then the other, till it was free again.

The moon came up about ten that night and we were well into Devil's Canyon by that time. The old Model T's headlights were run off the engine's magneto which was built into the fly-wheel of the engine. When it was running fast, the lights were bright; when going slowly, they were very dim.

With that cut-down car, Hoover could get over the sandy roads very fast; but when we entered Devil's Canyon, the sharp, narrow curves cut our speed down to low and the lights got dim. Once he hit a rock that had rolled off the canyon wall into the road on the left hand side, and the front of the car bounced up, almost throwing us out. Hoover never stopped. I asked him why he didn't stop and see if the car was damaged. The only answer he gave me was, "She sounds all right and handles all right, so that's all right with me." I guess it was, for we arrived in San Diego "all right", about 3:00 A.M. next morning.

I visited with my family for four days, then boarded a stage one morning that went through to El Centro. I got off at Coyote Wells about 4:30 that afternoon, waited there until five, then put some water in my canteen and started the eight-mile hike to camp. It was still hot and I took it easy, taking advantage of the shade of the pinwood (smoke) trees and sides of the washes. It was dark when I got to the cut-off, where Dutch had cut across before. I climbed the bluff and started along the trail. I wanted to get over the bad places before it was dark, for there were several spots where one could slip off and drop twenty-five to seventy-five feet, maybe break a leg or be stuck there for some time before being found.

It was darkening fast and it seemed I had gone a long way, when I came to the brow of a hill. This hill I didn't remember. I couldn't see farther than ten feet ahead of me, because of the darkness, but I knew I was going in the right direction to cut the big Creole Wash leading to the camp.

Looking down from the top of the hill in the direction I wanted to go was like looking down a mine shaft at night. So I just sat down, took a chance on disturbing a few sidewinders, started sliding, and in a short time was at the bottom and walking again. I came into a small sandy place where I got down on my hands and knees to feel for car tracks, but found none. I did that three times and was beginning to think something was wrong. The next time I found them. I turned to my left and in ten minutes was in my tent. Everyone in camp had gone to bed.

We quarried a good number of the white-orange blocks of marble and piled them up on the opposite side of the little canyon, where they could be loaded when the time came to haul them away. Bill took his family back to San Diego and I took over the job of chief cook and dishwasher, tool sharpener, foreman, and what-have-you.

It would have been interesting if the quarry had been in a feldspar dyke or a deposit of pegmatite. But in a marble quarry like this, we encountered nothing in the line of gem stones or rare rocks. I looked in most of the old fault cracks but found nothing. It was only when Bill and I took time off to look around the mountain, that we found anything worthwhile.

We tried to trace back to its source some pinkish-violet colored calcite we found on the northeast side of the mountain on the mesa flow, but were not successful. Some fair colored petrified wood was found over on the southwest side but in no great quantity. We found nothing in that line on the Carrizo Creek side of the mountain.

Bill Trenchard, Wiley Hoover and I were discussing the fault lines that ran through the marble, when Bill suggested driving over to a big fault he knew on the north side of the mountain. We decided to get up early next morning and get over there before the Old Fire Ball got too high in the sky. It was beginning to warm up, and the boys were commencing to feel the heat even in those canyons. Some hours during the day, it was too hot to work - the temperature running up to 135 degrees, or higher.

Bill, Hoover and I lit out early the next morning, drove down the Creole Wash to the old Butterfield Stage road and turned left in a westerly direction. We crossed the Carrizo Creek, went on up the northwest bank within a short distance of the old stage station, parked the Ford, walked across the creek in a southeasterly direction. We could see ahead another cliff striking off in the direction we were going. Soon we were at the foot of one lower down. On the right, the land seemed to have the appearance of having sunk. At this point we measured the height of this cliff, which we found to be ninety feet. There were scorings on its face which looked as if they were made yesterday. We could see other cliffs to the southeast that looked higher, but we didn't go over to them.

In some of the cracks and vugs in the face of the cliff, we found some rusty cubes of iron pyrites. When broken open, they showed very beautiful insides. The outside portion of the cube was only a shell. Some natural chemistry had taken place which had broken down the interior of these pyrite cubes and lined the interior with thousands of microscopic crystals of beautiful velvety colors of blue, yellow, orange and green. The cubes we found were from one-fourth to five-eighths inches square. We did not investigate the other cliffs as our time was getting short.

Forty years have gone by since we made that trip. I regret very much that I didn't mark the cliff at a certain point - say two feet above the bottom so now I could tell if there had been any movement, either up or down, during that time - for we have had some pretty hard shakes and earth movements in Southern California in those intervening years. Since both top and bottom were of stone, at points where we took the measurements of the heights of the cliff, I believe one could get an answer to the movement question even now. In April, 1953, a friend, Hugh Rogers of Salana Beach, and I drove out there; going in by way of Carrizo stage station, and then on down to what I thought was the place we entered. After a half day's walk I found it wasn't. There were too many clay hills to go over, and I knew we didn't cross many. I believe we didn't follow down the creek far enough. Anyway, we didn't get into the right wash. We had little time for that's a U. S. Air Force aerial target range and we weren't supposed to be there. Maybe, some day, someone will get in there and measure that cliff.

One day, while Bill was taking a short cut back from a sulphur claim he had at the southeast of Hell Camp, he saw an old saddle at the base of a large ocotillo. Under the saddle was a man's coat. On the inside coat pocket was a letter written by Worth Merritt to his wife, while he was at Coyote Wells, possibly forty-eight hours before it was placed under the saddle. Close by were the remains of a rope where he tied his horse. The horse evidently had broken loose and wandered down the little draw, to perish.

All this was in 1906. It was his horse's skeleton that I once found near our first camp.

Worth Merritt stated in the letter found in his coat, that he was writing in the shade of a mesquite tree, dressed like Adam. He said he intended to go on to Brawley, a town on the Southern Pacific Railroad branch in Imperial Valley that evening and would start away from Coyote Wells that afternoon.

The next we heard about him was from my old school friend, Frank Webb, who at that time was camped at Pelican Lake, one of the lakes formed by the overflow of the Colorado River, and by rainfall. Frank said he tried to get Merritt to stay the night there with him for it was dark and he might lose his way. Merritt said he would give the horse his head and he would stay on the road. But the horse didn't.

Merritt had procured the horse at Campo, a town forty miles east of San Diego. When the horse felt free to go where he wanted, he no doubt made a wide turn to the left and started back to Campo. It is possible Merritt dozed now and then; thus giving the horse a chance to head back west. When Merritt discovered he was going wrong, he was well above the Narrows, in the Painted Gorge of the Coyote Mountain. He turned the horse around and climbed out of the wash, up the right bank, as you head down the wash. When we were there, the tracks were still visible in the lava bank.

Merritt rode only a short distance, dismounted, tied his horse and took off the saddle. It must have been warm, for he took off his coat and put it under the saddle. He also had a box of 38-caliber pistol cartridges in his coat pocket. There he was, standing where he could see country he had looked at the afternoon before, and only five miles from where he had written the letter at Coyote Wells. He might have followed down the wash, where I had found what was left of his horse, for that would have led him right to Coyote Wells. Surely, he expected to come back for his horse, saddle and coat! But he didn't. They found Worth Merritt's body on Superstition Mountain, ten miles northeast of where he tied up his horse.

Bill and I figured all the angles we could think of and decided that he may have seen some smoke from the Southern Pacific train at Westmoreland or Brawley, and started to hoof it across the worst desert he could have tackled.

Doc Wilson and Burr Porter in Garnet diggins, Devil's Canyon

Dr. Waldemer T. Schaller, expert Gemologist and Geologist.

CHAPTER XV

QUITTING THE QUARRIES AND LOADING MARBLE

The days were getting hot and the men were showing signs of wanting to quit. We could hardly blame them. The quarry was a furnace from eight in the morning till five at night. So Bill said, "Fred, let's take a look over the claims, check on the work done, and then shut down for the summer."

We took a canteen apiece and some lunch and drove around on the southwest side of the mountain. We ran across some old fossil shells, some of them quite large, sand-dollars and other kinds, all embedded in marbleized sandstone. Most of the rock-boring clams made their holes in the blue marble. Why, I couldn't say - other than probably the blue marble formed the edge of the sea at that particular time. We have found these rock-boring clams still in their holes, and could not detect any wear on the shell. This led us to believe they must have been able to exude some kind of acid that would dissolve the limestone. They must have gone in and out of their holes too, and so kept them the same size to keep pace with the growth of their bodies.

We had three men on the job at that time, besides Bill and me. Bill let one man off and kept Bodendick and Hultz. These boys owned two burros each, so Bill hired them to pack some Siena marble down the trail to the floor of the Gorge, where it could be hauled away in the Model T pick-up.

We had moved the Creole Camp over into the Gorge wash, about eight hundred feet above the Narrows. When all the Siena marble we had collected had been packed down the trail to the Gorge wash, we started hauling the equipment and tents back to San Diego.

After eight months on Coyote Mountain, ending up in a temperature of 135 degrees, I was glad to get back to the coast, but it wasn't for long. Wiley Hoover, a Director of the company, came to me with a proposition to help him haul the marble blocks we had quarried, down to the terminus of the San Diego and Arizona Railroad tracks, which terminated two miles east of Coyote Wells. .

We set up our camp a hundred yards up the wash from the Narrows and in the Gorge. Next morning we drove both Model T's and scouted out a road to the railroad terminal, four miles from our camp. Then we drove back to the quarry and each took a load of marble, about twelve hundred pounds, down to the railroad, to a suitable place where it could be loaded onto a box car. We worked together most of the time. When we didn't, we checked on each other every two or three hours, for it was very hot, especially in the quarries and the Gorge.

We managed to make two trips to the railroad a day. On the last morning, on our first trip back from the track that morning, Hoover twisted an axle on his Model T in the deep sand of the Narrows. I towed him up to our camp. While he was taking the broken axle out of his car, I made one more trip to the foot of the trail for the Siena Marble in the Painted Gorge. I don't know what the temperature was up there, but I got very dizzy and had to wrap a wet towel around my head until I got the car loaded. Not a breath of air was stirring. It was the hottest temperature I had ever experienced.

When I returned to camp, Hoover had the axle out and we drove on down, leaving my load at the railroad. Then we drove on to El Centro. Hoover got another axle, then he ordered a box car spotted at the railroad terminal where we had deposited the marble. The railroad officials promised to spot the car for us within two days. This gave us time to move the rest of the marble, and our camp, down to the rail terminal.

The first night in our camp at the rail terminal, was a beautiful one. The stars hung down so one could almost reach up and touch them! The air was balmy as one could find any place. We laid our blankets down on the sand and sprawled out on them, enjoying the relief from the day's intense heat.

The morrow was the day the car was to be spotted for us. We bounced out of our blankets early, cooked our breakfast, loaded all our stuff in the cars, and waited. As the morning wore on, the temperature climbed higher and higher. The country around us was flat and sandy and took up the heat at once. No train smoke was in sight, so we ran one of the cars alongside the other, with a five-foot space between. Then we threw the tent over both of them and crawled under. As the sun moved to the west we moved to the east, and by the time the sun set back of the Laguna Mountains, we were out from under and on the east side of the cars.

The next day we used the same routine and we went through the same watchful waiting. The third day, we waited till almost ten-thirty A.M., when we decided to find out what caused the delay.

We took the car I was using and started for El Centro. It was a lucky move that we started when we did, too; for it was REALLY getting hot, and we had gone only a mile or so when we could make out two men, walking slowly, going east on the old Butterfield Stage road. I don't think they saw us till we were close to them. I don't believe they could have made it for another mile.

I'm sure, if we hadn't come along when we did, it would have been the end of them!

From the expression on their faces, one would think they couldn't believe their eyes when they saw us. They had already walked about five miles that morning, and now the heat was about to get them. We put them in the back of the car and lit out for Dixieland, the nearest town. They told us their car had broken down a little east of the Carrizo Stage Station. They had some rusty water they had taken out of the radiator, but it wouldn't have been enough, anyway. The heat would soon have cracked them.

They were from San Diego. When they found out we expected to go back to San Diego, as soon as we loaded the box car, they asked to ride back with us, offering to help us load the marble for the ride back. They said they would rest up and ride out on the train with our box car. We didn't expect too much help from these fellows. It all depended on "how" they rested up.

We were given another two-day promise by the railroad official, who said they would send the car out sure, this time. We filled the car tank with gas and lit out for camp. When we were getting supper that evening, a little kit fox came and sat on a little hillock about fifty feet away. We talked to him for a while, but he wasn't as tame as some, and soon left.

The next day was as hot as ever. We rose early and made breakfast, then started our migration eastward, under the cars. That was the toughest day we experienced. We didn't expect the box car, so we didn't look for smoke. All we could do was sweat it out - which we did. How glad we were when that old fire ball went down behind the mountains!

There is something about the desert on a summer's evening that is restful, provided one's tongue isn't swollen and that one isn't out of water. The desert offers companionship to those who want to listen to the scores of little wildlife and their music. If one happens to camp near a Kangaroo rat's nest and to have some soda crackers, he can put in an enjoyable evening.

One afternoon, along in the fall of 1939, and about four P.M. Mrs. Rynerson and I camped just above the Narrows in the Painted Gorge on Coyote Mountain. We expected some friends to arrive that evening about nine. Around dusk, we built a small fire and toasted some bread for cheese sandwiches. After we had eaten, we discovered a small Kangaroo rat that would come up close to us and stand there wiggling his little nose in all directions.

I got out some soda crackers and threw him a small piece,

which he immediately carried away. He did this several times. Then a big Kangaroo showed up and drove the little fellow away, but not for long. Back he came. I threw him another piece of cracker. The little fellow dove for it, and so did the big one. But the little fellow got it, and the race was on. It didn't take the little fellow long to ditch the big one, and he was back for more in two minutes, lashing his little tail. I threw in another piece. This time the big fellow dove after the little one, but he dodged out of the way, ran in and picked up the cracker.

This kept up for an hour or more, and the little fellow had that rat wild. I don't think the rat got one piece out of the lot! At last the rat followed the little fellow away and out of the camp. We had about given up seeing them again, when the little fellow showed up. By nine P.M., when our friends arrived, he had maneuvered about all our crackers away from us. With a piece of cracker as a lure, Mrs. Rynerson got the little fellow on her hand. But he forgot the cracker for an instant and took a taste of her thumb, with the result that he found himself on the sand! That ended the day for the rats.

To come back to the marble camp; next morning we got up early, had our breakfast and loaded up the cars before the sun warmed things up. This was the day we hoped the railroad officials would not fail us, for we were getting tired of waiting.

It was about ten-thirty A.M. when we first discovered train smoke around the town of Seeley. It seemed to get closer, and soon we could see that it was heading for the end of the line. Sure enough, the two men we had picked up three days before were in the box car with the brakemen.

We had a two-wheeled truck, like those used in freight depots. We passed a one-inch rope through the front end and the two men in the box car took an end apiece. Hoover and I loaded the truck and got it headed up the gangplanks. Then, with all of us pulling and pushing, we loaded the whole eighteen tons in about two hours. Leaving the truck, gangplank and rope in the box car, the brakeman sealed it up and we started for San Diego; Hoover taking one of the men and I the other. We arrived in San Diego about sundown.

It was in 1935, twenty-two years later, that I was standing in front of an assay shop on Eighth Street in San Diego, when I noticed a well-dressed, heavy-set man standing in the doorway of the store next door. I noticed, too, that he kept watching me. A thunderstorm had come up in the east and the clouds were black overhead. I made the remark to him that it looked as though it were going to rain. He replied that it sure did, and came over to where I was standing and said, "Is your name Rynerson?"

I said, "Yes."

"Do you remember me?" he asked.

I said, "I don't believe so, but there's something familiar about your face."

"Well, you saved my life once." he said. About that time, I thought he was crazy.

Then he went on, "Do you remember you and a Mr. Hoover picked up two fellows on the road between Carrizo Springs and Dixieland? Well, I was one of those fellows, the one that rode back to San Diego with you.

We had a long talk over those few hours when we first met, out there in the heat. I had forgotten his name, also his partner's, and haven't seen them since.

Sam Cameron, old-time Campo (San Diego Co.) pioneer.

CHAPTER XVI

WORKING THE ESMERALDA. OLD FRENCH CHARLEY. THE BIG COYOTE

The old Esmeralda Mine had produced very good pink crystals of tourmaline, as well as pink beryls, or morganites, when I was interested in them in 1905. I had in mind to prospect the west end as soon as I left the marble company.

I had taken on some cutting for a Mr. Tom Quin who wanted some tourmaline buttons cut Chinese style. I had in the past sold Mr. Quin many pounds of pink tourmaline; now he was in the market for many more. I told him it might be possible to get some out of the Esmeralda if we could get a lease from Mrs. Nickelson, who owned the property. He told me to see what I could do about it and we would go in together on working it. I looked up the address of Mrs. Nickelson in Los Angeles and got a lease from her.

There was only one place on that vein that I thought might throw a pocket and that was at the west end. I had a few hand drills and hammers and, with some powder, grub and a tent, I had a man haul the lot over to a small creek a quarter of a mile from the mine. In the meantime I had made arrangements with Fred Angel to help me with the work.

We put in about a week running a cut across the vein, but that was enough. The vein was very blank and completely crushed, indicating a pinching off of the vein. All we found that was interesting was a big rattlesnake, one morning, coiled up near the breast of the cut.

On the day I decided to quit the work, Fred Angel had quit at noon and had ridden his horse home. I put in the afternoon, until about three, looking over the vein, then walked over to my tent. As I topped the hill where I could see my tent, I saw a man leave it and walk toward a road close by, in a direction away from me. I knew this man, but not his name. I whistled to him, and also called, but he paid no attention. He turned to his right and entered some thick brush.

When I arrived at the tent, I found he had left a horse-hair quirt and two matches on the floor. He had searched through my bed, from head to foot, taking a tourmaline watch fob, made of two bi-colored tourmaline crystals, green and pink, about two inches long and three-eighths inch thick, mounted in eighteen carat gold - also my flashlight.

It was too late then to go after him, for he could easily lose me in the brush. I had intended to go over to the Mesa Grande store for my mail and stay the night at the Angel ranch. So I tied up the tent and started walking up the trail to the ranch house about three miles away.

When I described to the Angel boys the man I had seen leave my tent, they at once told me his name and where he lived. They also told me I had a phone call awaiting me at the store. Borrowing a horse of one of the boys', I rode over to the store and found that the phone call was from my friend Tom Quin, who wanted to know what I thought of a lease on the Himalaya Mine. He said he could get a fifty-year lease if I thought it would pay. I told him to get it. He asked me to come down to San Diego next morning, but I told him I had a little matter I wanted to straighten out before I could come.

I was a little worried about losing my tourmaline fob. This fellow who took it was pretty smooth. He could pass it on to someone else, or hide it. As I was the only one to see him leave my tent, he could put up a good fight. By the time I had come back to the Angel ranch, I had made up my mind there was only one way to get my fob back.

Everything, including the weather, played into my hands, for during the night it rained, and continued through the next day and night. I stayed at the Angel ranch that night. The next morning I borrowed a 30-30 carbine from Newton Angel and started out afoot for my fob. It was a long walk and I soaked up a lot of water for I didn't have my slicker with me. I was sure, though, that I would find my man home in this kind of weather.

His house was located in a little clearing on a ridge, not more than three-quarters of a mile from my tent. Smoke was coming out of the fireplace chimney, which was reassuring. I made my way around to the blind side of the house and came to the door. In answer to my knock, an old man opened the door. I asked if Pedro was home. He opened the door wide and pointed at Pedro sitting in front of the fireplace.

On hearing his name, Pedro turned towards me and I pointed the rifle towards the inside of the room and told him to come out, I wanted to talk to him. Picking up his hat, he came out at once. I showed him the quirt I had found on the floor of my tent and asked him if it was his. He said no, it belonged to one of two boys that I knew. I told him I had seen him coming out of my tent and I had picked the quirt up from off the floor. But he still said it belonged to the other fellow.

"All right, we'll go see this boy." I said. But he didn't want to go because it was raining. I told him he'd better come, or I would take him to San Diego. That seemed to do it, for he made no further objections. On the way, I filled my pipe and asked him for a match. He gave me the same kind of match I had picked off the floor of my tent.

When we came within two hundred feet of the boy's home, and facing the door, we paused for a few minutes in the timber. I told him to take the quirt and go to the door, but not to go into the house, or it would be too bad for him. He was to ask the boy if he owned it and then come back to where I was standing. I told him to get going and pointed the rifle toward the house.

He slipped out of the brush into the clearing and walked to the door and knocked. One of the boys opened it and Pedro held up the quirt for him to see. I saw the boy shake his head, meaning no. After a little more talk, the boy backed inside and started to close the door. Pedro turned and walked back to me.

"He says he does not own it," Pedro said, and he was shaking like a leaf in the wind.

"Pedro," I said, "I knew all the time that boy didn't own that quirt. You own that quirt and you know it! Now, I'm going to give you one more chance. Bring that watch fob and my flashlight back by tomorrow noon, or I shall take you to San Diego and they will compel you to go some place you don't want to, when they hear what I have to say." I never saw a man more frightened, when he left me.

Pedro puts me in mind of a Borneo native who was captured by whites. One of the white men had lost one of his own men and felt sure this native knew where he could be found. After being questioned for some time, and denying any knowledge of him, a white started to tie a rope around his neck. The native asked the interpreter what they were going to do. The interpreter told him the whites knew that inside of him he had the knowledge of where the lost man was, but wouldn't tell, so they were going to hold it inside him while they cut open his belly and get it out. The native quickly told them what they wanted to know.

The next noon, Hector Angel and I arrived at the camp to get my tent and things and move them over to Vance Angel's ranch. Twenty feet from the front of the tent lay a rolled up grain sack, tied with a string. I picked it up and felt my flashlight inside. On opening it, I found my fob wrapped in some paper. Whoever brought it back rode up on horseback fifty feet away and threw it over to where I had picked it up. So I didn't have to take Pedro to San Diego with me. That was in 1914. I understand he has been dead for some years. I learned that Pedro wasn't his real name.

In the fall of 1914, Sam Cameron of Campo, San Diego County

brought me a dark heavy rock and asked what it was. It was quite heavy and since tungsten was one of the principal minerals wanted at that time, I thought it might be wolframite. Sam was going back home that day, so I told him I would let him know what I found out about it as soon as I saw the assayer.

The assayer told me it was tungsten ore. So two days later I boarded a stage for Campo, fifty miles east of San Diego, near the Mexican border. I walked north to Sam's ranch at La Posta, arriving about 2:00 P.M. I had known Sam since the latter part of 1895 but had never visited his ranch. Sam told me that it was the old home place his family had settled on in 1866. It was an adobe house of four or more rooms. The kitchen, dining room and living room were one, with a big fireplace in the east end. Jane, his sister, had never married and neither had Sam, so both stayed on in the old house.

That evening Sam played some old time tunes on his violin. Jane brought out her big Colt 45, with its six-inch barrel and white bone handle. Now don't think Jane couldn't shoot that 45!

A young man rode up to the house that evening, rigged out with a six-shooter and knife. The gun was one of those suicide guns, about six inches over-all. Sam said he was from the city, and asked him what he could hit with a gun like that. So he set up a tomato can on a post, saying, "See if you can hit that."

After the stranger had taken two shots at it and missed, Sam called Jane. When she came he said, "Get your gun and show this feller how to hit that can."

Jane disappeared into the house. When she came to the door again only her head and arm showed. She took a quick shot at the can and it flew off the post as if a cannon ball hit it. Jane ducked back into the house and Sam said, "Now, that's the kind of a gun to have. You can't hit anything with a gun like yours."

But Sam didn't count himself in on that. I had a little automatic with an even shorter barrel, which Sam took and put three bullets into a four-inch circle, twenty-five feet away. That was one-hundred per cent better than I could do.

Later Sam had some work and couldn't go with me to the place where he found the wolframite. He gave me instructions so perfectly that I had no trouble in finding the spot, three miles from his house. The ore was in little veins, one-quarter to an inch in width, in the massive granite, and not in one large vein. I collected a few pieces and left. I told Sam I didn't think it would be worthwhile to mine. I found afterward it was mostly iron, and not wolframite.

Sam Cameron and his brother Charley were tough fellows. I do not mean in character, but in other things. Through the many years I have known them, I could always depend on what they said. Charley was on the Mexican border as an immigration officer for years; being finally retired by Uncle Sam.

One day, Sam and his brother George were driving across a creek near home when Sam fell out of the wagon, breaking his leg. He told George to take hold of his leg and pull it. Sam then set the bone and George tied some sticks on four sides of the leg to hold it in place. Sam told me afterward that it didn't knit correctly and had to be broken and re-set again.

Sam, Charley and George brought to me for cutting many of the local native stones, and some from Mexico. Most of them were very beautiful.

One time Sam left his ranch home at La Posta, rode his horse to a place called Boulevard, and on down into Carrizo Gorge. He said he was riding along a trail when he happened to look up on the side of the Gorge and saw what looked to be a cave. He rode as near to it as he could, then dismounted to make the rest of the way on foot.

He found quite a cave with a sandy floor. In the middle of it someone had left, sticking in the sand, an old Spanish cavalry sword. It had been there a long time. The blade had been thrust into the sand about eighteen inches. Sam believed some Indian or Mexican had killed a cavalryman, or had stolen the sword and, not wanting to be caught with it in his possession, had left it in the cave. He said he made a combined butcher knife and hunting knife out of it.

Sam told me he hired out as a guide to a small detachment of soldiers and surveyors who were working the Mexican line across the desert, east of Campo. One morning the lieutenant said, "Sam, let's ride along ahead into these hills." As they rode the lieutenant said, "Sam, let's wrestle!"

Sam didn't know what the lieutenant was up to, at first, then the lieutenant told him he liked to wrestle, but didn't want his men to see him.

Sam was most afraid that one of the soldiers, after not seeing them for some time would decide to look them up. If it was his turn to be on top - and Sam said he could throw the officer easily - he might take a shot at him, thinking he was killing the officer. Sam said he wouldn't have blamed the soldier, either; for who but a crazy man would be wrestling out in that country!

Blue tourmalines were good sellers in those days. I heard that some had been found at the head of Rincon, on the north-west side of the Warner Ranch. I thought, as long as I was in Mesa Grande, I would go over and have a look-see. Fred Angel was willing to go with me, so we got together some provisions and blankets, a rifle and shotgun, climbed on a horse apiece, and lit out.

We arrived at the old ranch house in the Rincon about noon. A small boy was there who told us French Charley was sick in bed and he had just brought him something to eat. The boy, not more than seven years old, said he lived over near Dead Man's Hole, on the north side of the ranch, six or seven miles away. He didn't stay long, but mounted his horse and rode away.

We went into the house and found Charley on a bed about four feet high, no springs. It was simply some hay on boards, with a canvas over the hay, an old comfort to lie on, and two blankets to cover him. This was well along in the fall of the year when the nights were cold. No fire had been in the fireplace for some time, or in the kitchen stove. All the food in the house consisted of some corn starch. I told Fred I would go back to a slough we passed coming over, and get a duck or two to make Charley some soup. It was about a quarter of a mile back, so I took the shotgun and started walking.

When I got within a hundred feet of the slough, the banks of which were five feet high, I could hear the ducks. I got down as low as I could and crept within forty feet of the bank, then raised up. The slough was full of ducks! I picked out a bunch of canvas-backs and let them have it. When they rose into the air, I gave them the second barrel. When they flew away around the bend of the slough two hundred yards, seven remained on the water in the slough. With a long willow pole I retrieved the lot and started back to the ranch house.

Fred cleaned the ducks while I cleaned up the kitchen, built a fire and got things ready to cook the ducks. I never saw ducks so fat. When I got through cooking them, I had about a quart of duck fat, or grease. I made some gravy out of some of it. The rest, we put into a can for Charley's later use.

When Fred was cleaning the ducks, he had a hard time keeping Charley's dog from stealing them, he was so hungry. The only animal around the place that had plenty of food was Charley's horse. He had a whole barn full of hay and was as fat as he could be.

Charley paid us little attention up to the time we brought the duck soup. He just lay there cussing himself. After he had eaten some soup and a piece of duck, he sat up in bed. In the meantime,

Fred had built a fire in the fireplace, and the room got warmer and more cheerful. About an hour later, Old Charley climbed out of bed and sat in an old rocking chair by the fire. He started to talk, telling us all about his boyhood days, herding sheep and then, cattle. His rich uncle in San Francisco wanted him to go to school, and then into business with him. But he wanted to be a cowboy, and this is where he ended up. He talked a blue streak till midnight, when we told him to get into bed for we were going to turn in. After we got to bed, I remarked to Fred it was wonderful what a little duck soup would do!

Charley said his stomach had been bothering him so I told Fred we had better ride over to Warner Hot Springs and get some medicine. The next morning we started. We left our guns with Charley, for they didn't allow rifle shooting on the ranch and we had enough meat for a few days, anyway. On the way over, the trail led along a wire fence. We hadn't gone more than a mile, when we saw a large wildcat on the opposite side of the fence, in a grove of cottonwood trees. Fred had two of his dogs along, Muzzy and Joe. Joe was a hound, no special kind. Muzzy was a shepherd. Fred started them out after the cat. We dismounted and ran after them for a ways, then lost sight of the cat while the dogs seemed to be interested in some other animal. I wasn't sure, but I thought the cat got into the brush on the edge of the clearing, so I stopped and sat down on a log.

Fred was up near the brush trying to get the dogs under control. Muzzy had gone into the brush. When he came out I saw a big black-shouldered coyote following, smelling of his tail. I saw Fred throw back his head and laugh. At that instant the coyote let out a sharp bark and turned back into the brush. We knew then what had bothered the dogs. Fred couldn't get them to do anything after that, so we started back to the horses. The dogs stayed within twenty-five feet of us all the way over, while that big coyote followed behind about a hundred feet, barking like a dog and trying to get the dogs to chase him. He was the largest coyote we had ever seen and we decided he was part dog. Fred said he knew where we could get the horses through the fence into the other side. When we came back from the Springs we would give that fellow a run.

We couldn't get anything for Charley's stomach at the Springs, so I bought a bottle of Jamaica ginger and started back. We kept in low places, out of sight of the place where we figured the coyote was. But shortly after we got near the fence, we saw five coyotes, one extra large one and four normal size. They were in a clear spot, an acre in size, opening out onto the cleared ranch.

At the upper end of this clearing it narrowed down to six or eight feet wide, then opened out again into an open spot about fifty feet across.

Now this old coyote was a General! All five sat in the lower clearing, watching us as we rode up to the opening in the fence. Two of the normal-sized coyotes went into the brush on the left side of the clearing. Then the other two went in on the right side, leaving the big boy sitting there scratching himself and paying no attention to us. It was no use for us to rush them for it was rocky in the brush. We walked slowly along to see what the old boy would do. As we got closer, he walked slowly up through the narrow opening into the upper clearing, not a hundred yards ahead of us, and sat there watching us. Seeing the dogs wouldn't follow, he too went into the brush. We went back and out on the other side of the fence.

Here the dogs ranged farther ahead. It wasn't long before we heard old Joe's voice. Fred said old Joe had something cornered - and he sure did! We pressed the spurs to the horses and soon saw what Joe had. It was a big, baldheaded skunk. Joe was wise and stood off ten feet barking at it. About that time, I saw Muzzy coming like a race horse. About twelve feet away he opened his mouth as wide as he could and made for the skunk. I saw the skunk turn about half around and send a stream the size of my finger right into old Muzzy's mouth. Talk about a bomb shell! Old Muzzy stopped in his tracks and went over backward, rolling and tumbling on the ground, acting as if he couldn't get his breath! Joe, about that time, closed in, getting a dose too! Fred got off his horse, saying something about having to live with those damn dogs. Getting a big rock, he killed the skunk.

When we got back to Charley, we found he had cleaned up the soup and was on his feet again. We left some Jamaica ginger with him. Taking our stuff, we moved on up to the head of the Rincon. This was late in the afternoon and we killed a few birds for supper, cleaning them near a small creek on the southwest side of the Rincon.

We made our camp seventy-five feet north of the creek, under an oak tree, beside a sloping bank four feet high. The lower branches of the oak on that side came down and rested partly on top of the bank. We finished our supper and were sitting around the fire, planning what to do in the morning. Muzzy and Joe were lying on the bank under the oak branches. We had heard some coyotes earlier and had noticed one had a very deep voice. We remarked that probably he was the big fellow we had seen that day. It wasn't long before we heard the coyotes scratching in the leaves near the creek where we had cleaned the birds. Half an hour later, we heard Muzzy growl, and then in another instant, he dove out from under the branches into the pitch black night. In another second, back he came. He must have made one big jump, for he came flying through those oak branches, almost sliding into the fire. He had his mouth wide open, with an expression which seemed to say, "Boy, that was a close call! I'm happy to be here!"

Joe hadn't moved during the whole fracas, except for a few growls and a bark or two. We didn't let Muzzy stay by the fire, either, but drove him back under the branches. He was still too "skunky" to have close around.

Next day, and the following, we prospected the veins over the surrounding hills and found nothing we cared to work. I believe the blue tourmaline came from the old Bill Dyche claim on Aguanga Mountain. The following day, we started back to Mesa Grande, arriving in a light snow storm. The next day I took the stage for San Diego.

Mrs. Beulah Rynerson standing by giant Barrel Cactus, on flat below Mt. Palms, San Diego Co.

Charley Camer on Border Guard, San Diego County.

CHAPTER XVII

QUARTZ AT TRIPP FLAT. THE OLD MEXICAN

On returning to San Diego, I found that Quin had closed the deal on the Himalaya Mine lease and it would be a few days before the papers would be in order. Quin asked me if I knew where we could get some crystal quartz, as he had an order for a thousand pounds or more - but it had to be clear and free from imperfections. I knew all the gem mines threw some quartz crystals. I thought of all the likely places and ended up with one Bert Simmons had told me about but which I had never seen.

I rented Wiley Hoover's Model T, and drove out to Bert Simmons' place at Oak Grove, which is on the road from Warner's Hot Springs to Temecula. Luck was with me. I found Simmons at home and told him what I wanted. He said he would leave with me the following morning for the place.

I stayed the night at Bert's. The next morning we drove down to Aguanga and turned right on the road to Coahuilla. After passing the Indian Reservation Settlement, we turned to the left and drove to ''Tripp Flat'', and camped in the old Tripp adobe house. We arrived there about noon. After lunch we took a pick and shovel apiece and walked in a southeasterly direction, a quarter of a mile to some low hills. We climbed about two-thirds of the way up the side and came to an old tunnel about twenty feet long.

The dump from these workings was full of quartz crystals. We gathered up some very fine ones - one water white, badly broken on the crystal edges, that would cut a good five-inch sphere perfect. We picked out of the dump, and also off of it, about a hundred pounds of first class material, some slightly smoky.

Sizing up the vein, I started in on a likely place to the right of the tunnel about three feet. I hadn't worked out but ten inches of vein (badly broken), when I ran into almost a solid mass of silica. I worked on through this and broke into a dry pocket containing very fine crystalized quartz. They lay like stove wood corded up, with the terminated ends pointed in a northerly direction. The largest crystal was fourteen inches long by three inches in diameter. They averaged around ten inches in length. I took about five hundred pounds out of this pocket, along with a few pounds of smaller crystals, three to six inches long, during our operations. We got out about three hundred pounds that afternoon, including those we picked off the dump, and packed them over to the house.

That evening Bert made some biscuits in the Dutch oven and,

along with some honey, bacon and coffee, we ate supper and called it a day. We cooked outside the house on a camp fire, but rolled up in our blankets on the floor inside the house.

The old adobe house hadn't been occupied for some time. No furniture remained except a homemade table, ten feet long. Near the end of the table, on the wall side, was where Old Man Tripp sat. When he had finished his meal, he would tilt back his chair against the wall and fill his pipe for his usual smoke, so Bert said. In doing this, his chair had worn a gash in the adobe wall two inches deep and eighteen inches long. It must have taken years, and several chairs, to wear a gash like that in so hard a brick.

Next morning, after a good breakfast, we climbed the hill and went to work on that pocket. I was in hopes I would find something besides quartz crystals there, but I didn't. It was strictly a quartz crystal pocket. There was one feature of this pocket that differed from other pockets I have seen. The roof, or lining, of the pocket was a solid sheet of silica. In some places it showed a rough crystalized shape, while the rest looked like slightly smoky, molten glass.

Other than quartz crystals, the pocket contained a dry yellowish-red clay that looked like coarse corn meal, and a large amount of mica balls, the size of a pea. Some of this mica was crystalized on the sides of the quartz crystals and the lining of the pocket - or was already there when the quartz crystalized.

I was told by an Indian who lived at Coahuilla that the tunnel was made by one "Petra", a lapidary in Los Angeles who was looking for beryl, but the tunnel was now owned by the Indian, from whom we got permission to work it.

The next morning we drove over to the old Fano mine where Bert said he wanted to show me some kunzite he had found in a little hole on the southeast slope, near the old workings. It wasn't long before Bert ran across the hole which was five feet long, two feet wide and about two feet deep. I could see very little of the vein, but on the little dump was a lot of small pieces and slivers of very light lilac spodumene. None that I saw would cut a faceted stone.

After eating our noon lunch, we started for Oak Grove, Bert's home. Looking towards the southeast, the whole country seemed to be afire, and Bert was anxious to get back. Passing a team and wagon driven by a man whom Bert knew, Bert asked about the big brush fire and was told that an armed Mexican was setting fire to the whole country. When we arrived at Bert's home, it was getting dark. Bert stopped and talked with some friends and

I drove on into the yard. After a while Bert came into the house and told me that Henery Bergman and his son had trailed the Mexican to his camp. After some parleying with him, the Mexican had said that the Insurrectos in his country had killed all his family and friends. It seems he had gone on a one-man war against Insurrectos and everyone else with whom he came in contact.

After supper at Bert's, I started for San Diego with my six hundred pounds of quartz crystals, the nicest lot of clear quartz I have ever taken out of a pocket. I have picked out some "all quartz" pockets, but none that threw such perfect material and clear cut crystals.

Next day at my home in San Diego, I culled the lot down to 400 pounds. It was shipped to China and fell into the hands of pirates-so we were notified. I went back later to look the quartz property over for a probable purchase. I again picked up Bert and we contacted the Indian who wanted $600.00 for the claim. After looking the whole vein over, I decided not to buy.

Returning to the car, I walked up a small ravine with Bert about twelve feet ahead of me. I passed a rock on my left, about twelve inches high where I saw a large rattlesnake coiled behind it. I stopped and called to Bert to look what he had just passed. Seeing the snake, he jerked both arms up alongside his body, as if shocked. I had seen him do that before. It seemed to be an obsession, or habit, with him. Why he should continue to be that way when he lived almost continuously around snakes, I never knew. He never was bitten, or he would have told me about it.

After a few days of lapidary work, I again drove up to Mesa Grande with tools and powder to start work on the Himalaya Mine. At that time, most of the mine workings were open. We worked all the likely places that promised quick returns. Vance Angel, who had been foreman of the mine for eight years, was the only man I had with me. Cleaning out around old pockets netted us some stuff with a nice lot of specimens in the matrix, which we broke to get the tourmalines out. Specimens, in those days, were practically worthless. They weren't worth hauling to town and holding until some collector came along to offer a few cents for them.

Facet cutting material was slow selling at the time we took over the Himalaya Mine, but the imperfect pink cabochon material (three-fourths inch in diameter) and, in sound condition, had a ready market in China or Japan.

Our first underground work of any importance was a drift off the old flag pole shaft at the top of the hill, where the vein leads over the ridge. We were down sixty feet from the surface and started drifting east off the shaft on a portion of the vein which was highly mineralized.

We picked up some tourmaline in small pockets of eight or ten inches in diameter, and then the vein became blank, with the vein almost all feldspar. This was still encouraging. After two or three days more of work, and ten feet of drift, we came to a more mineralized vein.

About time to quit work one evening, I thought I would investigate a small block of lepidolite on the side of the drift which we had cut through that morning. I hadn't picked into the side more than a few inches when I broke into a small pocket about two inches in diameter and a little over four inches deep. There, facing me, were the terminated flat ends of thirty tourmaline crystals about the size of a common lead pencil! They lay so close together I could hardly get the first one out. They were not all the same length, being three to four inches long. All were bi-colored, pink and green, with double terminations. I have taken out a good many of these small pockets, or "bugholes", but none as rich as this one. Some have only one tourmaline, or quartz crystal in them, while others have a few lepidolite crystals and, sometimes, a crystal of stibiotantalite.

Most of the pockets farther in on that drift, ran to the yellow-green side. As we were after the pink, we shifted our work to a place below the main tunnel on the west side. Here, some of the vein had been worked out, but this locality had been rich. Vance thought he could pick up the vein in a place which others hadn't disturbed.

We started a cut on an outcrop, but hadn't gone far before we came to the end of it, and then, onto the foot-wall, along which we followed. Some time in the distant past, a severe disturbance had taken place here. It might have been a quake, or a very wet period, or both at once; for the vein had slipped out, leaving the hard "gabbro" foot-wall in place. Of course everything on top of the vein went with it, for what we found on the foot-wall was fill that had washed in. After following this foot-wall about ten feet, we started underground in a shallow tunnel, keeping the foot-wall high, to give us more ground overhead. After sixty-five feet, we came to the vein where it had broken off and, as luck would have it, right across a pocket. This pocket hadn't a gem stone in it, but had dumped the contents when the break occurred.

The way the fill had been laid down on the foot-wall, we could determine the course of the vein's slip. We augered a hole some three feet, straight up in the roof of the tunnel. Close to the broken pocket, at the breast of the tunnel, we loaded it with a stick or two of powder, lit the fuse, and went outside to locate the end of the tunnel from the shot. Then we dropped downhill for sixty feet and started digging a cut toward the end of our tunnel. This cut was almost at right angles to the tunnel.

We hadn't gone far before we started picking up pink slugs of tourmaline, one and one-half inches thick by two and three inches long. We found none under three-quarter inches in diameter and no gem material at all. Material classed as gem stuff in those days was free from fracture or imperfections. The contents of this pocket must have been dumped out all at one time, for it lay in a bed of yellow clay two or three inches thick, strewn along for thirty or forty feet, and not over three feet wide. The bulk of the pocket contents must have remained in the side that pulled away, and then dropped out as the piece of the vein slipped along. We found no crystals any closer than five or six feet from the broken pocket in the tunnel, leading us to believe it must have been quite a jerk.

We used this new cut and continued on with the tunnel. Then we ran into a mess of boulders and water, also much broken vein matter, so we quit. We took out some thirty-five or forty pounds of pink tourmaline there, all of which was Chinese stuff.

In the meantime, I had been trying to get Vance to remember where his men took out the deep wine-red colored tourmaline with the blue caps and yellow collars. The next morning, after we quit the dumped pocket cut, Vance said he thought he knew where the red stuff had come from. So we went about three-fourths of the way up the ridge along the vein and started a cut. But after a couple of days, I could see we were wasting our time. The spot was blank. I quit then and went back to San Diego for a few days.

It was late in the spring of 1915 when I got an order for some blue tourmaline. Knowing of only one place where it had been found in quantity, I got my camp outfit together and lit out for Mesa Grande. The place I had in mind to work was an old prospect that was first found by Bert Simmons and later located by Bill Dyche - and later, given up. This large chunk of vein matter lies almost due south of the Mountain Lily Mine on Aguanga Mountain and is very much like the Esmeralda Mine in the Mesa Grande district, except that this vein lies almost flat.

Some very good blue tourmaline and blue topaz had been taken out here. The men who did the work, started a small tunnel and drove it in about twelve feet, then turned to the left and continued turning till they almost broke outside again, not more than fifteen feet from where they had started in. That was the extent of the work done when we got there, and that many years before.

"Doc" Wilson (with wheel barrow) and Fred Rynerson, in cut at Esmeralda Mine, San Diego County.

Old Thomas Car, with chain drive, at Pala Mission. Mrs. Rynerson is in front seat; her father, Buel Bonfoey, in back of car. Three Rynerson children are present, including Eugene, Elizabeth (now Mrs. Elizabeth Rynerson Wiltse), and Myrna (now Mrs. Myrna Rynerson Elsinger).

CHAPTER XVIII

CAMPING WITH NEWTON ANGEL. MAKING A STOVE WHAT A RAIN!

Newton Angel and I made camp at the foot of the trail on the north side of the Rincon, in the northwest arm of Warner's Ranch. The trail led up to Fir Tree Canyon, and was very steep. We had a small six-by-eight foot tent to sleep in. We expected to do our cooking outside.

We cleared away all the leaves from under an oak tree and set up the tent, then made a rock fireplace, with stones to cook on. That evening it looked like it might storm, so we put in the rest of the evening gathering wood. As our tent was pitched on a slight slope with the sides facing up and down the slope, I dug out a space length-wise with the tent, about two feet wide by six feet long and five inches deep on the up-hill side and two inches on the lower side. I then filled it up with grass and figured I had a pretty good bed. This bed was on the up-hill side of the tent. Newton slept on the lower side. That night we had a few sprinkles, just enough to wet the grass, but it still looked stormy, so we rustled some more wood.

About ten o'clock next morning, one of the Angel boys rode up on a horse and told us that the Angel Ranch House had burned down and they wanted Newton to come home. I told Newton to send over Henry Stenbock, if he could come. Henry was a miner who had worked in the gem mines and later, for me, and was a good miner.

This put a different slant to the picture. To save as much time as I could, I carried up the picks and shovels and looked the vein over, also put a location notice on it. Looking over the indications in the tunnel, I decided on a spot on the right side of the tunnel, about ten feet inside. Looking over the vein on the surface, I could see it was only a chunk that had slid down the mountain. Hence, my chances of finding very much stuff were very limited.

As I walked down the trail to camp, I could see that I might be in for some rain that night; but, as it had failed to come the night before, I thought it might clear up. Not far away from camp, someone had set up some bees and hunters had used the place for a camp spot. The bees were gone now and cans of all kinds were scattered about.

I was tired that evening after the long climb up to the diggings with that load. After supper, I sat by the fire about an hour, then hit the hay. I must have gone to sleep at once, for it seemed no time until morning and I awoke all at once to find myself lying in a pool of water. It had rained steadily during the night and had seeped into the hole I had made and filled with grass. I must have been dead to the world, not to know that I was lying in so much water.

Scrambling out of my blankets, I put on my pants, which were soaked from using them as a pillow. My blankets were wet too - and it was raining outside. I couldn't build a fire in the tent, or I would have to move out myself. After jumping around and warming up a little, I thought of the cans over at the bee camp.

I have always carried a pair of side cutter pliers and a few nails with me on all my trips. They are the handiest things to have on a camping trip, other than matches and bailing wire. I found two five-gallon honey cans in fair condition, and about ten tomato cans. Using my knife, I cut one end out of each five-gallon can and wired the cans together. I cut a hole for a door in the side of one can to use to put the wood in. Setting the cans on end, I marked a three-inch circle; then, from the center, I slit the tin several times back to the marked circle. This was in one corner of the top end of the can. I then pulled up the slit ends of the tin with the pliers.

I then cut the ends out of the tomato cans and wired them end to end; making a stove pipe. I wired one end of this pipe to the hole I had cut in the top of the stove cans. Then I placed the stove close to the door, or flap of the tent and extended the can stove pipe out the flap opening. I cut another piece of tin to hold the smoke stack away from the tent - and fired up the contraption.

In getting the material to make this stove, my clothes had absorbed a lot more water from the steady rain, and the temperature was dropping. It wasn't long before the tent was warm, however, and by night the blankets were only slightly damp. My clothes, too, were almost dry. It took very little wood to keep that tent comfortable. I cut a ditch around the up-hill side of the tent to drain the water away and keep it from seeping in. This I should have done in the first place. It was like locking the barn door after the horse was stolen!

I knew that Henry Stenbock wouldn't come over as long as the weather continued like this. So I just settled down to ride it out. The storm lasted three days, then it broke clear and cold. Henry didn't come that day. The next day I walked over to a spur of the mountain and made out a man walking away across the flat about where Lake Henshaw is now. Henry got into camp about 2:00 P.M. and we made over the inside of that tent so that the two of us could sleep in it.

We had some good weather after that, and got in some work on the gem vein. I found one very blue topaz crystal about one-half inch wide by one inch long, and some not-so-good blue tourmaline. As our grub was running low, and we were spending too much time going to and from the mine, we decided to come back later and make camp by a spring about two hundred yards below the workings. I told Henry to go on back to Mesa Grande and I would stay at camp. He was to send someone over with a buckboard to get our stuff, which was done the next day.

The following day, I left for San Diego and spent about a week there before returning to the mine in Mesa Grande. San Diego was experiencing a slight boom on the strength of the World's Fair being held there, which boosted sales. Salmons and Ernsting had the only gem mine exhibit there; exhibiting tourmaline, kunzite and numerous other minerals found in the Pala Chief and Tourmaline Queen Mines. They had a lapidary plant set up in the show-room, with Ben Boone cutting tourmaline. Rose Guatelli was the saleslady. She afterward became Mrs. Rose Gopel and was saleslady for Mr. Salmons in his store on Broadway in San Diego.

On my next trip back to Mesa Grande, I took a Chinese cook by name of "Y". He not only did the cooking, but helped around the mine and was a very good man. When he arrived at the bunk house, he looked all around at the wood hills and said, "This looks like my country, back in China."

After we unloaded our provisions and stuff out of the old Thomas car, he took the ax and cut an oak club about six feet long and five inches thick at the big end. When he brought it into the bunk house, I asked him what he was going to do with it. He said, "Maybe tiger here, like in my country."

The bunk room he was to occupy was only eight-by-eight feet and I was wondering how he was going to swing that size club in it - if he had to use it at all. I told him there were no tigers in this country - only mountain lions, and they didn't like Chinese meat, so he would be safe!

After two weeks at the mine, we decided to quit for a while as the weather was getting bad. It had rained several inches already since our arrival. The last two evenings the sky had cleared and Y told me, "In the morning we go." But when morning came it was raining. Several days passed that way, when one morning we awoke to find the skies clear and the sun shining warm.

I had put the chains on all four wheels of the old Thomas car and had everything ready. After a hurried breakfast, we started out. The roads were bad. In some places we had to build them up to get across washouts and creeks. We arrived at a creek, a tributary of the old Santa Ysabel Creek, about two miles east of the Mesa Grande store. Here, I stopped and walked ahead to look the crossing over. The road sloped down through a cut to the creek, which was six or seven feet wide, with a depth of twelve to fourteen inches, and moving fast. The road on the far side was in good shape, and seemed hard; but the side we were on, approaching the creek, for seventy-five feet back from the creek, shook like a lot of jelly when walked on. Others had thrown tules on the muddy road and it looked like a trap, but the old Thomas car was good at getting out of bad spots, so I thought I would try it.

Putting her into low gear and giving her all the gas I could, we made a run for the creek. We hadn't gone twenty feet when I felt her start to sink under us. Then a solid wall of mud and tules seemed to form on both sides of us, with mud flying in every direction, for we had no fenders. Just before we hit the creek, a large blob of mud and tules, about a dish pan full, came down partly on my head, but the most part on the steering wheel. I got a quick peek out when I had to shut my eyes as we hit the creek bottom - which turned out to be about a foot below the road level we were traveling on. We hit the opposite bank in a wave of ice cold water and mud and climbed out all right, going on about a hundred feet before stopping. I pawed the mud out of my eyes and looked over at Y. He looked at me and started to laugh, saying, "Pletty muddy haa, Fled?" Pretty muddy was right! I couldn't see skin on his face for mud. After scraping all the mud we could off each other, we used the canteen water to wash our hands and faces.

From there on we had no trouble and arrived in San Diego that afternoon about four, in a rain-storm. We were completely soaked, for the old Thomas had no top.

I stayed on in San Diego til the bad weather was over, doing some kunzite work and some cutting of my own, also some repair jobs.

After about a month, I drove back to Mesa Grande to work, starting a new tunnel. My crew dropped back down-hill about seventy-five feet to a spot along the vein that formed the breast of an old cut made by the Himalaya Company. After making a short cut we cut a mineralized zone. It contained nothing of value. We worked on the lower end of this zone and picked up a few crystals of tourmaline. From the looks of the layout, if there were any pockets worthwhile, they must be above us. So we drove on ahead a few feet, then started a "raise", where we put in a "chute" to load the mine car.

When five or six feet up, we cut the south end of a pocket, but continued on about ten feet. We then dropped back to where we first cut the pocket and started to drift west, taking out some tourmaline. Before the drift was three feet long, we were taking out plenty of tourmalines. It was a dry pocket; that is, one without mud, but dry, red dirt varying from ten to sixteen inches wide up and down, opening and closing for a distance of about twenty-five feet, and ten to twelve feet wide.

At times, I could take my candle stick and rake across the pocket and the tourmaline pencils would clatter out on the footwall like a lot of twenty penny nails! All the crystals were about the same color, light pink with a blue cap. They ranged in size from one-and-a-half to three inches long, down to one-fourth by one inch long. The majority ran one-half to two-and-a-half inches long. We took out five hundred pounds of tourmaline at this point!

I found a very rare specimen here, but lost it before I could take it out of the drift. I had been working out a small arm of the pocket. Some pockets are like a short armed octopus, having short cavities extending out from the main pocket cavity. I was cleaning out the tourmaline crystals sticking to the lining, when I came to one about one inch in diameter and one-and-one-fourth inches long. It was standing upright in a small cavity. The roof of the cavity extended over the top of the tourmaline about one inch, and from the top end of the crystal, there sprayed out hundreds of hairlike tourmalines; connecting with the roof of the cavity where they had sprayed out to about one-and-a-half inches wide.

I had cut around the whole specimen and had taken it out, laid it on a ledge near the entrance to the pocket stope, and continued on with the work. In about ten or fifteen minutes, Vance called to us that he was going to shoot, or blast. Vance was driving a drift east, and in an opposite direction off the same raise from which we were working. We got down into the tunnel when Vance called, "Fire!" and walked out on the dump.

After a little while the smoke cleared and we went back in. At that time, I remembered my specimen. Getting back to the ledge where I had placed it, I found it gone. I spent an hour looking for it. I looked at every rock in the drift, but was unable to locate it. Every carload we took out of that hole, we searched - but no luck! It is a loss like this that really hurts!

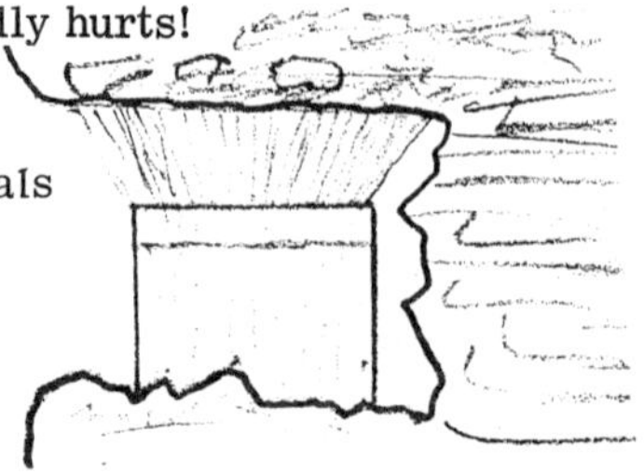

Tourmaline with sprayed crystals on top.

CHAPTER XIX

HENRY QUIN. A RARE SPECIMEN FOUND.

Henry Quin, one of the owners of the lease, was working with me on the pocket in mid 1915, but was working the lower part of it and twenty feet to my left. I was working the upper half. We would always clean up our own tailings, taking turns using the mine car.

One day Henry had pushed the car under the chute and said he was through with it. I had more than a carload pushed down below me and started to shovel it into the chute. As Henry passed me going into his workings, he said he was getting some nice sized stuff. When I got the car loaded, I pushed it out to dump it. When I got to the end of the track, I saw some tourmaline on the dump, under the track. Taking another look, I saw that the whole dump was covered with tourmalines from five-eighths inches in diameter and two-and-a-half inches long, down to small ones!

I walked back into the tunnel to the chute and called Henry, asking him if he knew about dumping all that tourmaline. He said sure, and that he was saving only the big ones! Before I dumped my car, we retrieved some forty to fifty pounds; three-fourths of them cleancut crystals with perfect terminations! Some fifteen years later, a lady asked me to look at some tourmalines she had and tell her what they were worth. She had twenty-five or thirty pounds in a grain sack. When I saw the stuff, I knew someone had been working that spot in the dump where Henry had piled the "not too big ones". They probably got these deeper down than we took the time to go after.

The small arm cavity where I found the rare specimen, proved to be an "extra special" one. Within a foot of the end, I saw a large crystal that almost blocked the cavity. At first I thought it was beryl, but after cleaning some of the white crystalline deposit from around it, I found it to be an apatite crystal, five-and-a-half inches long by two inches thick and three inches wide. It was broken into three pieces but still stuck together. It was a beautiful green on one end and a clear rose red on the other.

After taking the rest of the tourmalines out of this arm cavity, I ran into a green tourmaline about five inches long by one inch thick. It was firmly imbedded in the same white crystalline material. It too was broken into three pieces but still stuck together. What was most interesting about this crystal was what had happened to it before it got to its last resting place.

One side of the crystal was exposed and I could see that all the crystal striations were worn off, leaving it smooth. After removing the crystal, I found the other side was partly worn smooth also; leading me to believe this crystal had come from another locality in the mineral stream, before the tourmaline in the pocket had crystallized; for not one of them showed any wear. Even the apatite crystal showed no wear; and it would; for it is only "5" in the hardness scale (talc 1 to diamond 10).

After cleaning out that pocket, we quit the stope and drove the tunnel on ahead. It was sixty-five feet further before we cut another mineralized stream. We didn't locate anything big in the line of a pocket here, but a few bugholes which gave up some gem stuff. Some cavities had only one crystal in them while others had as many as a dozen. These bugholes sometimes occur along the mineral stream between the larger pockets, and sometimes isolated between streams.

It was at this spot that we found some mineral that took us eleven years to sell. We drove the tunnel on through the old Flag Pole Shaft that had been sunk by the Himalaya Company. On the east side of this shaft, we drifted in about twenty feet and took out some very fine Chinese quality stuff. What we classed as "Chinese stuff" was any size crystal above one inch in diameter and pink in color. Rose pink was the color most desired by the Chinese.

It was here I experienced a thrill. As a rule, when driving a tunnel, the vein shows up diagonally across the breast, or face of it. We generally put in three or four dynamite shots above the vein to soften the hanging wall, then we cleaned off about five feet of this, exposing the top part of the vein. One of my shots had gone off right on top of the vein, and cracked a round spot the size of a pie plate, and forced it down about an inch. Taking a small pinch bar, I pried the small broken pieces out and ran my hand down into the red mud of a pocket. It was like reaching into a large stone big-mouthed jug or jar. Every time I dipped my hand in, I brought out one or two crystals of tourmaline. This continued until I had taken out about thirty pounds of fine crystals, all pink; the largest about three inches long by one-and-a-quarter inches thick. About one fifth of the thirty pounds was gem material, and of good color.

It was getting along toward fall, 1915, and bad weather, so we shut down the work at the mine. I started cutting tourmalines and buttons, and a few kunzite for Salmons and Ernsting.

CHAPTER XX

GOLD ON THE COLORADO!

The latter part of November 1915 I again met Bill Trenchard. He wanted me to go with him over to the Colorado River and locate some placer gold claims. This was intriguing - anything in the prospecting field was to me. So I threw a few things together, rolled out the old Thomas car we had been using at the mine, and started for Yuma, Arizona by way of Campo, Coyote Wells, and El Centro.

We made it through to about three miles of the Sand Hills east of Holtville. Here, in passing over a small sand hummock we twisted off a small jack shaft in the transmission case. This was actually good luck, but it didn't seem so at the time! After burying our provisions and other things in the sand, I took out the broken shaft and both of us started walking to the station, "Gray's Well", on the west side of the Sand Hills.

We hadn't gone more than a mile, and it was getting dark when we saw the lights of an auto coming toward us. They said they would be glad to have us join them while crossing the Sand Hills, since they were on their way to Yuma. The car, as I remember it, was a 1914 coupe. We had to stand on the running board for a four-hour ride before we arrived at Charley San's restaurant in Yuma at 10:30 that night.

The road over the Sand Hills, at that time, was a plank affair, three 2" x 6" x 10's laid side by side, making a surface runway eighteen inches wide, on each side, for the wheels to run on. This plank road led across the Sand Hills for several miles. At numerous places it had been torn up and pieces used to pry cars back onto the planks again.

We got off those planks a dozen times, and it was lucky there were four of us to lift that coupe back onto the planks again!

Later, the road was again planked. This time the planks were laid across the road and placed in sections, with turnouts at points visible to the on-coming motorist. This was the last of the plank roads across the Sand Hills. It is now paved. Remains of the last plank road can be seen at several places along the route.

On leaving San Diego the first morning, we filled the gas tank (thirty gallons), but we could get only twenty-three gallons of gas into it. Bill said we ought to have left one gallon out, or tried to squeeze another in; for "twenty-three" was bad luck. That night, when we left Charley San's restaurant at Yuma, we got a room in a hotel across the street. Bill went outside for a while and when he came back, called me to the door and pointed to the number on it, saying, "What do you know about that! This room is number twenty-three!" I said, "Well, let's sleep in it and see what happens."

I don't think either of us moved once during the night, for it seemed we just got into bed and out again. Morning came in a hurry. We dressed and walked down to Charley San's for breakfast. Then I took the broken shaft to a machine shop and ordered a duplicate made. I told the machinist I would pick it up in a week. Then we looked up a livery stable and hired two horses and saddles, got some provisions, and started up-river. Leaving Yuma, we crossed over to the California side.

We arrived at a point west of Pot Holes, the Laguna Dam, and prospected part of the district. When evening came, we watered the horses at Pot Holes and then rode up onto a bench in the hills to the west and camped for the night. It was very cold in the washes and low places.

Next morning, we got started early and followed the west side of the river up to Picacho, a mining town of the early days. Before we came to the settlement, we rounded a spur of a ridge close to the river and ran into a stench, like rotten meat. We dismounted and worked our way through the thick willows and came to a clearing twelve feet across where the willows had been cut out. Scattered about were a half dozen mountain sheep heads. Someone had made a killing and dressed them out in this place. Why they didn't throw them into the river - twenty-five feet away - we couldn't figure out. They may have intended to come back later for the horns.

About three-fourths of a mile farther on, we met two men who had a small gas engine and pump. They were pumping water out of the river and up into a canyon where they had a small sluice box. One of the men told us they were doing pretty good there, but didn't have much gravel handy.

We stayed three days in and around the Picacho district and took some samples of black sand which we wanted to test out for values per yard of gravel or ton of black sand. This black sand is distributed generously through the gravels and carries much higher values on bedrock, or false bedrock.

We had some of our meals with a Mexican family in Picacho, whose name I have forgotten. However, I won't forget the food! We had some goat meat, tortillas, beans and coffee. We slept out by the barn near our horses. After supper on the third day, we saddled up and rode back the twenty-six miles to Yuma. It was a little past midnight. Again, we finished the rest of the night in room twenty-three, to Bill's discomfort.

Next morning we gathered our jack shaft and samples and boarded the Southern Pacific train for Nileland in the Imperial Valley. Here we changed to a branch line that ran down the Valley to El Centro. This was Thanksgiving day so we planned to have a big feed at noon in El Centro. When we arrived at Nileland, we found the train to El Centro wouldn't be leaving until 4:00 P.M.

Not having had any breakfast, we were hungry and started looking for a place for something to eat. We found Nileland to be almost a Ghost Town, but at last we found a man who lived near a grocery store, which he owned, and selling what was left of his stock. We bought soda crackers, a piece of dried up cheese, and sat on the curb of the main street and ate it. We could have sat in the middle of the desert so far as people were concerned, for not a soul was in sight. When we arrived in El Centro that evening, we had a good dinner, and everything was all right, regardless of Bill's twenty-three hoodoo!

Next morning we hired a garage man to take us out to the old Thomas car near the Sand Hills. When we arrived we found everything as we had left it. We dug up the stuff we had, put in the jack shaft and drove back to El Centro where we stayed overnight. The next day we drove to San Diego, arriving about sundown.

This being so near Christmas, I found my hands full of lapidary work. I got down to finishing that up, for we intended to go back to the placer diggin's after Christmas. We had taken our placer samples to two different assayers to have them assayed and get a check. Though these samples were not a thorough test of the gravels, they did prove accurate, as later proved. Most of the samples were taken about two feet deep, or just below the surface.

We left San Diego shortly after Christmas, with the necessary equipment to make a more accurate test of the gravels. We traveled by stage this time to El Centro, and by train, to Yuma and Pot Holes, where we made our first camp.

For a while we ate at the boarding house for the employees at the dam, until we got our camp set up. We soon started testing the gravels on both the California and Arizona sides of the river.

Before taking our samples, we weighed up twenty-five shovels full of sand and gravel, which gave us an average of eight pounds. For each sample, we ran sixty-three shovels of gravel through the drywasher, and the concentrates were used as a one-fourth ton assay sample. These concentrates were pan-washed and the free gold and the black sand was saved, weighed and put into a strong cloth bag, identified as to location, condition and depth of gravel bed.

When taking these samples, we would check on how much black sand was in a ton of gravel. This varied at different depths; becoming more abundant at deeper levels. The leanest we got was one ton of black sand to about sixty-five tons of gravel. This was gravel previously laid down and not in the washes. The richest ran about one ton of black sand to twelve tons of gravel. This was taken close to bed rock and on bed rock.

The free gold would give us a "thrill", especially when we would hit an ashy-looking spot in the gravel. From some of these ashy spots we would find, in the drywasher riffles two-bit nuggets and from that value, on down. This would bring the tonnage value up. Some of the ashy spots were eighteen inches under the surface.

An old Mexican came along and asked if we cared if he drywashed some of the gravel. (We had located two sections of claims in the district.) We told him to go ahead but to let us know what he got, so we could check on the location. Then we were put wise to the ashy spots. The old Mexican told us about them and how they got there.

He said he was here, along the river, in the late 1860's and early 70's, to do some placer mining. He related that miners worked most of the day gathering up their concentrates, which they would pan down by the light of their camp fires. They would pick out all the nuggets over the two-bit size, throwing what was left in the pan into the fire, or close by. He was an expert in picking out these places, even when the ash didn't show on the surface. Some days he would clean up $1.75 a day, and others only 75 or 80 cents. He generally showed up around seven in the morning and was gone by two o'clock in the afternoon.

One day we were taking a sample near the mouth of a big wash when we dug up a bluish-gray piece of rock that was full of flake gold. After looking the stone over, we came to the conclusion that some place along the river there had been a small bay or inlet where the thick, muddy water, heavily laden with flake gold, had settled to the bottom. Wherever this place was, it (or some of it) had been uprooted again and washed down the river. Some of these pieces ran $5000 and better to the ton. Not known to us at the time, this ore had been found near the same spot years before by a Civil War veteran by the name of Murray.

We walked over to Pot Holes one morning for the mail and were returning to camp by crossing over the hills west of Pot

Holes. We got half way when I discovered a quartz outcropping about six feet long and eighteen inches wide - barely showing above the surface. With my pick I knocked off the side a slab about half the size of my hand. I got the surprise of my life when I found the whole fresh broken side covered with gold in the form of little flakes. I called Bill, who had walked on ahead some hundred feet. We both got busy on that outcrop! We found it was only one piece and did not extend more than twenty inches below the surface. We got another surprise when we found very little gold in the rest of it. It seems I hit the jackpot with the first stroke of my pick! The quartz outcrop would probably assay high, if the whole piece were used, but it wouldn't have paid us to work it out. This piece of vein matter looked very much like the ore from the Picacho District, eighteen miles north of us.

Where we found free gold in the samples, we found the black sand to run about the same value, so we could lump all those samples together. If they came from one locality, we could call it a sample of that locality.

A dark velvety red mineral was found when we panned the concentrates. It was very heavy and always settled down with the gold. The largest piece wasn't more than 12/100 of an inch in width. Most of the samples were spherical in shape - and were very rare. We didn't get them in every sample, and rarely two in a sample. An analysis was never taken. An old prospector said it was rhodium.

On the Arizona side of the river lies quite an area of gravel. We spent one day sampling the surface, and beneath as deep as we could in the banks of the washes. We got no free gold, but the black sand ran as plentiful as on the west side of the river.

We had an odd occurrence that day as we were returning to the river. We had made a long half-circle trip to the east of the river and had returned to a point about three-fourths of a mile to the north of our starting point. We had come out of a canyon into a small open piece of country of about five acres, but not level. It had small hills here and there, about twenty-five feet high. As we had been going around in circles, in and out of canyons, I asked Bill which was ''north''. He at once pointed in the right direction. I took out my compass and to my surprise the needle pointed to the west and to a small knoll. Bill said it probably had a deposit of iron ore in it that had magnetized the needle. As we were gradually turning to the left, I noticed the needle still pointed to the little knoll.

Through the years since then, this knoll has come to my mind very often. Located as it was, in an old river bed, it may have been the center of a large whirlpool which had collected tons of the richest black sand, and possibly, GOLD. This being the only spot in that whole country that had so drastically affected the compass needle, naturally got me to thinking. Of course it could be a high point in an iron ore deposit. I didn't find out anything more, nor has anyone else to my knowledge. So, in 1951, I drove over there and, with a friend, Mr. Val Colby, who knew the country well, we started looking for it.

I found many changes had taken place in the last thirty-six years. A large canal from the new Imperial Dam had cut through the country and barred off our old route. I tried to go in where we came out, but the canal again barred the way. I am not sure I picked the same exit we made in 1915. We took one day to try and locate the spot. From where we were staying it was a forty-eight mile round trip drive to the locality. Knowing that if I wanted to locate it, I would have to make several trips over there or camp on the ground; and, as I had other places in mind to go, I never went back again. But the possibility of a treasure lying there still remains!

Sampling placer ground on Colorado River near Pot Holes, Calif., 1915.

Remains of second plank road over sand hills in Imperial Co., California.

CHAPTER XXI

BIG FLOOD AND ODD MINING EXPERIENCES

After the prospect trip over on the Arizona side of the river, Bill and I decided we had better stick to the California side, since transportation and access to the land was much easier on that side. We were very anxious to find where this high-grade bluish-gray ore we had found came from. Since we had found this in a wash, it was the logical thing to believe it came from up-stream. We put in days looking for the deposit. In one place we found a brown streak, or vein, of a material which resembled it, but carried very little gold.

To make a practical test of the gravels, we decided to put in a small sluice box about sixty feet long, set in a pump, and sluice some of the gravel in a spot that was about an average of the gravel as a whole. We built the sluice box, set up the pump and engine, but never sluiced a shovel full of gravel!

The past week had been rainy. We had heard that over on the coast around San Diego it had reached flood proportions. I had gone to Yuma in answer to a wire from San Diego, and that afternoon I heard that the river was rising and a high point was expected to reach Yuma that night. By the time I was to start back I found no trains were running up to Pot Holes, so I engaged a room at the same rooming house where "we" occupied Room 23.

I stopped in to have a talk with a jeweler I knew, and asked him if he had heard of the high water expected to hit town that night. He said he had, but didn't think it would amount to anything serious. I had been in the store about a half hour and had noticed a little more activity in the street. I told the jeweler I would go down to the Southern Pacific Railroad bridge and see how high the water was.

I found they had run flat cars loaded with lumber onto the bridge and the water was within five feet of the bottom of the bridge, and rising fast. I walked back and told the jeweler about it and that I had heard they expected a still higher crest before morning.

About 2:00 A.M. I was awakened by the sound of car horns. Cars were racing back and forth on Main Street. I tried to get some more sleep, and did manage to get about thirty minutes more, when I heard the steam whistle at the City's pumping plant start blowing. Anyone not able to see what was going on, would suspect the City was putting on a celebration of some kind. In the next fifteen or twenty minutes I could detect quite a difference in the power of the whistle, and knew then that the firemen had tied down the whistle cord and moved out.

About 5:00 A.M. I got up and looked out of the window, which gave me a view of the main street. Most of the cars were traveling on the west side and going south. The east side of the street is lower than the west side, and I couldn't see the curb on my side because the roofs were built over the sidewalks. I couldn't see the water already in the hallway of the building I was in! Across the street people were hauling sand bags and placing them in front of the stores.

I got dressed, and by that time, I couldn't hear any more automobiles running in the street. I stepped over to the window again and saw the street was full of water flowing north, very slowly, towards the river. There was hardly a ripple on it as it moved along. Soup dishes and other kitchen ware, rabbits and chickens on logs, and cordwood came floating down the street. Charley San, I was told, piled all his stuff in the restaurant as high as he could and then got up on the counter with a jug of whiskey and stayed with the ship until the water went down!

I walked out on the roof of the building next door and saw a man in a row boat heading towards our building. He backed his boat into the hall at the foot of the stairs, or rather, six feet from the foot, and I stepped in. He picked up several other men and took us up a side street, to the west. All got out.

I started looking around and ran across an old schoolmate of mine I had known in San Diego, Tom Harris. He was in the auto repair business and operated a garage. He had taken all the cars in his garage up on a higher street, above the flood, and asked me to share his camp fire that night, which I did, and also the next night. Most of what I got to eat was out of a bakery.

The third day, I walked over to the railroad tracks that lead up to Pot Holes. On the way up the tracks, I saw the largest barefoot track I have ever seen leading in the same direction I was going. Soon I came to an Indian woman and a girl of about twelve years. They were sitting on the ends of the railroad ties, two feet above the water, watching some chickens, on the roof of an adobe house several hundred feet out in the water. I walked past them, then turned and saw only two small piles of clothes on the bank. I waited to see where they would come up out of the water, and when they did, it was within ten feet of the adobe house. That was some dive!

I hadn't gone much farther to the break in the dyke, when I met my "big-footed" friend. He was a Yuma Indian with long black hair mixed with gray, a big man with big feet. This finely built fellow looked to me as if he were a runner, or had been.

I said, "Who Mow?" He stared for a second, and a slight smile lit up his face, and he said, "Who Mow." To my knowledge, "Who Mow" is not a Yuma word, but is used by the Mesa Grande Indians and means "All out." It is possible this Indian knew the meaning, and also, where I came from.

When I got back to Yuma, I met a friend who worked at the Pot Holes Dam. He had been brought across the break in the dyke by two Indians in a boat who were helping people that way. He said he was going back right away and would give me a lift when we got on the other side.

We walked about one mile, and then were taken across the break a half mile by two Indians in a row boat. A boy there with one horse gave my friend a lift. I was offered my friend's place on the horse, but refused and walked the twelve miles to Pot Holes. After telling friends what happened at Yuma, I had the hardest part of the trip back - walking two more miles to our camp.

The Gila River flows into the Colorado River on the north side of Yuma. The U. S. Reclamation Service has built a levee from Indian Hill to Pot Holes on the California side of the river. The Southern Pacific Railroad also built one on the south side of the Gila to Prison Hill. This forced both rivers between Indian Hill and Prison Hill so that the high waters of both rivers hit Yuma at the same time. The levees couldn't hold the river and Yuma and the low lands were flooded.

We were not the only ones experiencing a flood. A few days later a telegram came stating that we should return at once to San Diego because of flood conditions. We left a man in charge of our tent and equipment and boarded a train for El Centro. We stayed the night there, leaving early next morning on a stage with a woman driver. She was a small, slightly built woman, but all nerve, and she was a good driver. Since the Laguna Mountains were loaded with water she took the detours and flooded creeks as safely as any driver could. We were a full day in making it to San Diego.

My home town had more than its share of water too. Dams, bridges, and homes were swept away. I was anxious to find out what the water had done to the mine workings, but the roads were in such bad condition we couldn't go up there, so waited until they were sufficiently repaired. In the meantime, I went back to cutting and ran a lot of my own stuff through with the custom work.

By 1915, the gem prospectors had almost vanished from the

hills. Only those who lived in the mountains and along the desert would occasionally bring in a few gem stones.

Since about 1907, synthetic, then called "reconstructed" stones had been showing up in jewelry stores and, up to 1915 all the jewelers carried them. Some carried nothing in the gem line but synthetics. Many of these synthetics were sold to jewelers as tourmalines and other native stones. This practice certainly took away a large percentage of native gem trade. One jeweler told me, "Fred, you can't beat these stones! They're harder, we buy them cheaper and make more profit on them, than we do on your native stones. Besides, the customer gets them cheaper. They'll match anything you want and no one on the outside knows but what they are the real thing."

While waiting for the roads to become passable, I had the most diversified amount of lapidary work I ever collected. This consisted in cutting beads and cabochons, quarter circles of tourmalines for bracelets, polishing slabs of gold ore, tourmaline buttons and some tourmaline and kunzite facet cutting. Some of these were store jobs and some, like the beads, buttons and bracelet pieces, came from my own customers, the Chinese.

In April we made our first try to get to the Mesa Grande mine. The old Thomas car had a chain drive and was built like a railroad flat car. It was cut down like a "hot rod", with no sides and with chains on the wheels. You could grind through any kind of mud hole and ship a lot aboard, too!

The Cuyamaca Railroad, that ran from San Diego to Fosters (the end of the line), met Joe Fosters' stages and jerkline freight teams, carrying passengers and freight, mail and express to Julian and way points. This track had been washed out from the little town of Santee on through to Fosters, six or seven miles. Some parts of the highway were also washed away, but we made it through to the Angel Ranch by that evening. In the morning, with some self help road building, we got to the bunk house.

We found Herb Hill there. He said the water had rushed out of the five-hundred foot tunnel almost to its full capacity. After examining the tunnel, I found most of the timbers in bad condition, and much caved. The flagpole shaft, which connected with the end of the tunnel, wasn't damaged too badly, but was almost closed at the mouth. Where the tunnel connected with the bottom of the shaft, and on the left-hand side, a pocket of considerable size had been taken out and the vein at this point looked very good.

We never worked in here for the ground was unsafe along the

lower end of the shaft. Instead, we ran drifts off in several places up the shaft, and shoveled the muck down the shaft. We had no luck in striking a large pocket but struck several small ones and several bug-holes.

About this time I bought a 1912 model Hupmobile car, right hand drive, which is much safer and handier than the left hand drive, on the mountain roads. This car had a very low first gear and could negotiate any of the roads in that country at that time. It was just what I wanted and needed.

As the country was full of water and the roads were bad, we decided to discontinue work for a while. I went back to San Diego. Shortly after arriving there, my brother-in-law, H. B. Griffis, sent word that Henry Fenton needed a steam-shovel runner and asked me to come down to Otay, to do the job.

Since the lapidary business was not brisk at that time, I drove to the Otay plant and went to work. It was when the United States entered World War One. Some of the gravel we were digging was used for war work construction.

This gravel pit was of great interest to me, for it was a concentration of parts of all the rock formations in the eastern interior at that point. A story was out that a Mr. Denari, who owned a large winery up the valley, had kept $30,000 in gold in the wine cellar and that it had been lost when the flood of 1916 washed the winery away. The gold was in a buckskin sack that, in turn, was in a canvas sack, and the whole placed in an iron box and locked.

One day we were working on a bank of gravel about fifteen feet high when we uncovered an iron box about two feet long by ten inches square covered with rust. We piled off the shovel and hauled it out of the gravel, visioning a rich haul; but found it was an old fuel tank off of a stove of some kind!

There were rocks in this gravel not found in any place in the back country and were probably brought here as gravel by some ancient stream. What few agates I could find were not very good. Some of the rocks I saw in this gravel I have seen on the desert, and not on the west side of the mountain range. Probably they were washed here by the Colorado River which is believed to have flowed into the Pacific Ocean before this western range of mountains pushed up.

About every ninety days, I went up to the Mesa Grande mines and put in a week's work to hold our lease. Some of these trips were very profitable, others were not.

I was later sent out to the Spring Valley Quarry to run a "Thew" shovel. This quarry was on the outcrop of the big dike I had drilled into the old Otay oil well, at the 998 foot level. It was some time after the close of the First World War that I quit the steam shovel business and went back to mining at Mesa Grande.

We started an incline shaft on the east side of the ridge, along the vein. While working out the cut up to the breast, suitable for the incline portal, I found an Indian arrowhead. It was about four feet under the surface in reddish clay. It was made of opaque quartz, about one inch wide, one-eighth inch thick and one-and-one-fourth inches long. I was told it was very old. I know it wasn't shaped like the kinds I had found around the old Indian camp sites in that country.

Herb Hill left me to work elsewhere, so I got a man by name of Erle Fitzpatrick to help me. He had just returned from the First World War and was ready to make a stake. Fitz was a good scout. He was always working, doing something worthwhile. He shoveled rock, ran the hoist and cooked, sometimes. He could even steer a sled into a pine tree!

We were down to the twenty foot level when we cut through the north end of a pocket. We put in a station here, setting in a four-by-five-foot-by-one-fourth inch iron plate, or turn sheet, to turn the mine car on. Then we started drifting south on the vein. It was plenty rich along here, but we were much handicapped by the weather.

It was while we were working this pocket that it had rained three days and we had piled our tailings and muck back on both sides of the drift. Then the weather cleared a little and we started hoisting the stuff out. Waiting for the bell signal to hoist out the mine car, I noticed a line of tree ants going and coming through the hoist house. I killed a large fly and laid it near the trail. It wasn't long before several ants were over to it, trying to pull it away, or apart. I noticed one ant would whirl around and almost stand on its hind legs. After doing this several times, I surmised something was bothering it, so I got down a little closer and discovered a little gray fly, not any thicker than a fine human hair, alight on the back of the ant's abdomen and then prod it like a mosquito. Afterward I noticed quite a number of the ants were bothered in this way. No doubt these flies fed off the ants. These flies are similar to the ones we call ''No seeum flies'', or maybe the same ones. When they bite or sting, they raise quite a welt, which stings and itches for hours.

CHAPTER XXII

DOWN TO SAN DIEGO THE HARD WAY IN THE OLD HUPP

By the middle of November, 1920, it had rained for several days and all creeks and streams were booming. We decided to go to town if we wanted to spend Thanksgiving there. So we loaded up the Hupp about six A.M. with stuff we had mined and lit out during a lull in the storm.

Reaching the Indian Reservation, we had to build up the road a little to get across the creek, and again in several places on the road down Black Canyon to Ramona. When we arrived at Ramona we learned the Muzzy Grade was washed out. No one knew how good the road was leading down to Poway Valley, so we thought we would try it.

We had clear sailing and a fair road up to the pass on Mt. Woodson; after that point the trouble started. We had just started down on the west side when we pulled up to a stop. A stream of water had shot off the mountain above the road and hit the center of the road, washing out a V and out on to the edge of the canyon, four feet deep! Here we had our lunch and thought over the situation.

After lunch we found a large flat rock that spanned the narrowest part of the V, where the right-hand wheels would travel, and we started across. It was a narrow margin to get by on, but we made it! As the rear wheel got across, the sides of the V collapsed and the rock slab fell in. After another hundred feet, we found that the dirt had been washed entirely off the road, leaving rocks from one foot in diameter to two feet thick, to form the roadbed for two hundred feet. Fitz got down ahead of me and guided me over the rocks so I wouldn't smash the engine crank case. As the car bounded from one rock to another, it wasn't long before we were on a fair road again.

We passed a small ranch and then started down the grade into Poway Valley. We rounded a corner in the road and there sat a big rock about four feet through and three feet high. It had a flat bottom sitting firmly in the mud. The bank on the up-hill side of the road opposite was a large sloping rock. I figured if I could get the rear wheel hub against the inside of the rock on the road, by running the front wheels up on this sloping rock bank, and then let the front end slip off into the road, we could get by it. We had to get down some way, for it was impossible to go back.

I slipped her into first gear and ran the front end of the car up on the bank and succeeded in getting the rear wheel where I wanted it. Every time I eased forward a little, the front end would slip down toward the road. Fitz kept telling me to give her a little more, and a little more. The car was reared up so high in front I couldn't see what she was doing, when all at once the front end slipped off the rock down into the road; almost catching Fitz, who scrambled out of the way. It was a drop of five feet. If it hadn't been for the deep mud in the road at that point, we would have stayed there. I found afterward that I had cracked both front wheel spindles!

We were lucky that old Hupp was a right-hand drive, and not a left-hand drive in the mountains. We had gone a hundred and fifty feet and were straddling a deep gully in the center of the road, when we felt the whole car start slipping into the canyon, along with a portion of the road. I stopped the car and we both slipped out on the left side. We cut a hole through the bank on the high side of the rear wheels, then put the jack under the center of the rear axle, lifting the whole rear end, and pulling it over into the ditch next to the bank. We did the same thing to the front end.

It had been raining since we had left the V washout and while I was jacking up the front end of the car, a man in a slicker walked up leading a saddle horse. He had come up from Poway. I made the remark that we were having a little rain. He never gave me an answer or a look. Thinking he was hard of hearing, I repeated what I had said. Still no answer, so I said no more.

In about a minute or two, he asked, "How in hell did you get past that rock?" Both Fitz and I started laughing. I told him if he was going up that way he could see for himself. I asked how the road was ahead and he asked me if I had ever been on the road before. I told him I had, many times. Then he said, "If you can get past that rock, you can make it through."

That didn't sound too good. About two hundred yards farther on, the bank seemed to dissolve and flow over the road. Luckily no big rocks were in that pile of mud, sticks and brush. I followed as best I could where I thought the road was, and came out onto a good road in a short while. We now hit it off at about twenty miles an hour - fast driving for that day!

When I came to a road I usually traveled I found it was good and hard - and we TRAVELED! We passed a man not a hundred feet from the road, looking at us. In another ten seconds I turned the car sharp to the left and through a wire fence and stopped. Not thirty feet ahead, the road had been completely washed out to a depth of six to eight feet! We backed out and onto the road, then back the way we came in to where we could take a different road. The trip on into San Diego was clear sailing, arriving there about four P.M.

Our plans were to stay a week or two in San Diego, and then go back to the mine, which we did. I put in several days cutting some extra fine stones we mined. Most of it went to my partner in the lease.

We drove back to the mine by way of San Pasqual and Ramona and made it through with very little trouble. The mine weathered the storm very well, with very little water running down the shaft. Again, we started to take out tourmalines and some amber colored beryls. Some of these beryls were so badly etched they were almost honeycombed. They were spherical in shape. The largest was about an inch in diameter. This was a wonderful pocket. We got so tired taking out the stuff, we stopped working the pocket and built a roof over the entrance to the shaft.

I have heard people remark that it must be a thrilling experience to take gem crystals out of the pockets. Yes it is at first, and for a while afterwards. But there's no way of holding the vein up so that you can work the pocket out while sitting in a chair, so you sit on the cold foot-wall until your legs itch and your joints are stiff. After several weeks of this the thrill is gone and you wish you'd come to the end of it. Then a few days of making a new exploring hole, and the stiffness and soreness are out of your joints - and you are ready and anxious to be thrilled again.

This pocket contained considerable amounts of microscopic tourmalines, beryls and other minerals found in these pegmatites. I sent my friend, Ernest Schernikow of San Francisco, a twenty-five-pound powder box full of the contents of a portion of this pocket, after all the gem crystals (one-eighth inch and more in thickness) had been taken out. He told me that the most perfectly crystalized specimens were the microscopic ones.

We had emerged from the mine about four, one afternoon, to find the temperature way down. Off to the east a small cloud was scurrying along toward the north. I told Fitz we should get over to the bunk house and prepare for a storm. When we reached the top of the ridge we could see, to the southwest, a dark gray bank of what we thought was fog, down to the coast. The temperature dropped to almost freezing, so we quickly brought in all the wood the storeroom would hold.

It was the first time I had seen it start in to snow on dry ground. The storm was well on its way when we went to bed, and the temperature was under twenty degrees. We awoke next morning in an ice-box, with about eighteen inches of powdered snow outside. We made a lunch so we wouldn't have to walk back through the snow to the bunk house for dinner; then we fought our way up the mountain; sinking almost to our knees in the snow. We found the cut (twenty feet long and from nothing to ten feet deep at the portal) flush with snow. We shoveled some of the snow out onto the banks on each side, and the rest, over the dump.

Coming out of a comparatively warm mine was like walking through a freezer, passing through that cut. The vein along here was so full of pockets that in places the vein wasn't more than an inch thick above the pocket to the hanging wall, and two inches thick on the bottom above the foot-wall. In shooting dynamite above and below the vein, at times a great deal of the vein and pocket contents, would be scattered along the drift. This kept us busy searching every little lump for crystals of all kinds.

Several days after the storm, the snow settled down to twelve or fourteen inches, with a four-inch crust. Going down the mountain to the bunk house one evening, Fitz spied a good place to take a sled ride; so the next morning, which was Sunday, we made a sled, cleared off the runway, and got ready.

Fitz said he had steered a sled in Kansas, so he took that position on the sled and when all was ready we took off. About half way down the mountain there was a slight turn that wasn't banked. We hit this at a good speed, some brush in the snow helped us a lot in making the turn, maybe too much; for we headed for a big pine tree. I was on the front end and called to Fitz to fall off. Being fresh out of the army, Fitz probably thought he had better stay with the fort, and didn't follow me. Well, Fitz didn't hit the tree, but he did dive under the low, ice-covered branches, while one caught him under the nose and across the mouth and laid him out on the snow.

Those pine limbs are rough enough in warm weather, but take them when they are covered with ice and they are like a rasp. Fitz's face was pretty well marked up. He didn't give up, though. After a little time and study of the ''Death Curve'', we tried again. This time we made it and ended up at the bunk house, where Fitz got first aid (?) - mostly antivenom - to counteract the venom coming from Fitz!

We had been thinking of going to town, for we had a lot of material mined, and there were things we needed too. So one afternoon we walked over to the store to get the mail and look over the road. While there, I received a phone call to come to San Diego, and then to San Luis Obispo County to look over some potential oil land.

After getting a good supper, we loaded up the Hupp and started just at five o'clock. We made it out to the road, about seventy-five feet from the bunk house, and there broke through the snow crust. We would back up and push ahead about five feet, then we would shovel the snow from in front of the car. This was repeated until we arrived at the top of the hill, or about two hundred yards. It was then eleven P.M. and we had broken a new pair of skid chains five times!

The road leading down on the eastern side of the mountain was so full of snow near the top that I could hardly see where it was. Fortunately it became thinner as we descended the mountain. In the Angel Valley it was only six inches deep. There was only one place I was afraid of not gettingby. That was what we called ''Red Hill''. It was at the foot of the grade and was really a mud hill a hundred-and-fifty feet long with mud about ten inches deep. We were taking it on up the hill, with six inches of snow on top of the mud.

When we hit the bridge at the bottom of the hill, I gave the old Hupp all the gas she could use and made that hill better than any spot on the road! It just happened that the whole road along here was frozen solid. Arriving at the top of the red hill, we found the road wasn't very hard. A little farther on there was a sharp turn which, as a rule, is muddy. Fitz got out to give me a push around the turn, in case I needed it, but we got around without help, and I left Fitz behind a ways. I had to cross another bad place and thought I ought to do it while I was moving. Crossing over this place, I hit a rock, or something, which threw up the front end of the car and to the left; placing it crosswise of the road. The rear end was on the down-hill side, while the lower edge of the road was almost touching the running boards of the car.

Fitz came up with, ''What the hell you doing in there?'' I told him I didn't know, guess Betsy must be feeling good these cold nights! I was surprised how easily we pulled out of there.

We arrived at the Mesa Grande store a little after midnight, then went on down Black Canyon to Ramona, San Pasqual. Pulling onto the paved Escondido-to-San Diego road, just north of what is now Lake Hodges, we found the road so smooth that I dropped to sleep at once. If Fitz hadn't had his eye on the ball, we would have gone into the ditch. From then on Fitz drove and I got in some sleep. We arrived at San Diego at five A.M. - just twelve hours on the road! One can make it now over the same road in less than two hours!

We stayed in San Diego three days, then went on to San Luis Obispo. Returning to San Diego, I got in some lapidary work, mostly kunzite facet work, and some cutting of my own.

We had returned to the mine, and had put in about a week, when Fitz's father drove up and handed Fitz a letter from his brother in Kansas, stating that Fitz had a good position awaiting him if he wanted it. He offered to stay on with me, but I told him he should go, so he left with his father that afternoon.

I worked on alone for a week, when Herb blew in and went back to work for me. We took out some very fine bi-colored crystals, pink and green, also red and green. I noticed some of these crystals have the colors joining at an angle and a little lengthwise of the crystal. I have noticed too that where the two colors in these crystals come together, the joining is like a ball and socket, with the pink or red acting as the ball, in most cases. This does not apply to the junction of colors between the cap and the rest of the crystal. This, as a rule, is pretty clear cut across the crystal.

Fred Rynerson and Fitz (who guides sled) just before hitting pine tree.

Old Hupmobile that carried lots of tourmaline.

CHAPTER XXIII

FINDING TOURMALINES IN THE DUMPS

Tourmalines take on a static charge that makes them magnetic. At times, when we shoot out a pocket or bug-hole with dynamite, the crystals will scatter along the drift, or tunnel floor, and collect the gabbro dust and dirt to such an extent it covers them entirely. This causes a lot of extra work, peeling off all the lumps of dirt and retrieving the crystals. This ''shooting out'' of gem material is the cause of there being so much of the stuff in the dumps.

We had put in a round of shots just before noon, when Herb Hill went over to the store. After lunch, and before I went back to the mine, I walked around the base of the old tunnel dump. When I got to the north side, I noticed a broken piece of vein right at the foot of the dump and right beside it were a number of tourmaline crystals, absolutely clear and water white! The largest was about three-eighths inch in diameter by one-and-a-half inches long. I could see where they had come out of a piece of vein. They had no doubt been in a bunch of pocket clay, and the whole bunch of clay had dropped out on the ground and been dissolved by the rains; leaving the crystals clean. These colorless tourmalines are the only ones I have ever seen in, or around these mines, though I wouldn't say that they haven't been found here before. This was a real treasure!

After working for a few days, we began to see the end of our job. It had been a dandy pocket, about fifty feet long and not over twelve feet wide, with no short arms. The vein on the opposite side of the shaft showed indications of being productive, so I started in there. In four feet I uncovered a large stibiotantalite and a few fine morganites. The specimen of stibiotantalite was sold to my friend, Ernest Schernikow of San Francisco. It was of a dark yellowish color and comparatively rare. This seemed to be the north end of the pocket, for the pay streak pinched down and scattered. I knew it would be quite a distance before I would come into another pocket, so we continued on down with the shaft.

We hadn't gone down more than fifteen feet, when we came across a very interesting picture. The vein here was about twenty-four inches thick, a little thicker than where we struck the pocket. A chunk of the hanging wall, about four-and-a-half feet long by three feet wide and twelve inches thick at the base, had tipped out until the top end touched the foot-wall, but the lower end still retained its footing on the hanging wall. When this piece of hanging wall fell over onto the footwall, the end touching the foot-wall splintered, or broke; leaving some of the pieces on top of the slab. At the end, still touching the hanging wall, were more small pieces, probably broken off the bottom of the slab. The small pieces and the slab were, of course, decomposed, but the slab was in place, just as it had fallen out of the hanging wall when the hanging wall was hard rock. (See page 156.)

This is proof, beyond a doubt, that this fissure had been open at the time the piece of slab fell out of the hanging wall. It also disproves the theory which, as some claim, that the pegmatite came up in a thick magma of molten rock. If it had, it would have pushed those small pieces off the main slab, or pushed the whole piece out of place. If the slab had been in its original hard rock condition, I could have fitted it back into the place it came from.

When this slab of hanging wall tipped over onto the foot-wall, the fissure pitched in an up-and-down direction, lengthwise, with the slab. This also coincides with the mineral streams which came up from below, and in the same direction. I have found several such examples as this slab, but none so perfectly preserved. The slab weighed several hundred pounds. If it had fallen over when the fissure pitched at the angle and the direction it does today, the slab would not have stayed in place, but would have fallen down the fissure. Most of the bulges in the vein are on the hanging wall; leading me to believe pieces of the hanging wall had fallen out and down the fissure before the vein was formed.

Some time in the distant past, the whole land structure covering the mine area was forced east at the bottom, or west at the surface. Now, the mineral streams point northerly and southerly the same as the rock slab, and there are parallels I have run across in these mines. No one knows how many times this area had been moved, or how much. I do not think it has been moved much, for the vein is in good solid condition, and is not cracked or crushed from too much motion.

I told my long-time friend, Dr. Waldermar T. Schaller, about the slab that tipped over onto the foot-wall, and he said I should have taken a picture of it for it would have been valuable for mining school studies. I should have taken pictures of MANY things I have seen in the mines. There were wonderful specimens destroyed, in getting tourmalines out of them. I was guilty of this waste, along with the others. But we were after tourmalines, not specimens. Specimen pieces wouldn't bring the money the tourmaline crystals would when cut, and cutting was my job.

It wasn't until 1919 when I first met my good friend, Mr. Ernest Schernikow, that I did get a reasonable offer for specimens. I have broken tourmaline crystals one inch thick by four-and-a-half inches long, half pink and half green, selling the pink piece to the Chinese for more than I could get for the whole crystal, from others.

We continued down with the shaft to the eighty-five foot level. Here we again cut a pocket. This one wasn't more than ten feet long and five feet wide. The material was fair, but scattered. We drove on down to the hundred-and-eight foot level, where we hit another pocket, which was like the one above. We also struck water which stopped further work.

It was in 1924 or '25 that I dropped into Ward's Lapidary Shop on A Street, San Diego. Ward was alone and I was talking with him, when an elderly lady of about sixty years of age came in with a paper sack containing a dozen corundum crystals. The largest was about two inches long by three-fourths inch wide at the bottom and one-half inch at the top. All were reddish-brown in color and pyramid in type. She wanted to know if they were worth anything. At that time they were of no value, and we told her so. She said she lived in Riverside County and was coming down to San Diego to visit some friends. She brought these crystals to find out if they were of value. These crystals, she said, were scattered over the side of a small hill back of her house. She picked up a few to bring along. Four years later I had a call for that kind of material. I searched every known collection in Riverside County to find the location of that find. Being without the lady's name, or home location, I failed to find the place. Riverside County is a big country!

When I was running the steam shovel in the Otay gravel pit, my partner, Tom Quin, had his brother Frank and Herb Hill start a tunnel on the east side of the ridge, cutting the vein forty-five feet below the surface.

When I went back to the mine again, Herb Hill and I finished the drifts which had just been started north and south from the end of the tunnel. In the drift north, and about twenty-five feet in, we cut indications of a pocket that lay above us. We drove the drift on about six feet, then started to stope up, putting in a chute here to load the cars. After six feet of stope, we cut into the lower end of a pocket, which at that point was about ten feet wide. As this stope was like a bottle turned upside-down, it didn't take long to use up the oxygen in the air. So we went outside to sink an air hole to connect with our stope, which gave us plenty of air. After we had completed the stope to about eighteen feet, we started drifting north on the pocket. Hill worked the lower half and I the upper half, leaving pillars of pegmatite between us.

CHAPTER XXIV

POLLUCITE - - WHAT IT IS. SEVERAL VALUABLE GEM POCKETS.

This was some pocket we had found! The tourmalines came in a white crystalline material with lepidolite veins running through it. What a haul we could have made if we had known what that stuff would be worth in a year or two! I estimated the amount we took out of that pocket, conservatively, at about ten tons. Two years later it was worth $12.00 a pound!

This material was pollucite, a very heavy sandy rock or ore with tourmalines embedded in it in places. Other spots had nothing but pollucite, or cesium ore. The tourmalines from this pocket were of a very fine color. Some would fall into several pieces when taking them out of the pollucite. In each section there would be a fine nodule, the largest about five-eighths inch wide by three-fourths inch long, sometimes in two colors, one half pink and the other green, or yellow-green. Several cesium beryls of good color were taken out, not in the large pocket cavity, but in small cavities close to the ends of the main pocket, and sometimes above the outer fringes of the main pocket. The largest of these was about three inches wide one way, by two inches the other, and one-and-a-half inches deep, of perfect terminations, with all faces polished. The top of the crystal had a polished surface about two inches long and one-and-a-half inches wide in the widest places, and not a scratch on them! This crystal was almost perfect, with only two faint lines of webs running with the axis of the crystal. I offered it to a certain collector for $75.00, knowing he would find some fault with it. He said, "I would be glad to give you $75.00 for the crystal if you hadn't polished that table on it." I told him I was withdrawing the offer and didn't want to sell - that old Mother Nature had polished that table, not me! I cut up the crystal, getting two large rectangle stones and several smaller ones. I gave George T. Ward, a lapidary in San Diego, a piece out of which he cut a thirty-carat stone, which he later sold to Mrs. Rose Gopel, of that City.

The pollucite in this pocket took up about two-thirds of its area and was like a core, leaving three or four feet of normal pocket all around it. It was only in the pollucite that the nodules were found. In the outer areas of the pocket that did not contain pollucite, the tourmalines were in good, solid, well formed crystals.

I cut into two short arm pockets taking off from the main pocket on the upper side. The one on my right, near the south end of the main pocket, produced some deep wine-red colored crystals. The largest was about one inch thick by two inches long. About twenty pounds was all I took out of this arm cavity.

The second arm cavity was a few feet north of the first one. Both had extended easterly and at right angles to the mineral stream and opened out into the main pocket cavity. This second arm cavity contained about the same amount of tourmalines as the first arm, but they showed the usual tourmaline colors - pink, yellow and green.

In a general outline, this pocket had the shape of an arrowhead. On the south end it was about twenty feet wide, ending in a blunt point. It extended north, retaining its twenty-foot width for about point. It extended north, retaining its twenty-foot width for about twenty feet, when it started to lessen gradually in width till it ran into some large black tourmalines, the largest crystal being about two inches wide by four inches long. All were not in a sound condition. A few feet farther on, with the usual scattered beryls and rarer minerals, the pay streak finally played out.

Sometimes, these big pockets will come to an abrupt end, into a blank pegmatite, which seems to have been formed across the mineral stream. This is because, after some feet farther on, we will again see signs of the same mineral stream our last pocket was on. This leads me to believe that possibly the vein had been faulted at that point across the mineral stream, and after the pocket had been formed, or partially so, the pegmatite solutions filled the opening. Almost always there is a stringer taking off from this point, indicating a fault.

This was a very rich mineral stream, with five large pockets, to my knowledge. The first one was about twenty-five feet from the surface. The next one was in a shaft south of that point, the third I have just described; the fourth I will describe next; the fifth was on my property that Gail Lewis and I worked in 1907, and was cut into at the sixty-eight foot level. If an incline shaft were sunk on this mineral stream, it would run through all five of these pockets.

After cleaning out this pollucite pocket, we dropped back down into the north drift of the tunnel and drove that on another fifteen feet. We put in a round of dynamite shots, blasting at noon and down to the bunk house for lunch. After lunch, Herb Hill told me he had to go over to the store and would get back as soon as possible. We had no blower on this job, for, as a rule the powder smoke would clear out of the tunnel and stopes in a short while. When I got back to the tunnel, I lit two candles and went inside. Coming to the end of the tunnel, I found the drift north of the stope still smoky, so I turned back and examined the short drift turning south which was ten or fifteen feet long.

At this point on the property, with a drift running south, the foot-wall of the vein is about four feet high on the left side and at about floor level on the right side. Six feet into the drift, and on the left side, the vein showed many pocket indications. I went at once to the breast, or end of the drift. Here I found, near the lower right hand side near the floor, a small bug-hole containing several lepidolite crystals. They are a sure sign of a good pocket.

I got the auger and put down two holes, three feet deep above the vein, and two below the vein, under the foot-wall of the vein. I loaded them up with dynamite, fired them, and went back to the bunk house. Next morning we looked over the effects of our shots in the north drift and found we were cutting into another mineral stream, possibly a pocket, for we picked up several dark red tourmalines one-half inch thick and three inches long, with a dark blue, almost black, cap. Some of these crystals were actually three-sided. One of the three sides was wider than the others, and flat. After cleaning up the effects of the blasts, we went back into the south drift where I had put in the four shots. Here we found tourmalines scattered over the entire floor, almost to the tunnel. Herb Hill told me that Frank Quin had taken out some beryls here, not five feet from where I had put in the shots, just before he quit; and he quit about two feet from one of the richest tourmaline pockets I have ever taken out!

After cleaning up what the shots had thrown out, we went back into the north drift and worked there for a day or two. We found that the mineral stream was opening into a small pocket zone which contained red tourmaline, scattered through the vein in a close, thin pocket. We also made the discovery that this pocket zone was another mineral stream paralleling the one where we found the pollucite; thus placing the two streams twenty-five feet apart.

We left the north end and went to work on the pocket at the end of the south drift. Here we found we had opened into a large pocket of fine pink tourmaline crystals, the largest being one and three-eighths inches wide by two inches long. They had perfect terminations, and a bright pink color which we classed as top Chinese stuff with a value for that size of from $50.00 to $65.00 a pound.

About ten percent of the tourmalines in this pocket were perfect gem quality and facet cutting material. We did not class cabochon material (small crystal material suitable for polishing but not for cutting). Only the material that was free from flaws and imperfections was classed as gem stuff.

We followed the pocket in this drift toward the south, about sixty feet, when the vein came to an abrupt end. We had hit one of Frank Trask's old drifts when he was working for Gale Lewis and me in 1907. He had run a drift north from the shaft and we had run into the end of it about as true as if it had been surveyed. He had done some other work here too, probably some stoping, as he had back-filled the drift which was full of broken rock, pocket linings, and dirt.

How much longer this pocket was, I couldn't say, but I know Frank wouldn't have drifted north off his shaft without a pocket or mineral stream to work on, for when he stopped he was about on the line between our property (Gale Lewis's and mine) and the Himalaya Mine property.

This pocket had not been a wide one; only eight or nine feet at the widest part. Most of it had a width of five or six feet. About ten feet back from the end of the pocket, we ran a stope out to the surface, but found nothing other than a few beryls in bug-holes about ten feet from the surface.

Then we dropped back to where I had seen some good indications, just inside the drift from the tunnel's end. We ran a stope here about ten feet, then drifted north about the same distance; taking out some badly etched cesium beryls. Some of these were almost round and honeycombed, and an inch in diameter to just a sliver. Here, too, we found some columbite, and a poor quality of tourmaline. This was the north end of the big pocket we had just quit.

We didn't do any more work in the north drift, where we had found the three-cornered red tourmaline, as the weather was turning cold. As we had a fine lot of cuttable material, I decided I would take on a change of work, after almost a year of mining and batching. We made a heavy door and put it on the entrance to the tunnel and locked it. I never worked in that tunnel or the north drift again. The mouth of the tunnel caved in that winter, which was a wet one.

At noon the next day, I loaded up the old Hupp with the last two weeks' products of a very rich pocket, and started for San Diego. A tire on the rear wheel had given me more than average mileage, but I expected it to blow out before I could get out of the mountain country. I wasn't more than five blocks from home, when I happened to think of this and said to myself, "I wonder if I'm going to make it home on that tire?" "Bang!" the tire went, with a loud report, just as I said "tire". I didn't stop but drove on home on the flat. Those days we carried forty-five or fifty pounds of air in the tires and the ones I was using were 33 x 4 tires.

With much fine material of my own to cut, and that which had come in from my customers, I had my hands full of lapidary work. We had a lot of fine solid material suitable for bracelets out of which I cut a great number of the quarter-circle sections. These had to be cut out of good solid material. No pieces with checks or large flaws could be used. The buttons were different. They could hold many imperfections, providing they ran from top to bottom of the button and not sidewise through it.

Most of the two-colored crystals were cut into rectangular shapes, without which they were nearer round than square. To save material, all stones were cut as near to the rough shapes as practicable. Some of these stones were beautiful, when the two colors would blend at an angle across the stone. It is best never to let either color dominate the bottom of the stone.

If a round stone can be roughed out so the line between the two colors will split the culet, (flat base of a gem) you will have done your best. Some of these two-colored crystals about one inch long by one-fourth inch thick, I cut into long drops, with either color in the bottom or widest part of the drop. These drops were cut faceted into matched pairs for ear-rings, or lavaliere ornaments. Other crystals with two colors and from two to two-and-a-quarter inches long by one-quarter inch thick, I mounted rough, in gold, as breast pins or brooches.

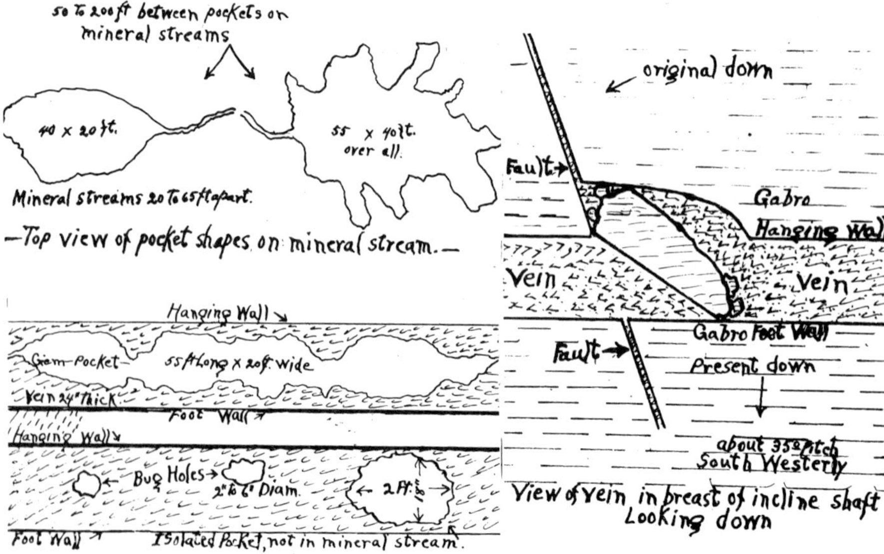

CHAPTER XXV

A GOLD HUNT IN WASHINGTON STATE. ADVICE OF AN INDIAN SCOUT

I had known for about four years a man by the name of Daily. He had told me several times about some gold he had found up in the state of Washington. At different times I had questioned him about certain angles of the story, but I always found him sincere in his beliefs. He was in San Diego, making his headquarters at Ward's Lapidary Shop on A Street, and was searching for a man by the name of "Keenen", who had sent him some good ceramic clays.

Dailey had some placer gold in with some black sand, also a piece of rock which he said he had put into a furnace for a temperature test. The result was a nice bubble of gold about the size of a small pea which appeared on it. One day Ward and I made a test of fineness of both the rock and the placer gold and found they were the same. Here is the story he told me about how he found the gold.

He was preparing to leave for Seattle when a friend asked him if, in case he ran across some iron ore or black sand, he would bring him back a sample; as he would like to test it for a certain kind of iron he was looking for.

Dailey said he had hired a guide at Port Angeles and had gone into the Olympic Mountains. The day he found the gold, he could look ahead and see a mountain peak, which he called a "goose neck". But before they made camp that night, they had lost sight of the goose neck and had descended into a deep canyon. They hadn't gone far before the guide picked out a sheltered place to camp. To get to this camp site, they followed a game trail along the face of a small cliff. As he (Dailey) was passing a crack about six inches wide in the face of the cliff, he chipped off a small piece and put it in his coat pocket.

Following the creek down along the face of this cliff, they crossed the creek and made camp fifty feet above it. Dailey said that while the guide was making camp he walked down to the creek to get a drink. He noticed a sand bar that split the creek at the point the trail crossed, and walked out on it. Getting down to get a drink, he saw some black sand along the edge of the stream and thought of what his friend had said. So he took a couple of handfuls of the sand to put into his canvas coat pocket, but then forgot it.

The next day they traveled down the mountain toward a river which they crossed in a heavy rain. They holed up in an old abandoned sawmill for several days, weathering the storm, and then stopped at a small settlement called "Fork".

When Dailey returned to Seattle, he was going through the pockets of his coat and found the rock and black sand. Dumping the contents out on some paper, he called his friend on the phone. The friend said he would be right over to get it. When he arrived he asked Dailey how much there was of it and Dailey replied, "Oh, probably tons." Dailey told me he had hardly gotten out of bed next morning when the phone rang. It was his friend again asking how much black sand there was where he had found the sample, for there was gold in it. Dailey told him he was joking about the tonnage part and explained how he had gotten it. Dailey said he put the rock chip into a ceramic furnace, and when he took it out found the gold bubble on it.

Ward and I had a talk over finding the place. We asked Dailey if he thought he could find the spot again. He said, "Well, we can get that same old guide, I'm sure." I asked him if he had seen anything along the way besides the gooseneck. "Yes," he said, "I saw some rocks with little holes in them about an eighth inch in diameter and an eighth to one-fourth inch deep, with white coating on the bottom of the holes. I remember, too, we stayed one night in a log house with part of the roof off so the smoke from the camp fire could escape."

After finishing some of the work I had on hand from the jewelers, I greased up the old Hupp and Ward, Dailey and I started for the State of Washington in the summer of 1924. We arrived in Seattle on the sixth day, picked up Dailey's brother-in-law in Seattle, and drove on to Port Angeles, arriving there late the following day.

Here, in Port Angeles we outfitted for our trip into the interior of the Olympic National Forest. We then looked up Dailey's old guide and found he had moved away. This was a very discouraging turn in our plans. Everything now depended upon Dailey's ability to follow his old route through the mountains. The Park authorities would not let us into the park without a guide at that time, so we hired a man by the name of Bill Stewart who was a trapper in that district.

The first day out I knew we had a slim chance of finding what we were looking for. I had noticed that Dailey was completely lost when he entered the timber. While we were on this trip we hired two other guides and walked a hundred-and-eighty-five miles on foot; carrying our blankets and provisions on our backs. Ward was a big man, weighing around two-hundred pounds; Dailey, about a hundred-and-seventy-five pounds, and tall; his brother-in-law, about a hundred-and-eighty pounds; and I, about a hundred-and-fifty-five pounds.

We had to return to Port Angeles three times for provisions. On our last trip back into a new section of the country, lasting eight days, Dailey, on the last day, acknowledged he was beaten and lost. He said he wouldn't have believed he could not have found the place again.

For breakfast that morning, we ate all our grub; making sandwiches out of the last of the flapjacks and bacon. Then we started the long eighteen-mile hike from 7,000 foot elevation down to where we had left the old Hupp. Dailey and Ward were about finished when we arrived at the car. Dailey was in bad shape. I had warned him about drinking much cold water. He couldn't, it seems, pass up those little ice-cold streams we crossed without a drink each time and the stuff had stiffened him up so he could hardly walk.

The advice given me by Mr. Burnett, the old Indian scout, when I was about twelve years old, served me well on these trips as well as others. He told me that if I had to make a long or forced journey on foot, to try and think of something I liked, such as finding a rich gold mine, or having a big cattle ranch. Or, if I couldn't think of anything else, figure out a way to fall in love with the Old Don's daughter! He said not to think of how long it will take to get where I was going - it was going to take me that long to get there anyway. Just keep my mind off the efforts to get there, and I will feel better when I arrive.

"Walk with your feet straight ahead, and not toed out," he said, "Let your weight roll off all your toes, and not off the big toe. When walking in sand, toe in the feet a little, and you will find it easier to walk, less tiresome. Don't wear heavy boots or shoes. If you do, take a lighter pair of shoes along and change to them when you get tired. You will feel better the last few miles.

"Never take intoxicating drinks at any time, before starting your walk or during the journey. Drink water only, and that, sparingly, and not too cold. If you are in a dry, hot desert country, drink plenty of water in the evenings, during the night and before breakfast in the morning; but leave it alone during the daytime. This will prevent you from having a feverish stomach, which will demand more and more water and end up with a sick spell.

"If the weather is cool or cold, and you want to rest, don't sit on the cold rocks or lie down on the cold ground. Try to keep standing and moving around a little; it will prevent you from getting chilled and stiff."

The above advice came from a Grand Old Man of eighty-five years, gentle and kind. He always had a smile on his face. It was hard to believe he had been through the Mexican War of 1848, the Civil War on the Southern side, the Modoc Indian War, and several other Indian wars. He stood about five feet, ten inches tall and was as straight as an arrow!

We pulled into the camp ground near Port Angeles about five P.M. and Dailey was so far gone he went to a hotel instead of camping with the rest of us. Dailey's brother-in-law, who had served as cook on the trip, bought a large piece of stew meat, and some vegetables, and we had the best feed we had gotten on the outside of in two weeks!

That evening I made the acquaintance of Leet Elliott, a timberman. After telling him where we had been, and about the gooseneck and other places we were looking for, he said, "I believe I could have taken you there. I can take you where you can see the gooseneck and the log house with part of the roof off." I asked him if he thought we could make it the next week, and he said the rains were about due now and we should wait until next year.

We had thrown up a canvas leanto, as we always did when making camp, and awoke next morning in a drizzling rain. As the morning passed, so did the drizzle, but it continued as a rain. Getting a late start and an hour's delay on the road because three fir trees had fallen across it, we made it to Tacoma before dark. Not a minute of that time did the rain stop. Here, the cook left us for Seattle.

Next morning it was still raining and it kept up until we arrived in Eugene, Oregon. The next morning we left in the same rainstorm. Before we crossed the Oregon-California line, we ran into a light snowfall. But it wasn't ten minutes after we crossed into California until the sun came out. We had sunny days from then on until we arrived in San Diego.

My reason for stating our experiences on this trip is to prove how some people can be so sure they can find a certain place and yet, when on the ground, don't see anything familiar and become completely lost. I believe Dailey was sincere in his efforts to find the place. He worked hard enough and looked like a starved mosquito when we ended the trip at Port Angeles.

I, of course, had my eye peeled for any gem stones that lay along our route, but only at one place did I find anything in that line. That was up in the Happy Lake district around 6,000 feet elevation, on what was called "Crystal Ridge." I found some small crystals of quartz which were of no value. I received several letters from Leet Elliott during that winter, and he promised to get me all the information he could about the trip

Dailey was on when he found the gold.

After a week at home, I loaded up the old Hupp with provisions and a fifty pound box of powder, and lit out for the mine at Mesa Grande. While I was away in Washington, the Chinese trade had picked up. They were howling for the Chinese grade stuff.

We went through all the old workings, and worked out all the likely places which netted us considerable Chinese quality stuff, including some good gem material. I was very anxious to get more bracelet material, for I could sell all I made up.

Just before Thanksgiving 1924, we quit the work at the mine on account of the bad weather. I went back to cutting again. The lapidary business was very good that winter, at least for me. But long hours at the bench, day after day, always gave me itchy feet. I had received a letter from Leet Elliott of Port Angeles, about once a month. About the last of June, 1925, I had a talk with Ward about going up to Washington and having another look for the gold. Ward said he didn't think he could make the trip again. I couldn't get in touch with Dailey, so decided to go alone.

I wired Elliott I would meet him in Port Angeles and boarded the Santa Fe train for the trip north to Seattle. From there I went by boat to Port Angeles. There I got in touch with Elliott and outfitted for the trip into the mountains.

We hired a man to drive us up to a ranch a little south and east of Port Angeles. This was the end of the road. Here we stayed the night, bedding down in a hay field. I had rented a sleeping bag from a friend of Elliott's. It weighed only six pounds, and was a "dandy", covered with waterproof silk the warmest bag I ever slept in!

We had hired a boy and a horse from the ranch nearby to pack some of our provisions. We put about two-hundred pounds on the horse and about thirty pounds apiece on our packboards. The trail we used when we left the ranch, led through some very thick timber. At one place we had to unpack the horse to get him between two trees, one on each side of the trail. It was impossible to get the horse around them. This trail was very steep. When we arrived at a little clearing, it was as far as we could go with the horse. This clearing was called "Coxe's Valley". Here was the log house with part of the roof off, where Dailey's first group built their fires.

We camped here two nights, for we had a hard pull ahead of us for the next three miles and a rise of 3,000 feet. This was a cold spot too. About four P.M. the ice began to form along the little creek back of the cabin.

The next morning we loaded up our packboards, each taking

about a hundred-and-thirty pounds! We never would have made it if we hadn't had the packboards. That three-mile trail took us eight hours to climb. It was so steep that all we had to do when we wanted to rest was to turn around and let our packboards lean on the trail!

When we got to the top, we camped in a little draw above the big timber line, where the trees were very short, about twelve feet high and not very numerous. Whistling marmots were everywhere. It was before we got to our camp site when Elliott pointed toward the west and said, "There's your gooseneck." And sure enough, it was just like Dailey had described it.

That night we slept twenty feet from a big bank of snow, ten feet high. And were we tired! We kicked up a fire right away, as the temperature was dropping fast. We had a big slice of ham, fried potatoes and, of all things for a southerner, "tea" and store bread, for our supper. Then we hit the sack. That was the toughest climb, and the heaviest pack I ever carried. At times we could go only twenty or thirty feet, and then had to rest.

Next day we moved over on Wolf Creek, but were so stiff and sore from the climb the day before, we decided to make two trips of it. We made camp in a sheltered, shallow ravine. Here we saw quite a number of deer and plenty of bear signs. We tied our bacon and ham up in a small tree close by.

Dailey said where he camped he could see the gooseneck, and when they started out next morning they crossed a large area of "down timber", partly burned, before they descended the mountain. There were three ridges leading down to the river (Elwaw), Dailey said. They went down the middle ridge and had just started down it when they made camp and Dailey found the gold.

We could see the gooseneck from the camp we had made after our hard climb up the mountain. When we moved our camp over on Wolf Creek, we crossed the patch of burned down timber. We also found the rocks with the little holes with white coating in the bottoms. Up to now, everything looked rosy, and we went to bed that night feeling pretty happy.

The next three days we covered every trail on that ridge and every place we could get through - but found nothing like the place Dailey described so many times. Dailey had told me as they had proceeded along, the gooseneck began to take the form of a peak. It appeared to do the same thing with us too, but it could do that from two directions. So we packed to the head of Little River, a mile from our Wolf Creek camp, and started westerly, keeping to the high ground.

This part of the mountain was very rough and showed very little mineral as we know it in the southwest. The last two weeks we tested every stream and every piece of formation that seemed different from the others, without finding any indications of gold. So we came to the conclusion that Dailey got the gold on another trip, other than in the Olympic Mountains!

Dailey said he had chipped off the rock, that he later roasted, several hundred feet above where he had picked up the black sand and gold. It has always seemed strange to me, that both the roasted sample of gold and the gold in the black sand were of the same fineness, which, in a way, ties them in together. Both tested between 20 and 22 carat. They could have been Calaverite. I looked the placer gold over with a glass and it was true placer gold.

Leet Eliott and our packs on our arrival on Hurricane Ridge, Olympic Mountains, Washington

Cabin in Coxes Valley, head of Morris Creek, Olympic Mts.

CHAPTER XXVI

MONEY IN POLLUCITE: QUARTZ CRYSTALS FOR NAVY

Arriving back in San Diego, I started cutting my own tourmaline material, as well as a lot of very small stones for Mr. J. W. Ware, a jeweler. These small stones were in two sizes, some one-and-a-half MM. wide by three MM. long, and some two MM. by three-and-a-half MM. There were only two colors used, dark pink and blue-green. I had delivered some stones to Mr. Ware, and had gone down to Skeats Assay Shop on Eighth Street in San Diego, and was told by the Assayer, Mr. Waggoner, that a Frenchman from Bakersfield told him he had received a cablegram from Paris, France, stating they had gotten a shipment of rock from "Pala-Grande", and some of the rocks contained "Pollucite".

Waggoner got down "Old Dana", (Dana's MINERALOGY) and looked up "Pollucite". It was described as a waxy, fractured, quartz-like material. I told Waggoner I believed I had some of it and went home to look over some boxes of material and scraps from the mine; coming up with only one crystal, one-half inch in diameter. I gave half to Waggoner to test and sent the rest to my friend, Mr. Schernikow in San Francisco. He answered that he had taken it to the Bureau of Mines, and they said it was Pollucite.

I hadn't been back from the Olympic Mountains more than two weeks, when a friend of mine, Mr. Nevell, from the State of Maine dropped in. He was stopping at the San Diego Hotel, but wanted to rent a house, as he had his wife and little son with him. I had a small house vacant at the time, and he moved into it.

I told Nevell what the Frenchman said about the Pollucite and he asked me a lot of questions concerning the material and wanted to know when I was going up to the mine again. I told him I was waiting to hear from my friend in San Francisco. Then Nevell broke down and told me he was representing a certain company in the east that wanted the stuff, and if I could show him some of the material out of the mine his company would pay us well for a lease.

Next day we drove up to Mesa Grande and looked over the mine. Only one stope hole was open that led down to the tunnel (where we took out the five-hundred pound pocket), which continued on through to the Flag Pole shaft. Water from above had poured down the stope, washing it badly and half filling the tunnel with mud. I tied a rope to a small tree and let myself down the stope. Coming to the tunnel I turned to the right, but ran into a cave-in that blocked the tunnel. I then turned and made my way in the opposite direction. Coming to a place about twenty feet from the Flag Pole shaft, I found the roof had caved down and slid on down the shaft; leaving a room about ten feet wide and twenty feet long.

The hanging wall on the upper side of the tunnel had slipped off the vein, leaving about five feet of the vein exposed, and cracked in one place about four inches wide. It wasn't hard to force the two pieces of vein apart, and there, exposed to view, about ten inches across, was some material I took to be pollucite, from descriptions Mr. Nevell had given me.

I had only a candlestick with me, so pried out what I could with the candlestick into my hat. Holding it by the rim with my teeth, I pulled myself up the forty-foot stope to the top. I handed Nevell the hat and he picked out a chunk the size of a small apple. He held it up and said, ''We'll go right to town and send this off to my people.'' He then told me the company was the General Electric Company, Schenectady, New York.

It wasn't long before word came that the sample was pollucite and he asked us to secure a lease. In the meantime, Quin bought the Himalaya Mine and I bought the San Diego Mine, joining and on the same vein. Shortly before we were ready to sign the lease, Mr. M. F. Westover, Secretary of the General Electric Company showed up. We leased both properties to the General Electric Company for five years, under certain working conditions, for $10,000 cash. Work could be stopped if less than $5,000 worth of pollucite was taken out the first year. The lessor was to retain all gem stones and all minerals other than pollucite.

At the time we signed the lease, storms and heavy rains swept over the country, washing out the roads and bridges so badly it was a month before we were able to do much work. During that time, I was put on the payroll to investigate all known gem deposits in Riverside and San Diego Counties, for pollucite. This was a job! The weather was at its worst. I did manage to look at all the prospects and deposits I knew of, and in only one did I find some pink material I thought might be pollucite. It was. Yet it was unlike what I found at Mesa Grande.

Up to that time I had little knowledge or experience in locating or mining pollucite. I had only a word description of the stuff. I had no means of telling accurately what material was or was not pollucite, and a spectrographic microscope, to test the different rocks.

The only other place I found pollucite, other than Mesa Grande, was a little west of north of the Pala store, and halfway up the side of the mountain. The claim was owned by Doc Trotter and a partner. Very little work had been done over the twelve years Trotter said he had owned the property. No gem stones, other than quartz crystals, had been found. I could see that the vein was only a piece that had broken off a portion above, but it was quite a large chunk and could contain a large amount of pollucite.

I asked Trotter what he wanted for the property and he said, "$5,000". I told him I would have to send the samples away and as soon as I heard from them again, I would see him. Trotter hadn't known what I was looking for, but suspected something was up.

Shortly after we had signed the lease on the Mesa Grande properties and Mr. Westover had left for the East, Mr. Nevell came down with a bad case of measles. I mean "down", when he wasn't walking around delirious. When he became well enough to travel, I drove up to Trotter's mine to show him the property. It had rained considerably a day or two before and, on our way to Pala, we met Trotter who was repairing the road. I introduced Nevell to him and told Trotter I was taking Mr. Nevell up to his mine to look it over.

All at once he became very angry, telling us he didn't want us or anyone else around his mine. I said, "Doc, you're making a mistake. I've known you for a long time and I know you don't mean that." Trotter said, "All right. Go ahead. But my old price is off. I want $10,000 for it now!"

I had the piece of pollucite on Trotter's mine, in the cut he had made before he started underground with his tunnel. It was in the mineral stream that ran a little east of north across the cut. The cut ran northerly and southerly. This mineral stream extended a considerable distance in a northeasterly direction up the mountain. Very little was exposed in a southwesterly direction from the cut.

When Nevell and I arrived at the mine, I could see that the recent rains had caved in the banks, or sides, of the cut and washed out the floor. Search as I would, I couldn't find another piece of pollucite; nor could Nevell locate anything like the piece I found.

We did not prospect the mineral stream farther north, but only around the cut. I believed the cut had been made across the southern end of the enriched portion of the mineral stream. In cases where a portion of the vein has broken off from the larger main portion, it has done so along a mineral stream, or a line of pockets in the stream. Sometimes the pockets will follow or cling to the portion of the vein that has broken off and moved away. Or, the piece of vein will move away; leaving the pocket matter close to the break or clinging to the main vein.

A similar instance was that which occurred at the point of discovery of the Tourmaline Queen Mine near Pala. Here the vein had broken off the east edge of the mineral stream, dumping a portion of the pocket at the point of break. Here is what old Bill Clark, storekeeper at Rincon, a few miles east of Pala, told me:

"I had prospected on the lower slopes of the mountain and had seen this large dike far up, through my glasses. I made up my mind I would look it over in the morning. A friend and I drove up to the foot of the mountain, on the east side. Leaving the buckboard and horses, we walked up to the large dike. After looking for and finding some small tourmalines and quartz crystals, we decided to locate it, but found we had come away without location papers; nor did we have any paper at all - not even a pencil.

"I had noticed a large spot of white ash-colored material about twenty feet east of the vein breast, which covered an area ten feet square, but had never investigated it. We decided to come back early next morning we found a monument there with a location paper in a can. Someone had been watching us, and after we left had located it. The ashy spot was worked out and later I heard several large tourmaline crystals and smaller stuff had been taken out of it." That was Bill Clark's story.

When I was at Trotter's mine the first time, I got permission from Frank Salmons to look over the Tourmaline Queen and Pala Chief mines. While at the Queen mine I could see what had taken place there which left the ashy deposit where Bill Clark saw it. Most of the pocket had clung to the upper portion of the vein and dropped off later, or did not move away with the portion that had broken off. Most of the pocket was back of the broken face of the vein.

This Tourmaline Queen Mine vein is badly broken and lies almost flat, dipping a little to the west at this point, with the mineral stream running in a northerly and southerly direction. Much time and money were lost here in working out this pocket, done mostly by main strength and awkwardness. All the dump rock and dirt was carried up-hill in a wheelbarrow, and dumped outside. I did not find a sample of pollucite in this mine. I wouldn't say that it did not occur in this vein, but I did not find it. My search through the Pala Chief kunzite mine, and the Steward lithia mine at Pala also proved fruitless.

In 1934, I again visited Trotter's mine where I found the pink pollucite. Someone had continued on with the tunnel forty-five to fifty feet, when he came to a clean break in the vein, and into the gabbro, or wall formation. The break was not along a mineral stream but through a blank portion of the pegmatite vein. This was understandable, for I had noticed in the tunnel leading west in the Tourmaline Queen Mine farther up the mountain that no mineral stream had been cut in the tunnel, which was seventy-five feet or more long. The same condition existed in the Old Schyler Mine on the west side of the mountain. Both veins are comparatively level, with the tunnels running toward each other, so that no doubt they are on the same vein.

Back at Mesa Grande Herb Hill and I started an incline shaft that we hoped would lead us down to the mineral deposit Hill had run into when he worked for the old San Diego Tourmaline Company. As he remembered, it was similar to that we had found in the big pocket on the Himalaya Mine. He told me he had taken out a car load of the stuff, but there was plenty more left. In this material he had found some large green tourmaline nodules without flaws, the largest about three-fourths inch in diameter.

I put two other men to work running a tunnel to connect with the bottom of our shaft. I walked down to the tunnel every morning and afternoon to see how they were getting along. After they had faced off the portal to the tunnel, I noticed the work slowed up. When they were underground about six feet I happened one morning to find both men standing outside. Asking what the trouble was, they told me they were quitting, as the work was too dangerous in there. I walked into the tunnel and examined the roof and walls, but couldn't see anything wrong - and told them so. I paid them off. I found out afterward they had been imagining a lot of things that might happen to them in that tunnel and this had scared them out of a job. That tunnel was never finished.

I picked out a location south of the old Flag Pole shaft on the Himalaya property and had Vance Angel and an Indian boy, Valentine Lachussa, start a shaft. They got down to the thirty foot level without finding pollucite, and very little tourmaline. Then the Indian killed a mountain lion in his back yard and went to San Diego to collect the bounty.

Later, Vance and my sons, Buel and Eugene, ran a tunnel easterly on the west side of the mountain; following the vein in from the surface. Here, they cut through a small deposit of material that looked like the pollucite samples I had, but under the spectrographic microscope, proved not to be pollucite. No amount of tourmaline was found in this tunnel. I believe though, that if we had continued fifty or sixty feet farther we would have cut a mineral stream I had known about several years before.

Hill and I were down in our shaft about fifty feet when we ran into trouble. At this point, we crossed the old San Diego Tourmaline Mining Company's tunnel running north. Here they had cut into a series of mineral streams, not ten feet apart, that were loaded with tourmalines! They had taken out so much of the vein that it had weakened the hanging wall over quite a large area. This made it tough for us. We had to use a false set of timbers always ahead of us, and drive our lagging, little by little, until we came to more solid ground. The cave portion was about twenty feet across at this point.

At the seventy-five foot level, we put in a station and started a drift north to get under the locality we were heading for. We hadn't gone more than twenty feet until we broke into another cave. This was a humdinger! The roof was in bad shape. With a flashlight we could see in some places as far as forty or fifty feet. The roof being so loose, we doubted if any timbers we had would hold it up, if it started to move. The next day, Saturday, we thought we would go a little farther in and take a better view. We hadn't gone three feet before we gave it up as too risky, and luckily too.

I drove to San Diego that afternoon and back the following Monday. During the warmer days of the year, we had to blow the shaft out with an air blower to rid us of the powder smoke and other gases that collected in the shaft sometimes during the nights or Sundays. We had decided to drive the shaft on down another twenty feet. That Tuesday morning Herb took a candle and started down the shaft to see where the ceiling of the gas laid. He went ten feet before he reappeared, saying it was almost at the top of the shaft. This was an unusual amount for so short a time. We started the blower and in about forty-five minutes the shaft was clear of gas.

This gas is carbon-dioxide coming from the rotten timbers in the old workings. You cannot smell it, and without a candle or other flame, or scientific instruments, the only warning you would get is a sudden spell of sweating, then drowsiness. Then one should move fast - or he will stay there!

I had an experience one afternoon when I walked into an old shaft to get some fish (flat metal) plates off the track. The sun was shining into the hole. The plates I wanted were five feet down the shaft, measuring along the floor level of the cut. I had taken my candlestick and candle along and jabbed the candlestick into the foot-wall, or floor, putting the light out. Since the sun was shining down on the very spot I was going to work on, I needed no other light. I hadn't been kneeling more than half a minute when sweat started pouring off my face. I grabbed the candlestick and rushed up into the cut. Re-lighting the candle, I waited two or three minutes, then again started down the shaft, slowly; holding the candle in front of me. When the candle got to floor level it started to dim. I stood very still, about three minutes. I could move the candle up or down two inches, causing it to burn or go out completely. The shaft was full of gas and it acted the same on the candle as if the shaft were full of water. To get my fish plates, I had to take a grain sack and fan the top of the shaft for fifteen minutes to get out enough gas to do the work.

When we cut through the old tunnel that crossed the shaft, we took out some of the old timbers that had been in there since 1907, or more than eighteen years. In one of the caps we found some large white ants, or termites. Some were three-fourths inch long with a large black head and a light yellow body. When dumped on the ground outside the mine, they died in about thirty minutes - whether from the light or too much oxygen I couldn't say. After many years, I suppose they become immune to the gas, or maybe change over to Carbon-dioxide, when oxygen gradually gives out.

While we had been blowing the gas out of the shaft, we decided that some movement had taken place that had caused a freer flow of gas into the shaft. When the shaft was free enough of gas to allow us to descend, we both walked down the incline inspecting the timbers. When we got to the place where the old tunnel crossed, and where we had to drive through the cave, we saw that the timbers were taking on a tremendous load, forcing one end of the caps into the posts. Then we decided that we would pull the track and get out, rather than go to the expense and work of replacing the timbers to catch up the cave ground. So we pulled all the inside spikes in the cross ties, hitched onto the upper ends of the track with the hoist cable and pulled it out, while both of us were on top taking off each joint, as it came out of the shaft.

We had used some very good white oak caps in timbering this shaft and didn't like to see them covered up and lost. So, tying a half-inch wire line to the three-fourth inch hoist cable, Herb went down to the weakest set of timbers and very gingerly made it fast to the cap, giving me a two-bell signal to hoist slowly. The hoist cable ran out level to the lip of the incline shaft. There it passed over an eight-inch shive, or pulley wheel, and then on down the shaft.

I let the hoist take up the slack in the cable, then started to pull. The cable came off the ground, and then fell back as if it wasn't pulling anything. With the hoist going, I couldn't hear what was taking place in the shaft. Not getting a signal from Herb, I started to take a look-see. About half way there, I saw Herb backing up the shaft. Then I heard the rumbling. I called to Herb but he motioned me to look down the shaft. Because of the light outside, I had to go ten feet down the shaft to see. I ran back and stopped the hoist, then on down the shaft. What I saw was a great waterfall, only it was dirt and rocks instead of water plunging down the shaft! At times a boulder would come roaring down, hit the shaft and bounce on down to the bottom. After an hour, it had filled up the shaft to the cave-in timbers, and there caught itself up. And that was that! We saved twelve good oak caps and started looking for another place to work.

Afterwards, we often thought, how easy that cap was pulled off. The whole set of timbers must have been ready to go, on a trigger tension, so that any jolt, like a falling rock, could have released it. The extra amount of gas got us thinking, but I doubt if we would have missed seeing the condition of the timbers, especially near any known caved ground, for we were always looking for weak timbers whenever we entered the mine. I was sorry this had to happen in this shaft because we could have driven a tunnel to connect with the bottom of the shaft at the hundred and-twenty foot level and come up under the section where Herb Hill had taken out the green nodules in the white material.

We then moved south along the vein about seventy-five yards and started another shaft at the end of an old cut which we cleaned out and faced up with a good portal. The vein at this point was about three feet thick, with small, light pink tourmalines and lepidolite in it. At this time, I received a letter from Mr. Westover, secretary of the General Electric Company, stating that my year was up and I had not produced the $5,000 worth of pollucite necessary to continue the work for the next four years. This I expected, but Hill and I continued on with the work.

At the fifteen-foot level, the vein pinched down to about two feet thick and was blank pegmatite with no indications whatever. We took this to mean we were between two mineral streams. The top one had been in the cut and had been taken out by the San Diego Company. At the forty-foot level we ran into a little mineralization ten feet wide, but with no pocket cavities. This indicated we were between pockets, north and south of us, on the mineral stream.

We didn't drift off the shaft either way at this point, but continued on down with the shaft. Before we cut across the old San Diego Company's tunnel, we cut the upper side of a pocket, the largest portion of which had been taken out by the San Diego, and was, no doubt, the lower part of the rich section leading to the surface, which was taken out in 1907. This was the top end of what Gail Lewis and I cut through when Frank Trask worked on our first shaft in the same year.

I don't remember the quantity we took out of what was left in this pocket, but it was considerable! We drove on through the old tunnel, and down to the eighty-five-foot level, through a highly mineralized section of vein, no doubt the southern end of one of the richest mineral streams that we ever cut on the surface.

Here we started to drift north, squaring up the bottom of the shaft for a station. While cutting out a footing for one of the posts on the upper side of the floor, or shaft floor side, I hadn't gone six inches when I cut into a pegmatite vein. Calling Herb, who was getting some timbers, we investigated and found it was the lower vein where it had branched off the main vein and outcropped on the surface farther down the mountain side. We found the vein below our station to be fifty-nine to sixty inches thick, just about double the thickness we had been working. As this new vein had taken off at a lower angle of twenty degrees, it wasn't as productive as the main vein that angled at forty-five degrees at this level, and was more perpendicular.

We didn't run the drift on this thick vein, but just above it on the upper or main vein. As a rule, where a vein or stringer takes off from the main vein, there will be a pocket close by, more likely above the junction, and not in the mineral stream. There are not likely to be large pockets like the ones that make up in the streams. It all depends where your shaft cuts through the junction of the two veins. The vein at this point, and above the stuff that we found in bug-holes, was not productive.

At this time, a young man, William Burnett, came up to the mine and wanted to know if I had any crystal quartz. I told him I had, but it was in San Diego. He told me he worked in radio for the Navy and wanted the crystals to make radio frequency plates. I told him I would see him when I came to San Diego, which would be in four or five days.

Stormy weather blew in while I was leaving, and I figured I should get out before I was caught there for several weeks. Loading up the old Hupp with what we had taken out the last week and a half, I slipped and slid down the mountain and on down to San Diego. The following day I spent looking over the material we had mined. I found I had some very good crystals of tourmaline, and some light pink beryls, enough cuttable material to last me through the winter.

Going out to the Cholla Heights Navy Radio Station, I again met

Mr. Burnett and we talked over his needs for radio transmitting crystal plates. This, as I remember, was in the fall of 1929. I had decided to try my hand at cutting these radio crystal plates along with my lapidary work. After a few instructions from Mr. Burnett in regard to sizes, thicknesses and angles, I sawed out several plates one afternoon along with my other work. Taking them over to Mr. Burnett, he expressed surprise that I had cut them out of the crystal in so short a time, so I asked him how he had cut them. He said he had used a hack saw with an abrasive. That certainly was doing it the hard way!

I had no knowledge of radio, other than tuning in the various radio stations, so all the frequency calibrating was done by Mr. Burnett. In the meantime, we had formed a partnership. We hadn't finished more than half a dozen "Radio Ham Crystals", when we sold one to Mr. Elden Smith, who was working for the Western Air Express in Alhambra. Through Mr. Smith we sold our first broadcasting crystal to the KGFJ Radio Station, Santa Ana, California.

We had no calibrated standard to check by, so Mr. Burnett got permission to borrow the Navy radio frequency checker, which was calibrated at room temperature. That is how we turned out our first broadcasting frequency plate. We then got busy and ground out a standard crystal. Mr. Burnett finished this himself, checking it against the Bureau of Standards radio frequency standard signal. Then he built up an elaborate radio frequency checking station, not only for checking the frequency of our plates when we made them, but also those that were in operation in the broadcasting stations.

Beulah Rynerson and Isabella Smith, at Tourmaline Mine, Mesa Grande.

CHAPTER XXVII

FIRST WESTERN AIR EXPRESS CRYSTAL

When in Los Angeles on other business, I noticed a newspaper article stating that Mr. Herbert Hoover, Jr. was taking over and managing the radio equipment of the Western Air Express Company. I went to see Mr. Hoover at once. Entering his outer office, I found a dozen men also wanting to see him. At first I thought I couldn't wait my turn. The lady in the office told me to sit down, if I cared to wait. I did sit down. Everybody in the room seemed to act as though he was waiting to be shot. Not a peep out of anyone. Then I got an idea. I took out one of my lapidary cards and wrote, "Radio transmitting crystals" on it and laid it on the lady's desk. She picked it up, read it, got up, and went out of the room. When she came back, she said, "Mr. Hoover will see you at once." and led me to his office several doors down the hall.

Mr. Herbert Hoover, Jr. is a fine man. I don't believe I ever liked a man so much in so short a time. I made it a rule to let these radio technicians and experts know I didn't know the first thing about radio technology. This was to avoid answering embarrassing questions. I explained to Mr. Hoover that I knew nothing about radio, but was a lapidary by trade and my partner, Mr. Burnett was a radio technician for the Navy and did the calibrating, while I cut and ground the plates, and that both of us worked together. He seemed pleased and said, "Well, I'll take one and if it is satisfactory we'll take more."

We did the best we could on that plate and got the job of supplying the company with crystals and holders as they gradually equipped their stations with radios. We made it a rule never to send a plate out unless it was perfect in workmanship and quality. It paid off. One technician would tell another, and soon we had considerable work on our hands.

I received a request to see the manager of Radio Station KFVD, so drove out to see him. His name was "Swallow". I asked him if he was related to a man in San Diego, a Charley Swallow, and he said, "He's my father." I told him I had known Charley Swallow for years and that he was one of the old timers interested in the gem mining business in the early days of that business.

Swallow called in his technician, and did he throw radio technical questions at me! After he got through, I told him I didn't know a thing about radio. I then explained to Swallow how Mr. Burnett and I worked - not having had time to do this before he called in his technician. Mr. Swallow said he had heard we were putting out some good plates, and he would take one calibrated to a 1,000 K.C. zero beat at 50 degrees centigrade.

Several weeks after they had received their plate, we got a call from the technician saying he was in trouble with the plate and to come up and see what could be done. Burnett couldn't get away so I drove up there. When I met the technician, all his former belligerence was gone. He said, "Am I glad to see you! Look," he said, "I wanted to look at that plate and, taking it out of its holder, I dropped it on this cement floor and chipped off a small flake, and now the frequency has gone up. Is there any way to get it back on the right frequency?"

I have forgotten what change was made in the frequency, but when I saw the plate I was surprised that it hadn't made a bigger change. This was an X-cut crystal plate. Sometimes just a slight nick would make a big change, or then again, a very little. This was one where the frequency moved very little, and then only a very few cycles higher. I told him to raise the temperature in his crystal oven a degree and we would check it when I got home and wire him. He said he hoped it would work, as $65.00 would about floor him. Those were the lean days of 1931 and '32 when we were commencing to feel the effects of the depression. I fixed that one, but later on we sold them another crystal plate, in case they had trouble with the chipped one.

We had some difficulty with the Western Air Express too. I had delivered a plate to the Alhambra terminal of Western Air Express, when a young man with a very important air, handed me one of our crystal holders and said, "What's the idea of selling us a crystal that won't work?" I asked him for a screwdriver and we walked over to a bench where I opened the holder. Before I touched the crystal plate, I could see a full thumb print on the surface of the plate.

I asked where the plate had been used and by whom. He gave me a vague answer about Arizona or New Mexico. I asked for some carbon-tetrachloride to clean the plate. Then I again installed it in its holder and told him to try it out. He of course registered much surprise and wanted to know what had been wrong with it. I told him someone had taken the crystal out of the holder and, not knowing how to handle it, had gotten it soiled so it wouldn't oscillate.

I had a suspicion about that time that some of the men in the employ of Western Air Express were trying to make trouble for us, but of course couldn't prove anything. One day the chief technician of Western Air Express at Los Angeles (Mr. Hoover had been transferred in the meantime) came down to San Diego and told us he was sorry, but the powers-that-be in the company had decided to take up a proposition offered them by an electric company, that if the Western Air Express would install its equipment in their radio transmitting and receiving stations, they would service it for a year free. This was quite a loss for us, but we continued along on smaller orders.

We had been using quartz crystals from Brazil, and a few pieces from Mesa Grande, California. The material from Pala and from Tripp Flat in Riverside County, showed too much twinning, which caused changes in frequency at different temperatures.

Two men from the Los Angeles Police Radio Division came to my home in San Diego one day after lunch, and said they had heard I had a quartz crystal mine, and if I had any stock to sell they would like to buy some. I had been thinking of going up to the mine to get a few crystals myself, so invited them to go with me. I told them we would start early next morning.

One of these men was the chief technician of the Los Angeles Police Radio Department. After I had told him to whom we had sold our radio frequency plates he said, "We expect to ask for bids on some radio crystals soon and will inform you when the time comes, so you can send in your bid." We were notified shortly after that, sent in our bid, and got the job.

About ten months after we lost the Western Air Express business, the technician for the company came to Mr. Burnett's laboratory where we calibrated our frequency plates, with a crystal plate which had been issued to them. He wanted us to calibrate it and tell him what was wrong with it. Mr. Burnett checked it and found it started out on one frequency and then jumped to another, and was very erratic. On examining the crystal plate, we found it very poorly made. No effort had been made to turn out a good plate, it seems. The technician, Delmar Wright, told us they had considerable trouble over the past months with these crystals but hoped to see us again as soon as the year of free service was up. This he did with an order for crystals and holders amounting to $1300.00.

After filling this order, I had other business to look after and turned my interests over to Mr. Burnett. He has since built up an accurate calibrating and experimental station in San Diego and is at the time of my writing this employed by the Navy.

CHAPTER XXVIII

CHEMICAL PROJECTS AND PROSPECTING TRIPS (GOLD, SILVER, OPALS)

Two assayers and chemists, Skeats and Waggoner, another man, Norman French, and myself got our heads together on a plan to extract minerals from the rich veins of pegmatites in Riverside and San Diego Counties. We located several claims below Banner, near Julian, and several near Mesa Grande. The Depression came to the West Coast and our plans were dropped.

Gold seemed to be the only worthwhile metal, or mineral to look for at the time, so Mrs. Rynerson and myself, at every favorable opportunity, went on prospecting trips that took us to the north side of the San Gabriel Mountains, along the south side of the Mojave Desert, and along the west side of the Colorado River. Along the hills near Vincent are the remains of what look like old mud springs. Some are ten to fifteen feet across. In some are found opalized material, also agates. One can spot these places by the growth of bottle grass on a brown clay formation.

From 1891 to 1898, "Bonnie" (Mrs. Rynerson) lived near Acton, California, and knew the surrounding country well. In 1935 we parked our car about one and a quarter miles south and one mile east of Vincent in a little valley. It was as far as we could go with the car at that time. Then we walked east to a long canyon that led on down to the desert. On our walk back to the car, I walked along the north side of the valley and close to the foot of the hills while Bonnie chose a lower level. I hadn't gone more than three-hundred yards when I jumped a fine big buck deer. He had bedded down under a small juniper tree and probably watched us when we came up the valley fifty yards below.

Our car was parked near the foot of a large alluvial flow (of silt) from a small narrow canyon. While walking across this silt flow toward the car, I saw what I took to be a good chunk of gold ore. Picking it up, I could see that it was just that. Knowing that it was a float and had been washed out of the canyon with the rest of the rocks, I marked the spot and walked on to the car. As it was late we drove on to San Gabriel.

The next day I assayed a part of the ore, which showed no free gold. Later, I found that it ran $104.00 to the ton. The piece I had left showed quite a lot of free gold and some small nuggets the size of a pin head. If I had assayed the whole piece, it would have run into several thousand dollars per ton!

We threw camping and prospecting equipment into the car and hightailed it out to that place. We managed to get the car up to that place. We managed to get the car up to the mouth of the little canyon, which spot proved to be a fine place to camp. Then we searched back and forth across that alluvial flow to the bottom. I don't believe we missed a foot of it, but never found another piece. . . (This would be a good start for a lost mine story!)

Next morning we contoured that canyon from top to bottom without success. Then we got to looking around our camp site and found several remains of camp fires. Bonnie found a stone core from a core drill. This started me thinking. This place had been used many times as a camp spot by prospectors. Probably the piece of ore I found, and the stone core, had been dropped by them while packing their burros.

In most cases the old prospectors knew very little about geology, but would carry specimens of rich ore to familiarize themselves with their looks, or to compare with other rocks. We found later that the ore I found was almost identical with that of the old Governor Mine, about five or six miles to the west.

Not having heard from Bill Trenchard for over a year, I learned from a friend that he had sold a gold property to some people in Los Angeles and was still camped near the property, directing the work. This friend gave me Bill's address at Yuma, Arizona, so I dropped him a line. Back came an answer inviting us over to visit them. I sent Bill a letter stating when we would be over, for he had said in his letter he would meet us in Yuma and lead us to the camp.

Putting our camping equipment into the car, we drove down to San Diego, stayed the night there, picked up our son Eugene and wife, and lit out for Yuma. We arrived about one in the afternoon, met Bill and drove up on the Lead-Silver district road to a point about opposite Picacho, on the Arizona side. Bill and Hanna Trenchard had a nice camp pitched near a wash in a very picturesque locality. Bill led me over the surrounding country and told me he had discovered some placer gold in a small ravine. Following up this ravine, he found the source of part of this gold, while much of it came from little stringers of quartz containing calcite.

Mrs. Trenchard and Bonnie put in most of their spare time painting the beauty spots. At one place near camp, was a high rock bank, almost sheer. This threw considerable shade, so Bonnie parked herself and easel there. A little above her head was a two-inch crack in the rock running parallel with the ground. After a short time, Bonnie heard a noise above her and looking up saw the heads of two chuckawalla lizards protruding from the crack. While proceeding with her painting, she talked to them, as she does with wild things. The largest of the two kept moving farther out of the crevice, eyeing her all the while, until it tumbled to the ground and scurried away among the rocks. I told Bonnie her picture must have looked pretty real to that lizard to have caused him to leave his old home and try to move in!

As I remember, I saw no gem stones of any kind in that locality. Once when I returned to camp from Bill's mine, Mrs. Trenchard told me that Bonnie had walked over a low hill and had been gone for some time. She was afraid, in that rough country, that Bonnie would become lost. Picking up her tracks, I followed them for about a quarter of a mile and found her sitting under a large bush in plain sight of the camp.

Bonnie had selected a high place, so I sat down beside her. She had picked up a rock from which she said she would pan gold - and she did just that. When we started to leave, we hadn't gone more than twenty feet, when I saw a small outcropping about ten inches high with some calcite intersecting the top. Taking my pick, I cut the top half off, and put it into my pocket. It all amounted to about a double handful.

When we returned to camp, I panned my find and when finished, had a nice string of gold halfway around the pan, which would amount to several hundreds of dollars a ton. Bill said he believed he had found all of it. I panned a nice showing out of Bonnie's rock too. About two P.M. Bill took his prospecting drywasher and we went back to the spot where I found the outcropping. Bill sampled all around the place, but only got a color or two in some of the niches, or gullies. Several years afterward, Bill told me he didn't believe any of the veins in that locality penetrated very far underground.

The country showed terrific results of erosion from torrential rains over a long period of years. This locality is about six miles by airline, in a northeast direction from the old mining town of Picacho, which is on the California side of the Colorado River.

Our next trip was after opals, near Midway Well, about thirty miles north of Ogilby, on the Southern Pacific Railroad in Imperial County. Here were some nice places to camp, also good water and plenty of country to look over. About a quarter of a mile west of the well, we found some geodes, some very pretty, but small, some plain white opal, and a couple of pieces that showed color.

Bill had a hole started where he had found an excellent specimen of opal. He didn't want to leave it when I told him next morning I was going to walk due west till noon, and then return to camp, just to see what the country was like. After breakfast, I started walking. To my left lay the Chocolate Mountains. All the rainfall on the northeast side of these mountains drained into the Milpites Wash to the north some five or ten miles away. I crossed dozens of washes, both large and small; jumped several deer, but didn't see them; only their hurried tracks.

When twelve noon came, I stood in an open, bare locality - a poor place to enjoy lunch. I had seen, about one-half mile ahead, a large green tree, so decided to go on and eat my lunch there. When I came close to it I was surprised to see the largest ironwood tree I had ever known. One limb taking off about five feet from the ground, was twenty-four to thirty inches in diameter. Deer beds were everywhere under this tree. Most of the other ironwood trees had been cut down for fuel for the steam-boilers at the Paymaster Mine, and the river boats.

On my return to camp, I swung to the south one half mile, and turned east again. In a short distance, I cut the old road leading to the Paymaster Mine. This I followed back to camp. Along this road I picked up small pieces of lead-silver ore, which no doubt had dropped off the old ore wagons years ago.

The next two days, Bill and I ranged over the country east of Midway Well, a distance of about two miles, but found nothing but an opal mine location someone had made on an old lava outcrop, where we picked up some small pieces of milky opal.

Not far from camp, I found a large, round growth, about twelve inches in diameter, on an ironwood limb. The limb itself was about three inches thick. Curious about what caused this large growth, I sawed off the limb ten inches on each side of it and lugged it back to camp. When we returned to San Gabriel, I put it down in the cellar under our house to cure. Then I forgot it. A year afterward, I was moving some things out when I ran across it. Looking it over, I could see that it was pretty well cured; so I sawed through the ball portion, parallel with one side of the limb. This exposed a pretty wood of yellow and dark brown, with dark brown veins running through the yellow. The stock on Mrs. Rynerson's rifle was broken, so I decided to replace it out of this wood. The job took me a week, for I found that the inner portion of the ball wasn't entirely dried out. When finished and mounted, it was very pretty and made an excellent gun stock. The cause of this ball growth was a worm, which had eaten out a cavity one and a half inches across. The cavity was filled with droppings, but the worm had departed.

CHAPTER XXIX

THE LOST GOLD MINE

I had received a letter from Bill Trenchard stating he wanted to look over some country about twenty-four miles, airline, north, and a little east of Yuma on the Arizona side of the Colorado River. Of course we couldn't pass up a trip like that, so it wasn't long until we were well on our way to Dulzura, a little place on the old San Diego to Campo road. There we met Bill and his wife Hanna, stayed the night, and lit out next morning for our destination, stopping at Yuma to stock up with provisions. We then drove up on the east side of the Colorado River about twenty-five miles by road, and made our camp.

Next morning, Bill and I took a lunch with us and started walking up the wash which led north from the camp. Bonnie and Hanna decided to stay in camp and paint some pictures.

While walking up the wash, Bill told me why he wanted to come up into that country. He said that a young man had come to Yuma from Kansas and inquired for work in a mine. Someone told him the old Castle Dome Mine was being worked and he could get a job there, so he started walking up to the mine; arriving there the third evening, to find only the watchman. This watchman told him he hadn't heard that the owners were going to start work again, and told the young man he should stay there a couple of days and rest up before starting the long walk back.

He told this chap he might get work at the Laguna Dam, as they had a large force of men working there. Before leaving, the watchman told him to strike a straight course in line with Picacho Peak, to the southwest, and he would come to the river on the second day.

Taking a gallon jug of water and some food, he started out. It had been pretty hot that day and he holed up in a little gully for the night. Taking off his shoes, he placed them on a ledge of rock that outcropped across the gully, built a small fire, and went to sleep.

Next morning, when he reached for his shoes, he saw some small yellow colors the size of wheat in the white rock. Not knowing how much gold comes in the rocks, he thought he would take some with him and find out if it were gold. Knocking off a few pieces, he filled his pockets with them and started for the river. He hadn't gone far when he sighted a green patch to the southwest of his course, so he turned to the left and, along about sundown, he arrived at the river. He had used up his water so made camp there for the night. Next morning he filled his jug with water, ate what was left of his food, and started down the eastern side, keeping as close to the river as possible. He arrived at the dam in the late afternoon.

He wasn't successful in getting work at the dam, but he did get something to eat, then went on to Yuma the next day. At his first opportunity, he went to a bank and showed his specimens to the bank president, who told him the wheat-shaped yellow particles were gold. The banker offered to finance him in locating and working his find, but the young man said his people back in Kansas had money to help him and all he wanted was a job to get money enough to go home and show them what he had. Bill said that the banker was successful in getting the young fellow a job on the city or county road system, where he worked for some time. One day he turned up missing, and was never heard of again.

Bill told me this young man had given the banker some of this ore and he (Bill) had seen it. The ore, Bill said, was a sugar quartz with small wheat-size gold nuggets in it. The banker, it seems, spent considerable money looking for the spot where this young man told him he had found it; but without success.

That day, Bill and I walked six miles north, and then covered thoroughly about a square mile of likely looking ground in a section where, Bill said, the formation would likely throw a vein of ore. He dry-panned all the little gulches but never got a color, except the usual colors one gets in that country where so much of it is placer.

We had decided on another place to look over in the morning, and then started the long hike back to camp. We hadn't gone more than two-hundred feet, when Bill picked up a nice white piece of sugar quartz. It was only float and there wasn't any gold in it either.

We ended our search five miles from camp. During that last mile back to camp, I drew on all the advice old Mr. Burnett had given me, about thinking of our hopes of finding fabulously rich gold veins the next day. Tired, and with good appetites, we pulled into camp just in time for supper.

Next day we covered the ground planned, but found no gold ore. In some spots or localities, the lava is exposed in little faults or shrinkage cracks. We found oolitic marble with blue, red and green coloring, which was very pretty when slabbed up and polished. Some petrified wood of poor color was found, yet there was considerable colored agate scattered about. Nearer the river were numerous remains of old Indian camps, and broken pottery, but we found no arrowheads.

On the walk back to camp we dropped into a wash about seventy-five feet wide, with walls almost sheer. Hearing a few pebbles fall from my side, I looked up to see a fox; not the regular desert fox, but the gray fox we have in the mountains or on the Pacific Coast. Up near the top of the wall, or side of the wash, was hidden a den. It wasted little time getting into it!

The rest of the country we wanted to look over was too far from camp to walk to but we couldn't get farther up the wash with the cars, so we decided to go back and camp near the old Lead Annie Mine which was worked in the 1870's. Here we found a stringer of lead-silver ore out of which we collected about fifty pounds in nice specimens. We also found not far from our camp about one hundred pounds of oolitic marble with five colors; blue, light yellow, brown, black, and pink.

We had a campsite here with plenty of firewood. There were several kinds of cactus; some had beautiful deep red flowers. Several single-stalk Saguaro cacti were standing near. The country formation was volcanic with little sharp reddish peaks, and in some places it was very rough.

We were in that camp five days when our water ran out so we moved back to the California side to a place called "Bard". For a few days Bill and I worked out of this place. We drove the car a mile west of Imperial Dam on the Colorado River, then left it and walked northerly four or five miles. Here we found some small geodes. We could see larger ones in the lava banks, but couldn't get them out whole. We found some fine crystal actinolite, and black and white laminated chalcedony which makes very good cameo carving material. Each layer was about three-sixteenths inch thick. After a day or two in Bard we drove back to San Gabriel, and home.

About this time, Bonnie and I bought a ranch four miles south of Pala, San Diego County. As there was an extra house on the property, Bill and Hanna moved in. Then the Second World War started and our prospecting trips ended. Most of our work after that was done around the fireplace in the evenings. This was hard on Bill and he was continually champing on the bit. I think it had a lot to do in breaking down his health.

Shortly after the war ended, Bill and Hanna moved over to Bard. We made only one trip all together after that and only for the day. Bonnie and I drove over to Bard and loaded Bill and Hanna into the car one day, and drove up to Picacho, twenty miles north of Bard. As we rode along I could see Bill was depressed. When we left Picacho he said to me, "It makes you a little sad and lonesome, doesn't it?"

I don't believe Bill was out on another trip. During the winter of 1949-50, when the snow was deep in the mountains, and covered the land almost to the coast, I received a telegram stating that Bill was very ill and wanted to see me.

We threw our sleeping bags into the car and lit out. Arriving in Escondido, we filled up the gas tank but found out we couldn't get through the mountains by way of Jacumba, so we drove back to the ranch and had lunch. Then I threw in my old chains, which were not very good, and rode through by way of Warners Ranch, Borrego and Kane Springs, down Imperial Valley to the Yuma road; arriving at Bill's house in late afternoon. Bill was in bad shape. When I took his hand he opened his eyes and said, "Fred". Then he started trying to talk, but I couldn't understand a word he said. He never regained consciousness and two days later he gathered up his prospecting equipment and moved his camp across the River. . . He was a swell camp partner. Burial was in Yuma, Arizona.

Bill Trenchard's camp in the desert mountains northeast of Picacho, Arizona. Left to right, Mrs. Trenchard, Mrs. Eugene Rynerson, Mrs. Beulah Rynerson, unknown boy, Fred Rynerson, Bill Trenchard, unknown man, and C. O. Johnson.

CHAPTER XXX

ALL ABOUT RATTLERS.

When Withem and Kelly took over our mine they built a bunk and cook house down in the creek bottom, not far from a small ranch house. One noon, when we (the two miners and myself) were walking down the hill to the cook house for dinner, I saw something I had never seen before or since. The day had been pretty hot. As we came over a slight rise about a hundred yards from camp, we saw a slight commotion in the grass on the right side of the road, about seventy-five feet ahead. We hadn't gone more than ten feet, when a rattlesnake thirty inches long sprang clear across the road; about five-and-a-half feet at that point. He landed near a small sumac bush close to the edge of the road and coiled up there, where we killed it.

What made it jump across the road, none of us knew. It first looked like a loosely coiled rope being tossed across. I have heard of their jumping, but that was the first and last time I have seen one jump that far. I have seen some strike their lengths, or seen the momentum of the strike or lunge carry them over their length. This, however, was when the snake became very angry.

When this rattler was first noticed, the grass offered very little cover. Probably it could see that the sumac bush and the growth around it offered more protection. If we hadn't seen it jump across the road we would have passed it by, for it didn't attract our attention by rattling and was well hidden.

Most people believe that a rattlesnake can strike only its length at most. This is probably true, but striking isn't jumping. Most strikes of the southwestern Diamond rattler are about eighteen inches long, or less. This gives it a quick recoil for another strike. If one surprises one or happens upon it when ready to strike at a rabbit, or if one takes what one has caught, the rattler often becomes very angry and will strike at you when too far away to hit you. I have seen a gophersnake do the same thing when a little rabbit was taken away from it. It would vibrate its pointed tail and strike at me like a rattler. All this was probably a bluff, yet if they do bite, their fine little teeth cut like a razor blade while the wound can become infected from food they have recently eaten.

There is no doubt in my mind about a rattlesnake having hypnotic influences over small game animals. When I was ten years old I shot rabbits for market along with a young man, Billey McDougal, who broke horses to carriages, wagons, and gunfire. I took along a 12 gauge shot-gun on the hunts.

My mother told me never to shoot a rabbit while it was sitting still, but always made it run so it would have a chance to save its life. This I tried to do, but several times I have come upon a rabbit that wouldn't run, even when I waved the gun up and down at it. I could get as close as 12 to 15 feet and then I would shoot its head off. In every case of that kind, I have always found a rattler within two feet or so of the rabbit. As I shot the rabbit, the rattler would make itself known by different degrees of rage.

A friend of mine, Martin Stenbock, a miner who worked for me in the tourmaline mine at Mesa Grande, was struck on the back of the hand by a large rattlesnake. He told me the force of the strike was like being hit with a singlejack hammer. Now a singlejack hammer is a three to six pound hammer with a short handle, used by a miner who handles the drill and hammer at the same time when drilling a hole. Martin lost two fingers on that hand while his arm was badly shrunken to his shoulder the last time I saw him, several years afterward.

When we first heard that Martin Stenbock had been bitten by a rattler, Mrs. Rynerson and I drove over to the old Black Eagle Mine property in Mesa Grande where Martin had been taken. His arm was blue to the shoulder and more than twice its normal size. He told us he had a dream that he was so thirsty he had put his arms around a reservoir, which was twelve feet across, lifted it off the ground and drank all the water out of it.

Martin made the mistake of holding his arm close to his chest with his other arm, and running a quarter of a mile to the Black Eagle property where his son and Newton Angel were. This exertion, coupled with the excitement, made the bite more deadly. What Martin should have done was to cut two slits with his pocket knife lengthwise with his arm and through each fang puncture. He should have made this slit an inch or more long, then whirl his arm around fast, windmill fashion, while he walked over to the Black Eagle. The centrifugal force probably would have forced the greater part of the poison out by the time he got over there.

The rattlesnake has an uncanny sense of locating water. On our ranch four miles south of the town of Pala, we kill several rattlers every spring and summer. The last few years the creeks have been dry and we have been irrigating, or where we have water in containers for our dog Shep and the cats (near the back door of our house), the rattlers sometimes come as close as twenty feet from the back door before we see them. We don't know how many come there that we don't see.

In 1951 there was a slight leak in the pipe line that carries our domestic water, and leads down through a dry canyon to the house.

This leak was only a wet spot on the pipe. At that point the pipe was fourteen inches from the ground. While looking over the pipe line one day, I found a large rattler coiled up by the pipe with its head reared up to the pipe. It was running its tongue in and out over the wet spot. It did this only when I stood perfectly still for a while, and was about twelve feet away. They can take a lot of water, too. I have killed them after they had been down to the creek for water and, cutting them open, have found as much as a cup of water in them.

Our neighbors, Mr. and Mrs. Terrell, whose property adjoins ours on the north, built a little cabin under an oak tree near what they call "Terrell Creek", which parallels our East Creek, about one-eighth mile to the south. During the summer they kill several rattlers on their property, and intimate they come from our East Creek Canyon.

Now we are well aware of our prize rattlesnakes that live in East Creek Canyon, and have sent the Terrells written notice that we do not restock the canyon each year with rattlers. If they persist in slaughtering them to the point of extermination, they will probably be faced with an invasion of rats, mice and gophers that will cause more damage than the rattlers. The last report on the doings of the Terrells, shows they paid little heed to our written notice!

We have had one dog killed by a rattler over the twelve years we have had the ranch. It was a little Chihuahua, but not hairless. It followed a friend of ours who was hunting up East Creek Canyon. This friend told us he heard it yelp some distance up the hill and to the right of him. Then it came running to him so he picked it up and carried it back to the house.

I was not at home at the time but when I did return, I found the dog had been struck squarely on the forehead. He must have walked right up to the rattler. The fang punctures were one-and-a-quarter inches apart. That snake was a big one. I searched the spot well but never found it. The dog lived about twelve hours. It was too small a dog to stand that almost perfect bite.

I was hunting one morning three-hundred yards east from the spot where the dog was bitten, and sat down on a rock to rest. I could look down East Creek to our house, but between Terrell's Hill where the brush was thin and myself, there was much heavy brush. The thought came to me that if I should get a pop on the leg by a rattler, I would have to exert myself too much in getting away and that would be bad!

I picked out what I thought was the easiest way through the brush and started down the hill. I hadn't walked more than fifty feet when I turned to the left on a small game trail and had taken my second step when I heard a slight "zip" - it was unmistakable. I stopped on the spot and stood perfectly still, first looking down at my feet, then all around. Hearing a slight noise where I had made the turn, I spied the rattler coiled up, not two inches from the track of my tennis shoe. I looked about for a rock. As I started to move, he took off down the hill as if scared to death. That was as fast as I ever saw a rattler move. Maybe he had encountered man before I came! I don't believe a rattlesnake will strike a human being just for the sake of biting him. A man is too big to eat, therefore the rattler must strike because he fears you will harm him. If you leave him alone, he will leave you alone.

Many times I have rolled up in my blankets in the brush, in rocky places, washes in the mountains and on the desert - but I never had a snake crawl into my bed. I have found both rattler and sidewinder coiled up so cold they couldn't strike, or didn't want to, when I held my hat close to their noses. But I would not advise anyone to believe they were harmless when in that condition.

Once in July, when the day was warm, I was crossing from one mountain range to another smaller one when I came to a gully about fifteen feet deep and too wide to jump across. I slid down through the brush to the bottom. When I landed on my feet, I was within four feet from a large rattler and he was mad! I suppose some of the dirt and rocks I had loosed in my slide into the gully, had hit him. He was striking in every direction. When I saw him doing that I knew what was bothering him. I sat my gun down, took a stick and killed him. The reason for his wild striking was he had started to shed his skin and it was loose over his eyes, causing a partial blindness. They seem to know this places them at a disadvantage, hence they put up an almost hysterical fight.

CHAPTER XXXI

WHAT IS PROGRESS?

People today still go looking for the sure-thing gold or uranium or gem mine. We probably won't hear of so many losing their lives from starvation and thirst today as we did fifty or more years ago. Airplanes fly everywhere now and many of them carry precision radiation instruments to detect the location of uranium-bearing ores. The "jeep" has replaced the old faithful burro. The old time prospector and his burro have been rubbed out of the picture, probably never to return. This is what we call "Progress". But sometimes I wonder about it, when they tell us that four large modern bombs would completely wipe out all life on the British Isles.

When one is so concerned with his present way of life, that he seldom thinks of his past, he surely misses a store of wonderful living. Some of that past, for most of us, was hard to take. Probably some of us wouldn't want to go through the experience again, but what wouldn't we give to turn back the clock and take another chance, to live again when this world seemed so young and there were so many things ahead of us to do!

One of the things I regret was my failure to record the many true happenings in the lives of my father's and mother's people. I believe everyone should do that for it would be interesting reading in anyone's language.

New usage of metals hardly known or used in the past, have found a place in industry. Some of the minerals we now have in abundance may probably change our mode of life. Most new scientific discoveries open doors to other discoveries. I believe there will always be something to find for those who love to hunt for them. Let us hope so! This old world has seen untold ages, only a few of which we know. This is without doubt the "Man Age" for he holds the power to destroy almost every living thing, including himself.

CHAPTER XXXII

BLACK, BUEL AND EUGENE -- CONTRASTED-- FOLLOWING BLIND CUES, AND ACTUAL MINING

When World War Two started, a man by the name of Black came to my home in San Gabriel and said he had been sent to see me about some quartz crystals. I told him I hadn't mined any for some time, and had used up or sold all I had.

He said someone had told him I knew where he could mine some, for I had taken several hundred pounds out of one pocket. I told Mr. Black who owned the property where I had taken out that quartz, and that I could show him the place.

He made me a proposition which I accepted. Next morning he picked me up and we drove out to Tripp Flat in the Coahilla district, Riverside County. When we arrived at the mine I found someone had done a lot of work there and moved nearly all the vein out, and had worked several other places along the ridge to the north. So Mr. Black drove back to the ranger station, where he thought he could get some information that would lead him to someone who had quartz crystals.

There were several young men there, besides the ranger in charge. When Black asked for the information, some told of seeing old workings around the country. One fellow, about nineteen or twenty, said a certain woman proprietor of a Motel at Keen Camp had a crystal about so long; holding his hands apart about eighteen inches; and about so thick; holding his hands about six inches apart. Black asked him how clear it was and he said, "Just as clear as glass."

On the way over there next morning, Black said he surely would like to get hold of a crystal like that. I told him I surely would too. "But," I said, "You didn't believe that fellow, did you?"

"Why, yes." Black said.

"Well," I said, "Don't get all excited over it. You won't buy it!"

When we came to the place, Black inquired of the woman if she had a large quartz crystal and she said, "Yes." She asked us into the living room while she got it. She was gone two minutes and then she returned with a chunk of quartz about seven inches long and not four inches through in the thickest part-and as clear as mud! Black asked her if she had any other pieces and she said "No."

Black asked me how I knew it wasn't worth anything. I said I knew the way that fellow described the crystal that he didn't know what he was talking about. Probably he had never seen the crystal. The description he received might have come through several others before he heard it; each one making it just a little larger than the original crystal. I have run down dozens of these stories for my friend Mr. Ernest Schernikow of San Francisco. Not one of them was what was described to me.

In April, 1947, our two sons, Buel and Eugene, sank an incline shaft to the depth of a hundred-and-fifteen feet on the west side section of a split in the main vein on the Rynerson Mine in Mesa Grande. This was the mine property that Gail Lewis discovered and sold to the San Diego Tourmaline Mining Company of San Diego.

They used concrete posts and caps to frame the shaft, instead of the oak or pine timbers; since wood timbers last only two or three years and then become subject to dry rot. This attacks the bottom of the post, then travels up the center; leaving an outer shell although one believes the posts are still in good condition. The oak caps last for years, since they do not come in contact with the earth, as do the posts. The boys had bad luck here. They hadn't gone far when they ran into a fault which traveled along with them to the bottom. They cut through several pockets but few of the tourmalines were in good condition. This is usually the case where there's a fault and where "An old fault" has cut through a pocket containing tourmalines or other crystals.

These old faults were made when the vein was still connected with the source of minerals that made up the vein, or shortly after the vein was made. Some forms of acid, either liquid or gas or both, have come up from below and caused the decomposition of part of the crystals, or even the entire crystal. I don't believe water from the surface percolating into the gem pocket or cavities will cause this decomposition, for where surface water has entered these pockets, not one of the crystals had been decomposed or altered in any way, in my experience.

Some of the tourmaline crystals were large; weighing three and four pounds, if they held together and were in good condition. A large number of morganites were found but they were badly altered; some completely into a soft white paste. A lot of albite was in the same condition. No red clay at all was found in these pockets. I have had this same experience on the Himalaya Mine which adjoins us on the north. The total amount of good material recovered was not more than fifty pounds.

I was told during the Second World War that radio transmitting crystals made from the tourmaline crystals were found to be tougher and better than the quartz. But getting a radio crystal out of tourmaline calls for material we would class as perfect quality, or gem material, and would be too expensive to produce for radio plates alone.

Tunnel opening on Himilaya Mine, 1927. Buel Rynerson and Vance Angel.

Two views of Rynerson Mine entrance in 1966.

CHAPTER XXXIII

TRIP UP THE AVAWATZ MOUNTAINS.

This last told trip brings to mind one I took in 1938 up to the Avawatz Mountains, about twenty-eight miles north of Baker and the same distance south of the lower end of Death Valley.

An elderly man, Sam Hoover, whom I had known for some time, told me he had gone once on a prospecting trip with two men into this area. They had walked up a canyon on the east side of the mountains and, when about one-half mile in, they came to the head of another canyon that led off to the right. At this point the two men with Hoover got into an argument and both decided to go back to camp. On the way back they traveled down the canyon on their right. When a short distance from the mouth of the canyon, they came to a large outcrop of red material. As they were traveling along rather fast, Hoover got a couple of pounds for an assay sample. When he arrived home he had it assayed. As I remember, the values were high and well worth the time to investigate further.

It was six years after Mr. Hoover found this material that I drove up there with him. Before we started, I asked him to tell me what he remembered seeing going in and out of the canyon where he found the red material. He described a cliff of dark rock on the left where the canyon on the right took off, and about three hundred feet below the red deposit. Right at the mouth of the canyon was a large white quartz outcrop.

I lived in the town of San Gabriel, California at that time. We took off in the early morning, arriving within three miles of the canyon mouth by 3:00 P.M. We made camp just off the road, for the surrounding country was very rough and rocky and our place had been cleared of rocks by someone years ago, probably for a camp site too.

We got away early next morning and walked three miles over an alluvial flow from out of the mountains we were headed for. This whole flow was covered with what looked like all grades of gold, copper, and silver ores. I examined several specimens but saw no free gold.

We arrived at the mouth of the canyon which, he said, was the right one, and started up. When we arrived at the "dark rock cliff", at the point where he had started back down the canyon on the right! I asked Hoover if he hadn't seen two black cliffs and this one was the first we had come to. But he said "No."

I had noticed when coming up the canyon that the sides were

composed of gravel. Some ore-like rocks were fifty to seventy-five feet in diameter and Hoover's "dark rock cliff" was one of them. The whole formation seemed one big dump.

I told Hoover we would climb the right side of this canyon, where he said he walked into the right-hand canyon. When we arrived on top, there was the other canyon, all right. It didn't take us long to figure out what had happened. It must have been "some cloudburst", that fell farther up on the mountain. Most of it had fallen to the north of the canyon we came up, and had carved a new canyon down to where our two canyons came together. Then the water turned down the canyon we intended to descend; piling up a wall of rock and gravel, seventy-five feet high, over four-hundred feet long, and three-hundred feet wide on top; completely blocking the canyon on the right and closing its entrance to the canyon on the left, or the one we came up.

So far, Mr. Hoover had been right. So we descended into the right-hand canyon and started down the wash. This canyon became much deeper than the one we came up, and the sides were just a pile of loose rock and enormous boulders. It wasn't long before Hoover pointed up to the left wall and said, "There it is. But it's almost gone. It once extended down to the bottom."

What was left of the red deposit extended ten feet across and seventy-five feet above the floor of the canyon. Hoover started to climb up to it but I told him he had better not for he might cause a slide and get covered up. I didn't have anything with me to dig him out, and anyway, there wasn't enough of it to bother with; so we continued down the canyon. Soon we came to the big white quartz boulder. I don't know how deep it extended below the surface, but it had stayed put while the rocks and other boulders had built the canyon out another three-hundred feet below the deposit.

About a month after the trip with Mr. Hoover, I went to Los Angeles to see a mining engineer on some other business and happened to mention the trip with Mr. Hoover. I told him the part of the mountain I was in looked like one big ore dump. He said he had several borax claims and a cabin on the north end of this range but had never found a vein of any mineral in place on the mountain.

CHAPTER XXXIV

JIM AND THE INDIAN WOMAN'S LOST MINE. THE GROCER'S MINE. MACK'S WILD GOOSE CHASE.

In the fall of 1915 when I was on the placers along the Colorado River an old man, "Jim" came to me asking if I had been along the west side of the Salton Sea in the country back about twenty miles from the shore line.

The twenty-mile distance made me cautious. I told him I had seen part of it. "Well," he said, "I know an old Indian woman called 'Lena'. She told me when she was a little girl her people, at a certain time of the year, would go to a spring at the foot of a small butte to hold their fiesta - away from the White Man. She said there was a big cottonwood tree growing near the Spring, also some smaller ones. While her people were enjoying their fiesta one day, she and a girl friend climbed to the top of the small butte. Looking around on the ground, she saw some little black rocks. Picking one up, the size of a walnut, she found it to be very heavy. She rubbed it on another rock and saw it was the color of ripe corn inside."

Jim said she wanted him to take her up there and she would show him some more of those rocks. But he said it was too long a drag through that sand with two horses and a buckboard wagon -and, anyway, he hardly believed her story. In later years she became tubercular and bed-ridden.

One day, two men came to him and asked if he knew of any coal in the country thereabouts. He told them he didn't, but then thought of Lena and told them he would see a friend of his and let them know, later. So he went to see Lena. She told him to bring a piece of coal for her to see. Jim took a chunk of coal to her. She looked at it a long while and then said, "Yes, I know where some of it can be found."

Jim told the two men what she had told him and that if they could rig up a bed on a wagon, she could lead them to it. This was done, and they started out. A day north of Yuma, the fellows thought they had been tricked, but Lena said, "Go a little farther." After a short time she told them to stop. Then she pointed out a place about a quarter of a mile from the road.

All three men walked over and found the coal, all right, but it was a very small seam and worthless as a commercial proposition. Jim said, "Maybe the old girl was telling the truth about the rocks, after all." But it was too late then to take her to find out. She passed away shortly afterward.

I don't know of any springs with that description in that part of the country, other than one that lies near the San Diego-Imperial Counties line, two or three miles north of the Borrego-to-Kane Springs road. This is not a running spring, but a hole two feet deep will reach water. When I was there last (about 1940), some small cottonwoods were growing there at the foot of a small sand hill; a long way from being a butte!

At that time I figured old Jim would liked to have gone on a good prospecting trip with all expenses paid. In a way, his story tied in with Peg Leg's. The coal tale kind of clinched the story and his plan might have worked if he had picked the right party.

I knew a man in San Gabriel who worked at one time in the old Hedges Mine in Imperial County. He owned a grocery store in San Gabriel where I often bought our groceries. He liked to talk mines and gems. One morning he handed me a rock wrapped in paper, saying, "Take a look at that!"

It was a collector's dream, a lot of gold in it - too good to be true! I asked him where he got it. He said an old friend had blown in from Nevada and wanted a little money for a grubstake to go back and locate it. I asked him how much he wanted. He answered, "Oh, about twenty dollars." And the way he said it, I knew he gave his friend more than that. He said, "My friend said he'd write me in about a week."

A week went by and I asked him if he had heard from his friend yet. He said, "No." Another week slipped by and he still hadn't heard. After a month passed, he said, "Something must be wrong." Months passed and he finally said his friend must have run out on him. It was the same old game, and the same old gold. Some can't resist the gold that glitters, and it DOES glitter to those willing to gamble!

I knew another man with more than average intelligence, who had worked as a court reporter, whom I shall call Mack. Mack met an old man in a city park. This old fellow had been a miner and prospector, had served in the Civil War on the North side and was living at Sawtelle, a home for old soldiers near Los Angeles.

After some talk, the subject turned to mines and ores. The old man said he wished he was able to make one more trip to a spot where he had found some very rich gold ore. He became sick shortly after being there and hadn't been able to get out there again since he was released from the hospital. This had cost him all his savings, so he had to go to Sawtelle to live.

Mack asked him how he was feeling and if he thought he could make the trip if he (Mack) would furnish the transportation and expenses. The old man said "Yes" he would go, but it would have to be a fifty-fifty proposition on the discovery. Mack agreed and set the day to leave.

Mack said he hired a horse and buggy, for the old man said the place wasn't far from the country road. He picked up the old man at the appointed time and they drove all that day, and camped alongside the road that night. The old man said it was about a day-and-a-half's drive. So about noon the next day, he pointed over to some low hills and said it was there.

Driving off the road a short distance, they unhitched the horse, tied it to a small tree and gave it some hay. After eating lunch, they started over to the locality where the old man said he had found the ore. When they came to a certain place, the old man looked all around the country, while his face seemed to brighten up. He stood for some time looking at the country, then he started looking over the ground. After a while he said he didn't seem to recognize the place, said he had thought sure this was the spot. The old man looked over the country again and, Mack said, from the look on his face, he was just reminiscing.

Mack said he had furnished the old man with everything, so when they got back within a block of Sawtelle, he let the old man out of the buggy. The old man, with a grin on his face, said he was sorry they didn't find it, and then walked away. Mack said he knew he had been taken for a sucker and wondered how many times the old man had gotten free rides into the country before Mack too had taken the hook.

Yes - I have taken the hook, too - once. It seems that all of us have an inherent desire to find what has been lost or hidden. The more valuable the thing, the stronger the desire. Some won't analyze a lost mine story but, if anything, will build it up a little. In some cases they will show you ore or crystals supposed to have come from these lost mine diggings, or an old map (which has been aged), giving directions to the property. I believe some of these people get so enthused over their own imaginings, they begin to believe them. I have a plaque hanging on the wall that reads: "We grow old too soon, and smart too late." This answers a lot of these wild-goose trips some people take, trying to find something purely of some man's imagination.

I have been told that many gems have been stolen from the mines at Mesa Grande and Pala and buried around close to the mines; but have never been found or removed from their hiding places. This, I do not believe! During the bonanza years of gem mining in Southern California, small quantities of the native gems were mined in several places around these larger producers but certain individuals in the bigger companies claimed all the stuff was stolen from their properties. This I know is not true.

Considerable amounts of gem material were lost in blasting which scattered the gem material; mixing it with the hanging and foot-wall dirt, so was hauled out and dumped. In some places in the dumps quite a number of crystals were found, probably leading the finder to believe they were buried there. Since the mines closed down in 1912 for the first time, hundreds of dollars' worth of gems have been recovered from the dumps.

About 1950, some three-hundred pounds of kunzite was mined by Charles Reynolds on the San Pedro Claim near Pala, after considerable expense and labor. Some of this material was very good so I cut several fine stones of different sizes, including one pear-shaped stone of 140 carats. Reynolds has also mined some very excellent morganites.

Most of the gem-bearing pegmatites, both veins and deposits, in Riverside and San Diego Counties, have carried beryls. No one place could you tag as a beryl mine, other than the John Mac Mine near Rincon, San Diego County. This mine produced more beryls than any mine I know of for the amount of work done.

It is strange why some people like to enlarge on things they see or hear; which accounts for most of the lost mine stories and tales of hidden caches.

Sign to "Hell Camp".

CHAPTER XXXV

OLD BOAT IN SALTON SINK. MYTHICAL LOST GOLD MINE. LOST URANIUM MINE

It was about 1888 I heard a story from the old prospectors sitting in my father's shop in Riverside, which had been going around for some time. It was about what some called an old Indian tale of a big bird with white wings that floated ashore in Salton Sink. In those days there was very little water in what is now Salton Sea. It was one vast salt marsh.

When the bird came ashore it opened its mouth and men came out of it and cut wood, and logs, and fed the bird wood. As I remember, that was the extent of the story. No mention was made of what became of the bird after that. Some people claimed to have seen something like a boat out in the salt marsh. That was all.

Then there was the tale of the Monster that had lived in Elizabeth Lake. This lake was fifteen miles west of Palmdale in Los Angeles County. The Monster was supposed to have come out of the lake during the night and fed on the cattle, then gone back into the lake. Oh yes, several people had seen it! . . . so I was told. One time it came out and traveled east. Several years later in Arizona, a large skeleton was found that was thought to be this Monster.

One of the old timers sitting in the shop had the key to the whole picture, I believe. He said, "Well, when we left Kentucky in the 1850's, we bought two barrels of corn liquor from a mountain man who sure knew how to make good liquor. There were ten or twelve men in our party. When we got to Californy, we had used up the contents of one barrel, so we knocked out the head of the barrel to use it for another purpose, but we found a plug of tobaccy a foot long by four inches wide, swelled up like a sponge and nailed in the bottom of the barrel!

"That was to give the liquor color and flavor, and I'm telling you, a couple of shots of that liquor in the morning would last you all day. I'm sure some of those fellows saw a lot of things they wouldn't have seen if they hadn't drunk that liquor. Now there was a lot of fellers come to Californy after we did; and they come from Kentucky too; so they must've brought a barrel or two of the same stuff along with them!"

It was in 1889 or possibly 1890 or '91, that folks noticed the water was rising in Salton Sink. As I recall, two government or newspaper men started from Yuma, Arizona with two Indians who claimed to know all about water getting into the Sink. Rumors at the time were that the water was entering through underground caverns and old volcanic passages.

The two men with their Indian guides floated down the Colorado River below Yuma to the Alamo River which takes care of some of the flood waters of the Colorado River below the Mexican Border in Lower California. They cut their way through the cat-claw and willows to the Salton Sink. There the two white men went ashore, paid off the Indians, gave them the boat and provisions, walked over to the Southern Pacific Railroad tracks, flagged a train, and went on their way.

We know now that the water flowing into the Salton Sea comes from the surplus irrigation water in the Imperial Valley and the flood waters of the Colorado River, if any. These in turn flow into the Alamo or New Rivers, both of which flow into the Salton Sea. Torrential rainstorms help too.

The most brazenly told lost mine story I ever heard came from an old man who came into Ward's Lapidary Shop on A Street in 1924. He said when he was a boy he remembered a man who discovered a large nugget of gold. It was the shape of a large funnel. The top was about ten feet across and extended down to a point about ten or twelve feet. It was so big he couldn't do anything with it, so he covered it up again. The old man hadn't heard of anyone else finding it! He said he remembered the place and could go right to it. As I remember, the old fellow said it was in the Wickenburg District in Arizona.

I told Ward that I remembered an old story that was told when I was just a kid, that whoever took a drink out of the Hassayampa River could never tell the truth again; and, if the old fellow lived in that part of the country, he sure drank a lot of that water!

I knew a mine boss who sold some very fine rose-pink tourmaline to my friend Ernest Schernikow; telling him he had taken them out of a new location he had made. He said he would sell a half interest in the claim for $500.00; the money to be used to develop the property.

I received a letter from Mr. Schernikow stating he had sent this man a check for $250.00 and was enclosing another to me for the same amount. I was to go and look at the prospect and, if I thought it worthwhile, to give the man the $250.00, or balance due of the $500.00.

When I got in touch with this man we went up to see the diggings. When we arrived he pointed out one of the poorest excuses for a pegmatite vein I had ever seen. I told him he did not get the tourmaline he had sold to my friend out of that vein. "No," he said, "I got it out down under that rock, but that isn't where I'm going to work." Then he showed me an equally poor vein. I told him neither was that vein worth working and that I wasn't going to pay him the money until he showed me a vein with more favorable indications of tourmaline.

He said, "Well, Mr. Schernikow promised to pay me the $250.00 and I'll write to him before he leaves New York." Mr. Schernikow was leaving for Europe in another two weeks. I said I'd be back if Schernikow agreed I was to give him the money.

About a week later I received a letter from Mr. Schernikow stating I should pay the man the $250.00 which he had promised to pay him, but for me to check how much work had been done in the meantime.

I sent the man word I would be up at the diggings the next Friday. When I arrived, he and a young man were working in the vein. I watched them for a while and told him he would never get a tourmaline out of that vein and that he was crazy if he thought so. Even if my friend had told me to give him the money I hated to do so and see my friend robbed. I gave him the check and asked him if he intended to work. He said, "Yes."

Next day I happened to pass the young man who had been working with this man, on the street in San Diego. I asked him why he wasn't working. He said, "Oh, I was only hired for that day." Then he gave me to understand the other fellow never intended to work the claim. The poor old chap was killed not long after that in a mine cave-in.

Now that uranium is in demand, there are those who are in the same old racket of selling claims. They will locate you a claim for a price. I have seen letters to that effect. Some of my friends say I take all the thrill out of these boom strike stories; but who gets a thrill out of being bunkoed out of his money? All those fellows have to do is locate you a claim, record the location notice, and send it to you when his end of the deal is completed. He won't guarantee you will find uranium on it. If he could, he could make more by holding it himself.

I prefer to take the grubstake deal. If at any time the prospector makes a strike, you can claim your share, unless he has notified you in advance that your grubstake has run out, but it seems they never do.

I was told by an old Montana miner that was the predicament that the discoverer of the rich silver mine in the Coeur de Alene Mountains of Idaho found himself in. He had so many grubstakers he had nothing left for himself. But luck was with him. He packed his burro and lit out across the Bitterroot Mountains and found the Anaconda Copper Mine in Montana. That time he had no grubstakers! This, of course, doesn't happen very often.

Bill Trenchard knew where he picked up a good rich piece of uranium ore, but no one else knows now where he got it. I do know he showed a piece of ore to me which might have been uranium, but I wasn't an expert on that type of ore at the time. He said he believed he had found a radium mine, but there was no market for radium then. Since I knew Bill and his ways pretty well, I don't believe he located his find; for that would show the spot to others. On the other hand, if it became valuable later, he wouldn't forget where he got it.

It was in the early 1920's that Bill put a trunk in storage. In this trunk there were some rocks he had saved, also mine location papers, and other things. When he went back to redeem the trunk, he found it had been sold for storage costs. He hunted no farther for it.

Some thirty years slipped by when a man showed up at the Colby Ranch near Bard, with a rich piece of uranium ore and a good Geiger Counter to prove it. (Mrs. Val Colby is Mr. William H. Trenchard's daughter). This man said that her father, Bill Trenchard, had given his sister a trunk. In this trunk Bill's sister had found the piece of uranium ore. Mrs. Colby told the fellow that her father's sisters had passed away years ago and she did not know this other woman. She also told him she knew about the trunk but not all that was in it.

This information seemed to confuse the man. It appeared the woman, supposed to be Bill's sister, had kept the rocks in the trunk and when the uranium boom started, she got them out. One of them proved to be what she was looking for. Whether the fellow made up the story about this woman being Bill's sister, or the woman told the man she was Bill's sister, we do not know; but whichever it was, it didn't give enough proof of anything to go prospecting on.

At the time Bill brought that rock to me, he had been prospecting all along the eastern side of the mountains in San Diego County and over on the Colorado River. For several years he worked for the Reclamation Project at Laguna Dam (sixteen miles north of Yuma, Arizona) and had charge of some part of the work there. During this time, probably eight to ten years, Bill could have gotten over a lot of country. When, during that time, did he find the rock that this man brought to Mrs. Colby? Was it the same piece he showed me or another piece he found? This information no one will ever know, for Dad Trenchard slipped across the river about four years too soon.

CHAPTER XXXVI

LOST PEG LEG MINE

One of the most talked of "lost mines" (or was it a mine?) was the Peg Leg Smith find. Some of these old men said they had known Peg Leg, but that he was such a damn liar and blowhard no one could believe him.

The story that was told those days, as I remember it, was that Peg Leg Smith left the Colorado River and traveled west, heading for Los Angeles. Some of these stories had him following the old Jackass Mail Route from Yuma to San Diego; a second, the Butterfield Stage Route; and a third, up the west side of the Salton Sea. But the crux of all the stories is the one where he climbed that little butte to locate an easy passage through the mountains and while on top of this little butte, picked up the black nuggets.

Some of the old stories had him riding a mule; others, a horse. I never heard of him having a string of pack animals, or even one pack animal. We assume he was riding a mule and left Yuma, going west. His first water, unless he used the mail route water holes, was the Alamo River, an overflow of the Colorado River into the Salton Sea. That would be a distance of forty odd miles, so he and the mule would have to have water in the daytime, though it might be done at night in the wintertime. As I remember, there is no record of how he crossed the Imperial Valley which was, at that time, one of the worst deserts in the West.

From the Alamo River to Yuha Springs, or Coyote Wells, would be thirty-five miles, and the toughest stretch of the trip for he would drop below sea level enroute. Now Coyote Wells is up close to the western range of mountains, while the only little butte around there is Yuha Hill. You can see as much of the mountain passes from the desert floor as you can from the top of this hill.

If he quit the old Mail Route at Coyote Wells, he could have traveled due west between Coyote Mountain and Dos Cabezas, and across Carrizo Creek. Then, following along the mountains on his left, he could cross the old Butterfield Stage road, heading through one of the big natural passes in the mountains.

If he had decided to go north from Coyote Wells, between Coyote Mountain and Superstition Mountain, he would cross the Butterfield Stage road again and follow it down into the Carrizo Creek. If he followed the Carrizo down past the point of Fish Creek Mountain he could turn to his left and go up into the lower Borrego Valley. That would be another forty miles without water, unless he found the Carrizo Creek running where he crossed it; which would depend on the time of year.

Besides water, his mule would need something to eat, for it was doing all the work. He carried old Peg Leg and his food and water, not counting his own food and water. If he had any, it would have been long gone by the time he reached the Carrizo. If he had come this far with his mule, there is some good native bunch grass the cattlemen call "Guyetta", that grows on the flats in the upper and lower Borrego Valleys.

Between the upper and lower Borrego Valleys is a low ridge called Borrego Mountain. Assuming this was the butte Peg Leg climbed to look for an easy pass through the mountains, it is very unlikely he found the black nuggets there. He could see two passes from the top of this hill; one through the Narrows, leading into the Grapevine Canyon and on up to Warner's Ranch, and another pass to the northwest up Coyote Creek to the Vandeventer Flat, then on to Hemet and points north. Coyote Mountain in the upper Borrego Valley, is almost at the mouth of Coyote Creek. If Peg Leg came that far, still alive, he wouldn't have had to climb that mountain to find a way through. I heard he stopped at Warner's Hot Springs. If he did, he no doubt traveled through the Narrows and up the Grapevine Canyon to Warner's - that is, if he came into the Borrego Valley.

After all, when he arrived in San Bernardino, he was a sick man and went to see a doctor. He had very little money, but did have the black nuggets, or nugget. As I remember the old story, he showed these nuggets to the doctor, telling him if he could get him well again, he (Peg Leg) would take him to where he had found the nuggets, so both of them would be rich. Peg Leg knew the Doctor would do his best to get him well, with a fortune as a fee.

Neither my father nor those prospectors he knew put any credence in Peg Leg's story. They figured he had picked up some pieces of rich ore or nuggets in or around a mine or placer and was using them to get a grubstake. Then, when he became sick, he worked the same game on the doctor. If the doctor cured him, it would be again a case of not being able to find the place again, and of course, at the doctor's expense.